Tropic of Cancer
ON TRIAL

Tropic of Cancer
ON TRIAL

A CASE HISTORY OF CENSORSHIP

by E. R. HUTCHISON

GROVE PRESS, INC., NEW YORK

Library of Congress Catalog Card Number: 68-17728

First Printing

Manufactured in the United States of America

The author is indebted to these writers and their
   publishers for permission to reprint copyrighted work:
Jason Epstein: "A Criticism of Commercial Publishing,"
   Daedalus, XCII (Winter, 1963); permission by the
   editors of *Daedalus*.
William B. Lockhart and Robert C. McClure: "Literature,
   The Law of Obscenity, and the Constitution,"
   Minnesota Law Review, XXXVIII (March, 1954);
   permission by publishers of the *Minnesota Law Review*.
Eric Moon: " 'Problem' Fiction," *Library Journal*,
   LXXXVII (Feb. 1, 1962); permission by R. R. Bowker
   Publishing Company.
Selections from *Publishers' Weekly* reprinted by
   permission of R. R. Bowker Publishing Company.
Kenneth Rexroth: "The Neglected Henry Miller,"
   Nation, CLXXXI (Nov. 5, 1955); permission by the
   publisher of *Nation*.
Stuart C. Sherman: "Defending the Freedom to Read,"
   Library Journal, LXXXVII (Feb. 1, 1962); permission
   by R. R. Bowker Publishing Company.
George Wickes (editor): *Henry Miller and the Critics.*
   Copyright 1963 by Southern Illinois University Press.
   Reprinted by permission of the Southern Illinois
   University Press.
Kingsley Widmer: *Henry Miller.* Copyright 1963 by
   Twayne Publishers. Reprinted by permission of
   Twayne Publishers.
William Carlos Williams: "To the Dean" (last stanza)
   from *Collected Later Poems.* Copyright 1950 by
   William Carlos Williams. Reprinted by permission of
   New Directions Publishing Corporation.

To Marian and Ray

FOREWORD

by Elmer Gertz

Just as it has been said that the conduct of war is too important to be entrusted to generals, the recounting of litigation is too involved to be left to the average pedestrian lawyer who writes a kind of jargon that, even when it makes sense, does not win literary prizes. Fortunately this epic story of the *Tropic of Cancer* litigation has been written by an inspired student of journalism, after protracted and resourceful research. The most casual reader will finish this book with some understanding of why the courtroom saga of *Tropic of Cancer* is so important a part of recent history.

If, ultimately, this nation gives viability to the First Amendment provisions for the freedom of utterance, it will be because of the battle waged over Henry Miller's pioneer autobiographical novel. This was a battle in which a proud and bright young publisher risked his resources, the very existence of his company, and, with the aid of lawyers interested in more than fees, was able to persuade unwilling courts in various parts of the country, and finally the Supreme Court itself, that a book which had a subterranean, if not a surreptitious, life could live, as it deserved, in the open, so that self-respecting Americans could read or ignore it, as they freely chose. Somehow, in this strange land, too few people are sure that the very persons who vote for our highest officials should have the right to select their own reading matter.

If one had been asked, prior to 1961, to name the one case that was most responsible for any progress made in advancing the right to circulate forthright literature, there is no doubt that the *Ulysses* case would have been singled out. The only differences would have been as to whether the Woolsey lower court decision or the Hand reviewing court opinion was the more significant. That was one case, one famous victory; but, like Blenheim, what did it really mean? Writer, publisher, distributor, and reader were little more free thereafter.

There followed isolated cases, and sometimes inspired opinions by great jurists such as Curtis Bok and Jerome Frank. The struggle over *Lady Chatterley's Lover* proved that the fight was not over, and that it could sometimes be won for a particular book—in one fell swoop. With the perspective of today, we can see that all that really happened earlier was that the nation was being prepared for the *Tropic of Cancer* litigation. *Ulysses* did not create a climate of freedom; it was merely a harbinger. *Tropic of Cancer* changed the climate completely. There could be ups and downs, temporary defeats; but henceforth American literature was as free as life. Hard-core pornography and commercial purveyors of it might have tough times, but material of any value could be sold, if its backers persisted and did not resort to crass solicitation.

Where earlier a single victory in any court, especially a federal court, put a halt to the censorship of the work that was involved, the *Tropic of Cancer* struggle illustrated that the censors were prepared to battle in every court, and in every city, village, and town. Thus there were over sixty legal proceedings involving the one book. This was Armageddon for the bigots and purists, and they lost.

As the lawyer in one of the early trial court victories, I followed the complicated developments elsewhere with the utmost excitement. Professor Hutchison's book puts everything in place; it makes one see the meaning of the classic campaign in a truer light than a mere participant could. The author is strongly opposed to censorship, and he has a great commitment to the truth. He tells everything. This book will both entertain and enlighten all who are concerned about the Bill of Rights and the great creative drive of mankind.

PREFACE & ACKNOWLEDGMENTS

Bookburners hot on the trail of Henry Miller's novel, *Tropic of Cancer,* have blazed a wide swath from Paris through England and across the United States. This study follows that trail, holding a mirror to it.

If the reflection repels some readers, if it offends those whose images are cast, then that is to the good. But I hope most readers will be more offended by the conditions of censorship that the book describes. I have tried to give enough detail so that the reader can check my conclusions against his own.

If in this telling, booksellers, librarians, law enforcement officers, judges, and newspapers are excoriated for lethargy, irresponsibility, illegal tactics, illiteracy, or professional lapses, then, for the general reader, there is solace in the thought that at other times and other places still other persons have reflected proper credit on themselves and their professions.

Lest the reader feel after reading this book that Wisconsin is a singular state where censors reign, I should point out that I do not feel this to be so at all. Though this state was personally convenient for such a study and I had many avenues of access into the labyrinthian censorship situation there, had my preliminary research into the censorship activities of this country indicated that Wisconsin was atypical in this respect and in terms of comparisons with other states' handling of *Cancer,* I would not have selected Wisconsin for a close-up study. Whereas Milwaukee, the state's largest city, may have more local censorship than many major cities in this country, I am by no means certain that it is a leader in censorship activities. The state's next largest city, Madison, has one of the most liberal climates in the country.

No. I believe Wisconsin to be more free of censorship than the majority of our fifty states. Certainly it is not besieged by censors in the way that Rhode Island, Georgia, Texas, and California are (to mention a very few). For this very reason, Wisconsin makes an excellent example of how censors can threaten even a liberal state. When *Tropic of Cancer* became an issue endangering the independent judiciary system in the Wisconsin Supreme Court election campaign of 1964, that simply provided the perfect climactic episode for this universal tale.

But this is more than just a story about *Tropic of Cancer* and Wisconsin. It is a story about a courageous author, a courageous publisher, and a book that had been for more than a quarter of a century the symbol of outlaw literature in America. Because of the United States Supreme Court decision on *Cancer,* this story about censorship in our society has a relatively happy ending.

And my book is meant to be more than a case study. Rather, it is a report on a war that is constantly being waged in America. Names of men and books may change from time to time, and battles may vary in size, but the aims and purposes of both sides in this war remain essentially the same. One side fights for freedom of expression, the other for suppression of this freedom in some manner or form. I have tried to describe how the battle rages on all levels and fronts—from top strategy posts to censor outposts on the front lines.

If this work falls short of its ambitious goal, then it is not because of the efforts of many friends, colleagues, and libertarians who aided me. They deserve only high praise—something I would like to shower upon them through these acknowledgments.

Though greatly revised, this study came largely from a doctoral dissertation written at the University of Wisconsin. Had it not been for Professor William Hachten I would not be writing this today. Professor Hachten suggested *Cancer* censorship as a dissertation possibility and then had the patience, forbearance, and intelligence to give me full rein in developing the subject. Later, as an adviser and friend, he carefully read what I wrote and made valuable suggestions—which I followed.

Professor Henry Pochmann can never know the deep regard I hold for him, for his understanding and guidance throughout my entire doctoral program. Charles Higbie also should be mentioned here.

Publisher Barney Rosset opened Grove Press files and correspondence to me. Certainly he must have been provoked to exasperation by my numerous inquiries. Without his help, this study could not have been completed.

Henry Miller gave up precious time to answer my every letter and request. Michael Vaughan of the Wisconsin legislative staff read the dissertation manuscript and was invaluable in leading me to information sources in the Legislative Reference Bureau and elsewhere. Elmer Gertz, the noted Chicago lawyer, faithfully corresponded about legal matters and contributed a generous Foreword to the book. Miss Judith Schmidt of Grove Press was so comforting in her reliability that I would be remiss in not thanking her.

Among the organizations that contributed to this work are the New York and Madison, Wisconsin, offices of the Civil Liberties Union; the Freedom of Information Center at the University of Missouri; and, through the efforts of Professor Hillard Trubitt, the Institute for Sex Research at Indiana University.

Generous beyond request were Charles Rembar, of Rembar & Zolotar; William Lockhart, dean of the Law School, University of Minnesota; Jack Ladinsky, sociology professor, University of Wisconsin; poet Karl Shapiro; Letha B. Rowley, indexer; and student assistants Robert Silvey and Phillips V. Brooks.

Such good friends as Professor and Mrs. David G. Clark of Stanford University and William and Priscilla Morse of Rye, New York, through conversations and hospitality, gave impetus and inspiration to my efforts.

Many others aided me. Too many to mention here. From red-faced librarians and officials to booksellers and public servants who willingly, and unwillingly, gave me golden moments. As their names appear in these pages, the reader will realize my debt.

Finally, there is no way to repay the sacrifices made by my wife, Marian, and my son, Ray, to whom this book is dedicated.

—E. R. Hutchison

CONTENTS

Tropic of Cancer
ON TRIAL

1
THAT OBSCENE HENRY MILLER

If in the early part of 1961 Elmo Roper had polled the best possible cross-section of Americans on their knowledge of Henry Miller and a book called *Tropic of Cancer,* fewer than one out of a hundred would have been able to answer him intelligently. Less than a year later, however, probably two out of three Americans could have filled in his questionnaire. By 1964, Roper would have had to climb the hills to discover a citizen who hadn't heard about the one man and the one book that had ignited the censorship holocaust searing the whole United States.

Scarcely six months after Grove Press published Miller's novel, the *Cancer* censorship campaign was described on December 11, 1961, in these terms by a Grove editor to Russell Lynes of *Harper's* magazine:

Dear Mr. Lynes:

As I told you on the phone today, we here at Grove Press think we are sitting on the story of what is undoubtedly the biggest single case of literary censorship in modern American history—yet nothing has been said or written anywhere to indicate the scope and extent of the current battle.

I am, of course, referring to our troubles over Henry Miller's *Tropic of Cancer.* In the past few weeks police intimidation, whether through threats or actual arrests, has resulted in *Tropic of Cancer* being taken off sale in a major part of the United States.

Cities such as Philadelphia, Cleveland, Chicago, Los Angeles, Dallas, Seattle, just to name a few of the larger ones, have no copies, or almost none, on sale. Entire states, including Massachusetts, Rhode Island, most, or all, of New Jersey, New Hampshire, have seen fit to ban the book. . . .

This censorship campaign grew in intensity until Henry Miller became the most controversial literary figure—and *Tropic of Cancer* the most censored novel—in American history. In those campaign years Americans who cared about such things learned a great deal about the man whose major novels had been banned from his native shores for more than three decades. And what they learned underscored the controversial nature of all of Miller's life and work.

One critic early called Miller the bigot's whipping boy.[1] The sobriquet reflects the attitude of Americans who sacrifice attention to Miller's literary merit to the excitement stirred by obscenity charges and Miller's so-called anti-Americanism. Though it is true Miller's attacks upon America have been violent, he loves his country. His anti-American statements come in part from the despair of believing that we ought to be and could be a better, freer nation than we are. And far from admitting to the obscenity slur cast on his novels, Miller believes them a prescription for the ills of the world, a world he described, in 1945, in this way:

> This world which is in the making fills me with dread. I have seen it germinate; I can read it like a blueprint. It is not a world I want to live in. It is a world suited for monomaniacs obsessed with the idea of progress—but a false progress, a progress which stinks. It is a world cluttered with useless objects which men and women, in order to be exploited and degraded, are taught to regard as useful. The dreamer whose dreams are nonutilitarian has no place in this world. Whatever does not lend itself to being bought and sold, whether in the realm of things, ideas, principles, dreams or hopes, is debarred. In this world the poet

is anathema, the thinker a fool, the artist an escapist, the man of vision a criminal.

Miller is capable of stating, "I want to declare that I am a traitor to the human race," and later saying to a foreign court, with some pride, "As a husband, a father, a neighbor, I am looked upon as 'an asset' to the community." He has excoriated Catholicism at one time and expressed sympathy for it at another. Abdicating traditional adult responsibility, Miller abandoned a wife and child, married another woman and fled to Paris to write.

His good friend Alfred Perles assures us that in addition to being a literary clown, Miller has sometimes been as much a clown in real life. But even that stern critic Kingsley Widmer concedes that Miller was "self-consciously organized, personally ambitious, and earnestly in search of broad self-improvement (even to the point of planning to steal books from libraries)." [2] Perles paints this character portrait of Miller: "Deep down in his heart he was so great an optimist that he saw hope even in hopelessness. [He] deliberately cultivated the rock-bottom situation. It seemed to respond to that curious masochistic streak in his spiritual makeup." [3] Philip Rahv, however, says flatly: "The final impression we have of Henry Miller is that of a naturally genial American who has been through hell." [4] Nonsense! Widmer would retort to Rahv; with the exception of Miller's flight to Paris, his "life has been the fairly ordinary one of a not especially adventuresome or profound literary bohemian—American style." [5]

There is one thing about Miller that has never created any confusion or controversy. He once said, "My great desire, before I ever so much as wrote a line, was simply to become a writer." No friend or enemy has ever doubted the sincerity of this desire. Miller's personal sacrifices in pursuing this literary ambition have been massive.

The key to Miller's writings is his life, because the subject of his writings *is* his life. Though he calls his works "auto-biographical romances," what he reveals in them is more than the vast majority of autobiographers care to reveal, and more than most biographers are able to reveal.

Born on December 26, 1891, in Yorkville, N.Y., Henry Valentine Miller spent most of his youth in Brooklyn. He was the only son of a lower-middle-class German-American family, and until he went to school, Miller spoke only German. He writes of a feeble-minded sister in *Black Spring,* his second published novel. His father, genial and weak-charactered, was a not very successful tailor. His extremely conventional and cold mother was the source of considerable emotional conflict.[6]

Miller finished high school in Brooklyn and enrolled at City College of New York, but he rebelled at academe and quit after two months. From this year, 1909, until 1913 Miller held a series of jobs, starting with the Atlas Portland Cement Company in New York City. He also entered a seven-year period of rigorous athleticism. At about the same time he acquired his first mistress—Pauline Chouteau of Phoebus, Virginia, a woman twice his age. Miller traveled west in 1913, working at odd jobs along the way. In San Diego he met Emma Goldman, the famous anarchist, who was lecturing in California at the time. This meeting Miller calls a turning point in his life, both intellectually and spiritually. Miller eventually dabbled in communism, but could not reconcile himself to the aims and discipline of the Party.

When Miller returned to Brooklyn in 1914, he worked for a while in his father's tailor shop, where he met Frank Harris, the first noted writer he had ever encountered. The best writing in *Black Spring* comes from his experiences in his father's shop. The characters he met there come delightfully alive in an almost Dickensian spirit. Miller married Beatrice Wickens, his piano teacher, three years later, at the age of twenty-six. A daughter was born to them in 1919.

In the following years Miller held various clerical positions and other unsatisfying jobs. Indeed, the variety of jobs he has held during his lifetime is impressive. He has worked as typist, candy salesman, insurance salesman, encyclopedia salesman, dockhand, ranchhand, beggar, dishwasher, bell hop, bartender, librarian, garbage collector, book salesman, gym instructor, secretary to an evangelist, proofreader for the Paris edition of the *Chicago Tribune,* gravedigger, and speakeasy owner. From 1920 to 1924, Miller worked for Western Union in New York City. For several months he was a messenger; then for three years, as messenger employment manager, he hired and fired more than 50,000 men, women, and boys. Miller's first and unpublished novel, *Clipped Wings,* was about twelve Western Union messengers, and his Western Union experience is relived again in *Tropic of Capricorn.*

In a Broadway dance palace in 1923 he met June Edith Smith. Soon afterward he left his first wife and their four-year-old daughter, Barbara. Thirty years would pass before he saw his daughter again. June Smith was devoted to Miller and as his second wife encouraged him to write, even supporting him financially and helping him sell his prose poems (*Mezzotints*) from door to door. She urged him to quit Western Union, and in 1924 he did. His writing career now began in earnest, and June Smith, the taxi dancer, became the alluring and haunting Mona and Mara and other heroines of his novels. This marriage lasted until 1933.

In 1927, in just one day, Miller compiled notes for a complete autobiographical cycle of novels, a trilogy that became *The Rosy Crucifixion.* In the same year he started painting water colors, and shortly thereafter held an exhibition in a Greenwich Village dive. (A Miller painting now sells at from $250 to $350.) Later, Miller and June ran a Village speakeasy of their own.

Just before the Depression, from 1928 to 1929, Miller and his wife toured Europe on money provided by a male friend of hers. The next year, without June (who joined him later), and with ten borrowed dollars, Miller returned to Paris. He remained there until driven out by World War II.

For the first two years in Paris, Miller, in his words, was literally annihilated. He barely existed through the hospitality of friends like Alfred Perles and Richard G. Osborn. With little left of the writer he had hoped to be when he left America,

Miller began *Tropic of Cancer,* and met Anaïs Nin. She herself was writing a voluminous diary, and she influenced and aided Miller immeasurably.

> I wanted to reveal myself as openly, nakedly and unashamedly as possible . . . [Miller later wrote]. My nature or my temperament compel me to do so. I am interested in life, all life, and every aspect of it. The one life I know best of all is my own. Examining my own life, describing it in detail, exposing it ruthlessly, I believe that I am rendering back life, enhanced and exalted, to those who read me.

Miller held off showing Anaïs Nin the *Cancer* manuscript in the first months of their acquaintance because he didn't want to be thought of as having a "dirty mind."

The period in Paris from 1930 to 1934 Miller calls a good writing period. He wrote *Black Spring* and also worked on his study, "The World of D. H. Lawrence." *Cancer* was published in 1934 by Jack Kahane and the Obelisk Press. *Aller Retour New York,* a long letter to Perles, was published in 1935; and Miller's correspondence with Michael Fraenkel began this year, to be published later as *Hamlet. Black Spring* bloomed, for Europe, in 1936 (but not for America, where it too was banned). His third major novel, *Tropic of Capricorn,* went into print in 1939. Both *Cancer* and *Capricorn* were immediately banned in England as well as in America. By 1939, the star writer for the Paris Obelisk Press was Henry Miller.

With the publication of *Cancer,* Miller was recognized as the spokesman for the "Left Bank." This was a later group of expatriates than the "Lost Generation," for Miller was never a member of the Lost Generation—never met Gertrude Stein. Arriving in France as the earlier group began returning homeward, Miller was of the Paris of the thirties, the Paris of the Depression. Describing Miller in these years, Perles writes:

> He was aloof, curious and detached—detached to the point of treachery. His best friends, who were prepared to go through fire and water for him, weren't safe from his treachery—an odd

streak of treachery that always stopped short of betrayal—
which was in reality only the manifestation of a bizarre sense of
humor.[7]

While he was traveling in Greece, World War II erupted,
and Miller returned to New York. The royalties from his books,
which had become substantial by now, were curtailed by the
war and Miller, nearing fifty, tightened his belt once again,
and kept on writing. A book about his Greek travels, *The
Colossus of Maroussi,* was published in 1941. *The World of
Sex* and *Quiet Days in Clichy,* along with the beginning of *The
Rosy Crucifixion,* were also written in 1940, though not published until later. Miller toured the United States in 1941, part
of the way with painter Abraham Rattner, and wrote *The Air-
Conditioned Nightmare,* an anti-American travelogue published
in 1945.

A passionate love affair precipitated a move from New York
to California in 1942, where he lived for a while in Los Angeles
with Margaret and Gilbert Neiman. Early in 1944 Miller moved
north to the Monterey peninsula, and here, in craggy, rugged
Big Sur, mellowed and melted by the California sun, the "boy
from Brooklyn" felt the first sense of home in his own land.

But this did not mean living was easy, by any means, as this
Easter Sunday letter from Big Sur shortly thereafter reveals:

> [Since my arrival in America] . . . I have made no more than
> four or five hundred dollars per annum. This past year was an
> exception, due to the fact that I had a moderate success with my
> water colors. What many of my friends do not realize is that,
> foolishly or not, I immediately paid out the monies which
> suddenly poured in from the sale of water colors—something
> like $1,400.00. I had naïvely thought it would continue ad
> infinitum. (I was an optimist and slightly delirious.) Now I am
> being absolutely honest when I say that all I got out of this
> sudden influx of wealth was three pairs of woolen socks, a plaid
> woolen shirt, and some good water color paper. . . . I didn't
> even get a good meal out of it. . . . I still owe roughly
> $24,000.00. This is what it has cost me to write as I pleased for
> the last twenty years.

Many Miller admirers gathered at Big Sur. And at Big Sur, while the greatest slaughter the world had ever seen was taking place, Miller became the spokesman for 5,500 conscientious objectors "settled" in West Coast camps. While other established writers kept their pens sheathed in deference to the militant patriotism of wartime, Miller courageously wrote the pacifist pamphlet *Murder the Murderers*.

Touring Eastern colleges in 1944, Miller once again exhibited his water colors—not in Greenwich Village this time, but at Yale University. Meeting Janina M. Lepska on this lecture tour, Miller married her in Denver, Colorado, and so ended nine years of what Perles calls "spasmodic love affairs." Janina was in her early twenties, Miller in his early fifties. They had two children, quarreled over the rearing of them, and separated after seven years of marriage. The children went with their mother after Miller made an unsuccessful attempt to keep them. Despite the family wrangling, Miller completed *Sexus* (1945), *Remember to Remember* (1947), and *Plexus* (1949).

By 1950, Miller was once again receiving a sizable income from his writing. More than that, his literary star was growing brighter. Some of its energy was supplied by the publication of his books in America, some from his Open Letters in the *New Republic* about the creative artist in America. More came when GI's bought his banned books in Paris after the war. But a more constant source was generated from his role at Big Sur, where he was reported to be leading a Greenwich Village–like bohemia in a revolt that was something more than a replica of the twenties.[8] As the sage of Big Sur, Miller became "the original beatnik and Zen saint—in this as in so many other ways thirty years ahead of his followers." [9] All this, however, would not have been so clearly seen by students of literature today had not Barney Rosset of Grove Press, starting with *Cancer* in 1961, published *all* of his previously banned books. *Cancer* then became the *cause célèbre* of artists and libertarians throughout America, and before the censorship furor had been quelled Grove Press was to spend more than $250,000 defending it.

The same year that *Cancer* was published in America Miller was separated from his fourth wife, Eva McClure, and from 1962 to 1963 he lived only intermittently in Southern California. He was healthy, wealthy, and a traveling celebrity. *Capricorn* was published by Grove Press. *Just Wild About Harry*, his first play, was produced. Most of his works now received wide distribution. He had finally arrived financially. But as Miller remarked, "In a way it's too late. The money should have been there in the beginning."

During the years of the *Cancer* furor, when most Americans were being introduced to Henry Miller's work, and some were obscenely equating both him and his writings with obscenity, what was Miller doing? For one thing, he started making silk screens, working with the nuns at Immaculate Heart College in Hollywood. For another, he was becoming more accustomed to the literary and spiritual halo that had begun to form over his balding pate.

Miller now lives with his two teenagers in a town house at Pacific Palisades, California. If you should receive one of the many letters he writes, chances are there will be, printed in red ink at the bottom of the letter, this sentence: "The time of the hyena is upon us." He is seventy-six years old, rides a bike weekly, swims in his pool, reads at night, and entertains primarily painters and musicians. He recently married a thirty-two-year-old jazz pianist, Hoki Tokuda. For these past fifteen years Miller has been able to live in a manner that by right should have been his for thirty years or more. A right denied him by censors.

In denying Miller this right, censors did more than inflict economic deprivation. The psychological effect of their actions must have been great. "No man in his right senses," Miller wrote at Big Sur, "would elect to be a poet in this land of kingdom come!" An understanding fellow artist, Orvis Ross, added, "Poor old Henry has been so much maligned, misunderstood, giggled about, blushed over, scorned, belittled and depreciated that it's a wonder he still has the stamina to pick up the pen." [10]

Not only had we banned Miller's books, we had banned their meaning and their intent as well. More than that, we had tried to ban the dignity of the man.[11]

To many Americans this treatment must have been puzzling, for a number of respected critics had applauded Miller's efforts. In 1958 he was elected to membership in the American Academy of Arts and Letters with a citation hailing him as a writer whose "boldness of approach and intense curiosity concerning man and nature are unequaled in the prose literature of our time." No less a poet than William Carlos Williams had written, in a stanza of a poem entitled "To the Dean":

> Miller, Miller, Miller, Miller
> I like those who like you and dislike
> nothing that imitates you, I like
> particularly that Black Book with its
> red sporran by the Englishman that does you
> so much honor. I think we should all
> be praising you, you are a very good
> influence.[12]

What is noteworthy about all this to American letters and life is that it took thirty years—in a country which prides itself on its freedom of expression—for a native artist to receive recognition for what he gave the world. And not, in Miller's words, "without some sacrifice."

2
THE MILLER MILIEU

In his role as artist, Miller holds the distinction of being perhaps the only American writer to reveal so fully and unabashedly the life he has lived:

"I take it you understand, to begin with, that what I am struggling to do as a writer, is simply to tell the story of my life, not out of egotism but because I am that sort of honest fool who thinks that the only one he can write about truthfully is himself." [1] Elsewhere he writes that he has been "utterly shameless" in revealing "every aspect of my life," but that "I am not the first author to have adopted the confessional approach, to have revealed life nakedly, or to have used language supposedly unfit for the ears of school girls." [2]

And he describes himself in *Black Spring,* a description that also includes a prediction of immortality:

For me the book is the man and my book is the man I am, the confused man, the negligent man, the reckless man, the lusty, obscene, boisterous, thoughtful, scrupulous, lying, diabolically truthful man that I am. I am thinking that in that age to come I shall not be overlooked. Then my history will become important and the scar which I leave upon the face of the world will have significance. I can not forget that I am making history, a history on the side which, like a chancre, will eat away the other meaningless history. I regard myself not as a book, a record, a document, but as a history of our time—a history of *all* time.[3]

If it is true that the autobiographer is in one sense an exhibitionist, and the more he exhibits the happier he is, then Henry Miller must be a most contented fellow, for it seems he has kept very little from his readers. After his mother died in 1956, Miller said: "Mother never understood or accepted me, right up till death—and I was very close to her those last three months of her life in New York. [She] never read . . . a line of anything I had written . . . [She] hardly ever acknowledged that I *was* a writer—[she] seemed ashamed of the fact. [She] was a block to me all my life. . . . When she died I felt a 'release.' " [4]

Being an artist meant freedom to Miller—a rebellious freedom from a petty society, a portal into a larger world. Using art as a stepping-stone to another, larger way of life, Miller set as his goal self-realization, and through his writing he attempted to attain it. "A man writes in order to know himself," Miller wrote, "and thus get rid of self eventually."

Throughout his books Miller weaves a theme of dehumanized man. For this man's salvation, Miller prescribes self-realization. A more widespread application of this prescription, Miller feels, would also minister to the ills of a "materialistic, hypocritical and meretricious America," [5] and he has unceasingly exhorted America to this self-realization. Before discussing *Tropic of Cancer* (and other major Miller books), we need to recall the social milieu in which that novel was written.

In their book *Pornography and the Law,* Phyllis and Eberhard Kronhausen used the term "erotic realism" to describe the frank and realistic treatment of sex in literature (in preference to the misleading terms "obscenity" and "pornography"). Erotic realism is a historical movement in art and literature that represents in part the artist's rebellion against social pressures which force him to exclude, minimize, or distort the sexual element in his artistic creation. Erotic realism is the counterforce against these social pressures which ultimately force the artist to falsify life. It expresses the artist's healthy demand to include, and in some instances to emphasize, the erotic aspects of life.[6] In establishing Miller's position in the American literary tradition, it is essential to glance briefly at this particular literary movement.

The "genteel realism" of William Dean Howells and Henry James of the 1870's and 1880's had given way to a more realistic treatment of life long before Miller typed the manuscript for *Tropic of Cancer*. In the early years of genteel realism, novelists merely engaged in some kind of human apogamy game, and lo, a baby appeared. Later, what Edward Weeks has called the "closed door policy" came into vogue. This consisted of the novelist's approaching the climax of a love affair, closing the door, and then tiptoeing gingerly away,[7] as if he were tucking a couple of babies in for the night.

By 1910, an "open door policy" had developed. Novelists revealed passions unleashed in their characters, and, incidentally, offered erotic stimuli to the reader. World War I then provided an impetus to prop this literary door open. Joseph Hergesheimer noted the significance of this to writers and the reading public: Here was a most extraordinary and new audience—clear-eyed, critical, and supremely invigorating. A great many trivialities had been secreted from their interests and needs. Now this audience was forever lost to the purely superficial, as writers showed the entire fabric of American life.[8]

When Freud and the new psychologists permeated the most exciting of all decades of American literature, the writers of the twenties removed the "open door" from its hinges, broke it into little pieces, and tossed it in the incinerator. Under the tutelage of H. L. Mencken, the young writers of the twenties rallied around Theodore Dreiser as a symbol of revolt—a revolt against Victorianism and Puritanism.[9] The twenties, and not without reason, were called the sexy decade.

Another influence on this period of American writing was the various sex hygiene books being published at the time. Mencken wrote:

> Whether these sex hygiene books increased or diminished loose living . . . I don't know. . . . But this I do know: they had a

quick and tremendous influence upon the content of American fiction. In the old-time novel what are now called the Facts of Life were glossed over and no one complained about it, for the great majority of fiction readers, being young and female, had no notion of what they were missing. But after they had read the sex hygiene books they began to observe that what was set out in novels was very evasive, and that much of it was downright untrue. . . . One by one the old-time novelists went on the shelf. . . . Their sales dropped off; they began to be laughed at. In place of them rose a new school, and its *aim* was to tell it all. With this new school, Comstock and his heirs have been wrestling ever since, and with steadily increasing bad fortune.[10]

Revolting against the tradition and the limitations under which they lived and worked, the writers risked prison by flouting the censors. They proclaimed homosexuality, incest, prostitution (male and female), miscegenation, impotence, venereal disease, abortion, and masturbation fit subjects for artistic treatment.[11] Assaultive writing came into vogue. America's muddling ancestors were berated and beaten. The novelists dissected man and isolated his libido. They raged against government bureaucrats, venal businessmen, and charlatan preachers. They destroyed the myth of small-town modality by exposing its underlying seaminess.[12] Censorship became an issue to be protested, battled, and cursed. And when it was all over, the writer had earned his Magna Charta, his Declaration of Independence, and his Bill of Rights.

American literature grew up in the twenties and so did the American reading public.[13] But not quite up to Henry Miller and *Tropic of Cancer*. Only after World War II, and after such novelists as Caldwell, O'Hara, Mailer, and Jones had been presented to the public, were those readers ready for such a novel as *Cancer*.

Miller had lived through the turbulent twenties in America and had experienced the first shock of the Depression. This, along with the chaotic experience of his own personal life, he brought with him to Europe. There he was confronted with still another chaotic world. Hitler and Mussolini were on the move. The League of Nations was dead. The Lost Generation was retreating to America from the world center of fine arts and literature. In Paris, surrealism was the rage. But even before surrealism arrived (in contrast to the American writing of the Depression), France had shifted away from literature as social expression and sociological document, to forms of writing in which the artist tried to be sincere with himself, to express his thoughts and experiences with maximum candor and honesty. According to Wallace Fowlie, this literary movement was obvious from the beginning of the century.[14]

The time and the setting were ripe for Miller to write a book which was at once a major attempt to be sincere with himself and an attempt to write a sociological document of major import. With the writing of *Cancer,* the wall through which the "open door" led was destroyed.

Roaming the streets of Paris day and night, many times jobless, hungry, sponging off friends, somehow Miller, motivated by hatred and vengeance, wrote his first major work, *Cancer.* The writing had a cathartic effect which was his salvation as a man as well as an artist.

"This is not a book," he wrote in the opening pages of *Cancer.* "This is libel, slander, defamation of character. This is not a book, in the ordinary sense of the word. No, this is a prolonged insult, a gob of spit in the face of Art, a kick in the pants to God, Man, Destiny, Time, Love, Beauty . . . what you will. I am going to sing for you, a little off key perhaps, but I will sing. I will sing while you croak, I will dance over your dirty corpse." [15]

In this now famous paragraph Miller announced that what followed would be something different. He was right. *Cancer* is "not a book, in the ordinary sense of the word." It is antinovel.

A series of loosely knit episodes, dreams and essays, *Cancer* taxes the patience of the conventional novel reader. And while the lyricism of the threnody tends to soothe that reader, there is much that is "off key." But off key or not, Miller does sing and dance as he describes the "dirty corpse"—his world, our world:

There is only one thing which interests me vitally now, and that is the recording of all that which is omitted in books. Nobody, so far as I can see, is making use of those elements in the air which give direction and motivation to our lives. Only the killers seem to be extracting from life some satisfactory measure of what they are putting into it. The age demands violence, but we are getting only abortive explosions. Revolutions are nipped in the bud, or else succeed too quickly. Passion is quickly exhausted. Men fall back on ideas . . . (p. 10)

And Miller wants to do more than simply describe this world in *his* Bible:

For a hundred years or more the world, *our* world, has been dying. And not one man, in these last hundred years or so, has been crazy enough to put a bomb up the asshole of creation and set it off. The world is rotting away, dying piecemeal. But it needs the *coup de grâce,* it needs to be blown to smithereens. Not one of us intact, and yet we have in us all the continents and the seas between the continents and the birds of the air. We are going to put it down—the evolution of this world which has died but which has not been buried. We are swimming on the face of time and all else has drowned, is drowning, or will drown. It will be enormous, the Book. (p. 24)

The artist, Miller reflects, is nihilistic. And once again, in *Cancer,* he says:

The task which the artist implicitly sets himself is to overthrow existing values, to make of the chaos about him an order which is his own, to sow strife and ferment so that by the emotional release those who are dead may be restored to life. (p. 228)

Cancer is about Miller and his first few years in Paris. About his dreams, his thoughts, his friends, his wife, his prostitutes, his escapades, his Paris. For the conventional reader, it is a shocking masculine world. The search—the continual, perpetual search—for sex and food in this Parisian world serves as a unifying element for *Cancer,* along with the recurring flowing images, and Mona—the absent second wife.

In this world—mad, syphilitic, cancerous—the male preys on the female. No love accompanies the many sexual acts.

There is no love in this world. There is a sentimental attachment to Mona by the artist-hero approaching love, but this readily dissolves when moments arise for more fleshly attachments. The moments do arise, time after time after time, and they are described realistically and in masculine language: four-letter words that are familiar to all men and to most women. This familiarity, however, does not prevent the words (as well as the scenes) from being shocking—for they are seen in print for the first time by most readers. These words and the sexual scenes are a major part of "the recording of all that which is omitted in books." This is one of the means by which *Cancer* is meant to shock and enrage the reader at the kind of society that has arisen from the cradle of civilization. Only through the sexual act itself is any sense of life experienced in this suppurative world, and Miller early announces what his role will be in it:

> By what he calls the better part of his nature, man has been betrayed, that is all. At the extreme limits of his spiritual being man finds himself again naked as a savage. When he finds God, as it were, he has been picked clean: he is a skeleton. One must burrow into life again in order to put on flesh. The word must become flesh; the soul thirsts. On whatever crumb my eye fastens, I will pounce and devour. If to live is the paramount thing, then I will live, even if I must become a cannibal. Heretofore I have been trying to save my precious hide, trying to preserve the few pieces of meat that hid my bones. I am done with that. I have reached the limits of endurance. My back is to the wall; I can retreat no further. As far as history goes I am dead. If there is something beyond I shall have to bounce back. I have found God, but he is insufficient. I am only spiritually dead. Physically I am alive. Morally I am free. The world which I have departed is a menagerie. The dawn is breaking on a new world, a jungle world in which the lean spirits roam with sharp claws. If I am a hyena I am a lean and hungry one: I go forth to fatten myself. (p. 90)

Although anti-Americanisms are voiced in various parts of the book, the attraction that his homeland has for the hero is explicitly symbolized by his concern about reaching the American Express Office every day for word from Mona. (Mona-Mara—the names are interchangeable—in *Capricorn* is equated with America.)

The humor in *Cancer* is scarcely mentioned in criticism, perhaps because it is the humor of the saloon, the army barracks, the factory—a masculine humor. Life and language in *Cancer* are rough—so is the humor. Once he is forewarned and attuned to it, though, the humor is there even for the unprepared novel reader: in Miller's scheme for cadging free meals; in the description of one of Gandhi's disciples in a whorehouse; in the description of Germaine, the whore; in the account of Fillmore's courting of the Russian princess, who dramatically reveals herself to be syphilitic.

This materialistic, insane world of Paris is fully depicted in the first two-thirds of the novel. The reader is not to think that life in this world is exceptional, however, for another is given as contrast—the life endured at Dijon by the artist-hero as a teacher of English. The Dijon institution, certainly the most representative of all that is sane in our society, seems more of a madhouse than the Parisian scene. The artist-hero quickly escapes from this monastic prison.

Throughout all of *Cancer,* however, he is optimistic and affirmative. It is enough to live. The hardships are a joy. The artist, as Miller has proclaimed, benefits from the bad as well as the good. Everything flows into his ink well. And Miller actually *lives* the life of the artist, or what he conceives to be the life of the artist.

What seems to be a proper evaluation of *Cancer* is given grudgingly by Widmer:

> Despite its muddle and artiness and basic fragmentation of sensibility . . . Miller did achieve a frequently vivacious prose, significant gestures of defiance, and an enlargement of feeling probably incompatible with the moral structures of bourgeois fiction and the decorous strictures of any more coherently controlled style and method. While some of this is derivative—Thoreau and Whitman, Joyce and Lawrence—Miller's fusion is sufficiently distinctive and intense to give the book a valuable

place, both for itself and for the literary and human directions
it points.[16]

But more needs to be said about this novel. Hemingway in
The Sun Also Rises gave to the American reader the high road
of despair taken by the Lost Generation in Paris. Miller in
Cancer gives us the low road taken by the bohemian artist in
Paris. And there are no distortions in the mirror he held up to
his road. In his delineation of lice-ridden people, of the hotels,
the refugees, the brothels, of the society in which he moved,
Miller recorded for the first time a type of life existing in Paris.
For this alone he deserves our gratitude.

The Parisian publication of *Cancer* in 1934 by Jack Kahane
proved to be more than simply a turning point in Miller's life.
The pattern for his future work, for his attitudes and his role
as artist was drawn here. Acceptance of *Cancer* by the public
served to brush away whatever lingering reservations Miller
may have had about his kind of existence. He would live as
he chose to live—not as society's conventions pressured him to
live. His interpretation of the world as sick and cancerous
changed very little in subsequent works. The anti-American
comments in *Cancer* increased in volume and profusion in such
later books as *Black Spring, Capricorn,* and *Nightmare,* and
toned down only when Miller settled in the idyllic Big Sur.

With *Cancer,* Miller discovered too that autobiography was
his forte. Never again would he approach literature from any
other viewpoint. He would be the one man who would tell the
whole truth about his life in his writing, and the rest of his
works would be dedicated to this aim. Miller's life story is the
source of unity for his works. The combination of narrative,
essay, anecdotes, episodes and dreams found in *Cancer* persists
in later works. The contradictions and confusion in *Cancer*
carry over to other works, too. Only the intensity of the
schizoid and surrealistic writing lessens.

The erotic realism of *Cancer,* part of the "whole truth" not
being told in books of that time, was amplified in *Capricorn*
and *Sexus,* along with the rough language. This realism is perhaps the most important reason for Miller's continuing popu-

larity. Another is undoubtedly his anti-American theme, which has been sweet music to many ears, both European and American. In the latter case, of course, fire-and-brimstone preachers since Colonial times have known that Americans like to be told they're going to hell. Miller, shrewd as he is, must have known how his iconoclastic and bombastic statements would be received.

Cancer is almost as fresh and full of import today as it was thirty years ago. When we consider that the novel received such favorable critical comment thirty years after the first edition, then we begin to realize just how good Miller was thirty years ago. *Cancer* not only ushered in a new life for Henry Miller, but with its publication in 1961 in this country it ushered in a new era of literature in America.

We should emphasize, however, Miller and *Cancer* do not so much break with the tradition of the artist and the novel of their times as mark the farthest advance up to now—an extension of the renaissance spirit of the twenties. Then as now, Miller's work could fairly be called extreme. Certainly he had forged ahead. In the 1960's Miller wrote of those years:

> I was sick to death of the lack of substance in English literature, with its portrayal of a truncated, partial man. I wanted a more substantial diet, the whole being, the round view you get in the paintings of Picasso, the works of Montaigne and Rabelais and others. So I rebelled, and perhaps over-generously made up for this lack and weakness in the literature of my time.

Cancer is one of Miller's three most important books, those which will carve their author's place in American literary history. The other two are *Capricorn* and *Black Spring.*

Black Spring was published after *Cancer,* once again by Kahane and the Obelisk Press, in 1936, in Paris, where it was simultaneously acclaimed and banned. In the second installment in the story of man—Henry Miller—he nostalgically recalls his Brooklyn childhood, alternating his memories with his Paris experiences. Although not so good as *Cancer, Black Spring* more solidly established the Miller reputation *Cancer* had earned. The self-liberation celebrated in *Cancer* becomes a little more pronounced in *Black Spring*. The novel is primarily "literature of the streets." With Millerian twists the reader is taken on a tour of French urinals, in a disjointed piece in the book entitled "A Saturday Afternoon," and then is transported to the Brooklyn sidewalks in "The Tailor Shop." No reader of *Black Spring* is apt to forget the billowing prose rhythms of either piece.

The third major segment of that great amorphous autobiographical book of Miller's was published by Kahane in 1939, promptly banned in England and America, and heralded elsewhere. *Tropic of Capricorn* is perhaps the best of Miller's work and, of the three mentioned so far, the most erotic. The purpose of *Capricorn* is not, as Charles Glicksberg writes, "to describe the sensual man as 'realistically' as possible," but Miller does suggest and describe in this work "the throbbing universe of sexuality, its physiological as well as psychic tensions, its anguish and aberrations, its ecstasies and satiated disgusts." And Miller dares to "tell the unvarnished truth about the sex-demented, copulating animal known as man." [17]

In a nihilistic rage Miller describes an insensitive mechanistic America where man is driven to sex as the only means of self-expression left to him. Central to this mechanistic society is the city. The kind of enterprise thriving there and making man its slave is exemplified by the Cosmodemonic Telegraph Company. Under similar regimented materialistic conditions a century ago, Herman Melville has Bartleby the Scrivener withdrawing into a schizoid shell and dying in prison, an apathetic enemy of society. In *Capricorn*, Miller, the artist-hero, roams the streets of New York venting his anxiety and frustration in a lusty, unsatisfying, sexual odyssey which somehow culminates happily with Mara—"The Woman whom you never hoped to meet."

Miller, in *Capricorn*, appears to be more in control of his subject matter than in either of his earlier books. A more mature Miller at war with our civilization is displayed. *Capricorn* marks the autumnal equinox of Miller's literary efforts. His writing deteriorates from this novel on.

The Colossus of Maroussi, published in 1941, received generally favorable criticism. But if *Colossus* is "one of the best
'travel books' on Greece ever done (the critics are unanimous)," [18] as Karl Shapiro professes, then either this is a
fertile field relatively untilled by the artist, or criticism is at a
nadir. More nearly correct is Widmer's appraisal of *Colossus*
as often "vague, strident, silly and sentimental," a product of
a devious, intellectually confused mind.[19] Shapiro and others
must have been overcome by the first evidence of another,
positive side to Miller's character as a writer.

The American companion piece to *Colossus* is *The Air-
Conditioned Nightmare,* which appeared in 1945. The major
criticisms launched against America in it needed airing. Nothing more need be said about it; on the whole, *Nightmare* is
absurd.

Big Sur and the Oranges of Hieronymus Bosch (1946) is
still another chapter in the history of Henry Miller, one which
depicts a more mellow person whose discovery of Big Sur has
led to ecstasy, even to a kind of humility. Twenty pieces, described as potpourri by Miller, make up the book. But life at
Big Sur is not portrayed convincingly or interestingly. As in
his two previous books (*Colossus* and *Nightmare*), the writing
is poor. *Big Sur* revives the reader momentarily with the vivid
portrait of a French astrologer and occultist, Conrad Moricand,
in Part III of the book, "Paradise Lost," but this comes too
late. As a whole, *Big Sur* is flat and unstimulating.

Writing about *The Rosy Crucifixion* to his lifelong friend,
Lawrence Durrell, Miller confessed:

> You may not like R.C. at all. In some ways it is a reversion to
> pre-*Tropic* writing. Much more conversation, direct and indirect.
> Many episodes, dreams, fantasies, throwbacks of all sorts. But a
> steady forward progression, chronologically, because I am fol-
> lowing my notes (written in 1927).[20]

The title, according to Miller, has this significance:

> If a moment ago I bemoaned my fate I am aware nevertheless
> that it is the result of my own doings. One spins his own
> web . . .

The Rosy Crucifixion, the very title . . . conveys this thought. It also conveys, I must quickly add, the idea of acceptance.[21]

In this acceptance, Miller goes back to his early days in New York and retraces his life. The three novels, *Nexus, Sexus,* and *Plexus,* which compose *The Rosy Crucifixion* have been called by Maxwell Geismar, "an epic work in personal, social, and esthetic terms." However, I believe Harry T. Moore to be more nearly correct in his remark that they are a dull, plodding and "wearying chronicle of sexual acrobatics." [22]

In broad summation of Miller's literary efforts, this may be said: As an apocalyptic artist, a prophetic artist, as an analyst of America's ills, Miller fluttered through the pages of his early books like a bright monarch butterfly. There is little discredit, under the circumstances, that Miller later covered much of the same terrain as a gray, heavy-bodied moth.

3

"A GREAT BIG SOMETHING" —THE BANNED INFLUENCE

"A great big something" was what an uneasy Tennyson called Walt Whitman. Aware of Whitman's greatness, Tennyson was still unwilling to call him a major poet. Most critics apparently have a similar feeling when they consider Henry Miller. Uneasy as the American critics have been about Miller, however, all credit him with at least three important novels and a major influence that has permeated Europe and America. The American influence has spread despite the fact that Miller's major novels were banned from American shores for most of his life.

Miller's influence abroad was registered in 1955 by Kenneth Rexroth, a poet and critic who is not particularly fond of Miller. In an article entitled "The Neglected Henry Miller," Rexroth noted:

> Henry Miller is a really popular writer, a writer of, for, and by real people. In other countries he is read, not just by highbrows, or by the wider public that reads novels, but by the people who, in the United States, read comic books. In the United States he has been kept away from the popular public and his great novels have been banned. Only the highbrows who could import them from France have read him.

. . . Miners in the Pyrenees, gondoliers in Venice, and certainly every *poule* in Paris, when they hear you're from California, ask, first thing, "Do you know M'sieu Miller?" . . . he has become part of the standard repertory of reading matter everywhere but in England and in the United States. If you have read Balzac, or Baudelaire, or Goethe, you are also expected to have read Miller. He is certainly one of the many widely read American writers, along with Upton Sinclair, Jack London, Fenimore Cooper and Caldwell.[1]

In one way or another, a great many critics have echoed the Rexroth line. "Though most of our own literary reviews wouldn't let you know about it," Walker Winslow asserts, "he is one of the American writers who is taken most seriously in Europe. He has been translated into most languages and his books have been distributed widely. In France, in particular." [2] George Wickes wrote that "Miller has received a good deal of attention from serious critics, both English and American, over the past three decades. Now, it is true that he is held in higher esteem in half a dozen non-Anglo-Saxon countries . . . we in America have only a dim notion of his international standing." [3]

George Orwell, of course, was one of Miller's first English admirers. During the war years Miller's name frequently crept into English magazines and periodicals and became well known among the cognoscenti even though his books were banned. Even before his first two major works were published in America, Englishman Lawrence Durrell had announced that "American literature today begins and ends with the meaning of what Miller has done." [4]

After World War II, Miller "was extolled in the French literary press as the most outstanding American writer." [5] By 1956 Miller was the third-best-selling American writer in Japan, after Hemingway and Steinbeck.

Miller's influence in America despite censorship was widespread. The *Saturday Review* noted in 1957 that Miller's central thesis is that "the world is a great womb, where life begins and then moves toward death. With such a thesis, of course, he has been paid the supreme compliment of imitation by more avant-garde writers than perhaps any other experimental writer now living." [6]

The two new major literary voices in the United States in the forties, Maxwell Geismar states, were Richard Wright and Henry Miller. In a sense, they were "underground writers." Wright brought the voice of the southern Negro into American literature, while Miller

> carried forward the sexual revolution in our letters. The celebrated "revolt of the flesh" which, in the history of the naturalistic movement, had assumed an importance equal to that of its social criticism, Miller indeed now extended to the point of a defiant and satiric sensuality which mocked at all our Anglo-Saxon and middle-class restraints and conventions, if not indeed at all the goals and values of modern society as a whole.[7]

Because they had instinctively chosen to be "subterranean writers," Wright and Miller were more powerful and authentic literary voices than such conventional novelists as John O'Hara and James Gould Cozzens.

> They marked the true ending of the great literary movement— call it naturalism, call it realism—which had lasted for half a century in American letters, which had done its work and left its mark. And perhaps, like the classic figures in the Greek Myths, they also felt the need to go underground in order to find new sources of life, and new directions for their work.[8]

Miller's influence has extended to such prominent Beats as Lawrence Ferlinghetti, Jack Kerouac, Allen Ginsberg, Gregory Corso, and William Burroughs. But many other, more sophisticated writers have written in the penumbra of Miller's literary shadow.

Since *Tropic of Cancer* was published in 1934, Rexroth remarked, its "form has become the foremost fashion in modern literature." [9] By 1961, Terry Southern could flatly state:

> Henry Miller is our culture of today, both in his work and in the image he has created of himself as an artist. A proof of this is that despite the extremely wide acceptance of another image— that of Ernest Hemingway—the young writer today rejects it

for that of Miller. These two images are antithetical, and the difference between them is, of course, crucial. It is the difference between a young man in a Brooks Brothers suit and a young man without a tie . . . it is . . . the difference between the would-be professional and the would-be artist.[10]

Much has already been implied or directly stated about Miller's importance in loosening the prose form. By ignoring the art forms, Karl Shapiro declared, by writing the auto-biographical novel, Miller furthered literature for all writers.[11] Even Widmer conceded:

Miller importantly contributed to the increasingly dominant and major poetic-naturalistic American styles—surreal, obscene, fantastic, iconoclastic, learned, colloquial, lavish, and desperate—which, in their mixing of low and high elements, provide an increased richness of language and awareness. Put another way, Miller's work—especially his early writings—have provided *ground* for such poetic-fantastic comedies of alienation as Algren's *A Walk on the Wild Side,* Ellison's *Invisible Man,* Bellow's *Henderson the Rain King,* and Heller's *Catch-22.* Miller's violent fantasies also appear to be having some direct effect on the early 1960's writing of Norman Mailer. And critics have rightly noted that a delightful bawdy comedy of American rebelliousness abroad, J. P. Donleavy's *The Ginger Man,* belongs to the *Tropic of Cancer* tradition of wild nihilistic humor. Miller's best work partakes of this major direction of our literature—the sardonic, physical, rebellious, and expansive tradition of American comedy.[12]

All of which seems an impressive enough list of influence-credentials for any artist. But the Miller influence has created ferment in two other areas, areas vital to the realistic writer.

In his famous Open Letters to the *New Republic* in 1943 Miller called attention to the plight of the artist in this country. By doing so he became the hero, and symbol, of the creative artist in America. This, along with his writings, has probably brought about more understanding for the artist than the efforts of any other American writer.

As Terry Southern pointed out, one of the crucial problems

in American literary creation has been how to construct believable dialogue without the use of four-letter words.[13] Genuine artists deplore and battle the censors' intrusion in this area which seriously hampers sincere and meaningful self-expression. Henry Miller's life and art have been consecrated to the overthrow of this tyranny over words. He is the seminal figure in this American stylistic revolution which has aroused the fury of the censors.[14] Given Miller's character and his desire to depict life as he experienced it, one would expect him to be in the vanguard of this movement. Concomitant with the publication of *Cancer* in America came a major breakthrough in the use of realistic language. And with the breakthrough, the idea that sex in literature when accompanied by four-letter words is obscene was also shattered.

In almost every art medium, when the form becomes so restrictive that it threatens and stifles the creativity of those working in that form, a steadfast, uncompromising artist appears to slash the bonds, once again allowing others to create freely. In our time, in literature, we were fortunate in having two such artists: William Faulkner and Henry Miller.

The difference between the two is that Faulkner fought the traditional literary battle that the young artist has to fight before he receives recognition in his country. Miller not only had to traverse this literary battlefield, he also had to contend with censorship on grounds of obscenity. Faulkner, though viciously attacked, was consistently published in the United States. Miller's work was viciously attacked *and* consistently banned.

Before proceeding, it might be well to examine briefly the positions manned by official and unofficial censors of Miller's works, and then look at the censors' foes, which include the United States Supreme Court.

The censors feel that the moral fiber of America is being rotted away by obscenity or pornography (they make no distinction between the two words), and that Miller's books are prime examples of obscenity. Quoting such persons as Clarence Keating of the Citizens for Decent Literature and J. Edgar

Hoover of the FBI, the censors hold that there is a correlation between the rise in both juvenile delinquency and adult crime and the ready availability in recent years of obscene materials. Censors ignore the attraction that taboos have for the public, and press for illegal and legal bans against readers of any age having access to what the censors themselves regard as obscene. Though they have gnawing fears for others who read such material, most suppressors of vice claim personal immunity to any such ill effects. In an American society and world situation which breed anxiety, it is no doubt a truthful observation that more often than not the censors' fears are founded upon their own compulsions and frustrations. But that does not lessen their effectiveness as censors—it merely adds a shrillness to their voice that makes it, many times, more appealing to the part of the American public that wants to be told what it should read.

Censors come in all sizes and shapes. Many are members of church committees, parent-teacher associations, Daughters of the American Revolution, American Legion, etc. Many are law enforcement officers. Whatever their backgrounds and associations, they are all censors—they are sure of what should be read or seen or heard, and through some channel of authority or influence they are able to enforce their views.

Facing these haunted foes of questionable literature are libertarians, most artists, and some newspaper and book publishers. Most would uphold the stand taken by the great defender of freedom of expression in America, the Civil Liberties Union. This stand is that the hallmark of American civilization is freedom of expression. What we have achieved, what we are, and what we represent to the world, we owe to freedom of expression. When this is appreciated, and when the dangers of an opposing policy are understood, then there can be no hesitation in taking the stand—No Censorship. Miller's faithful followers and allies, eyeing distastefully an American society teetering on a seesaw of sexual suppression and sexual exploitation, would support Karl Shapiro's observation that Miller is one of the few healthy Americans alive today, and that "the circulation of his books would do more to wipe out the obscenities of Broadway, Hollywood, and Madison Avenue than a full-scale social revolution." [15]

If one of the two clear stands on censorship (censorship or no censorship) were taken by each of the groups involved in this battle, the obscenity problem in America would be complex enough. But within the groups themselves are people and organizations who favor halfway or quarter-way measures. *Some* control, they believe, is necessary, if only to "protect" minors. And in some instances their belief in the necessity for some control stems primarily from their concern for children. (Trying to thrust from the mind, no doubt, that parents, ideally, should have sole responsibility for their children's reading.) No definition of obscenity, legal or otherwise, is acceptable to all persons in this battle. Add to this confusion of aims the various levels of control of questionable literature in our pluralistic society—from extralegal pressures by private groups through official actions by city, county, state, and federal officers —and the truly demoralizing and chaotic state of affairs begins to be seen. Mix in then what is known to happen all too often —when the word obscenity drifts in the door, unchaperoned, reason tends to fly out the window[16]—and you have a Molotov cocktail capable of setting fires in most American communities. And it has.

Shielding the libertarians and their right to read, especially from 1945 onward, is the United States Supreme Court. Before the Civil War there was little obscenity censorship. After the war, in the 1870's, Anthony Comstock, using the Hicklin rule, started a forty-year reign of terror that had even H. L. Mencken submitting manuscripts to censors for approval. The Hicklin rule came from an 1868 English court case, *Queen v. Hicklin*.[17] Under its definition of obscenity—anything that tends to deprave and corrupt those whose minds are susceptible—censors have ever since flailed purveyors of pornography and of great books. In 1873, Comstock engineered congressional passage of a comprehensive law (the Comstock Act) that barred obscene literature from the mails. (He then became a special agent of the Postal Inspection Service to help enforce it.)

Censorship activities by the Postmaster General and his forty thousand post offices were not curtailed until *Hannegan v. Esquire, Inc.* (1945) and the *Lady Chatterley* case in the Federal Second Circuit Court of Appeals, *Grove Press, Inc. v. Christenberry* (1960).

The Customs Bureau's role in obscenity censorship was upstaged when the Tariff Act was amended in 1930 to allow the Secretary of the Treasury to admit classics and books of recognized value. When Judge Woolsey decided in favor of Joyce's *Ulysses* in 1933, books of "recognized value" (but not *Lady Chatterley* or the *Tropics,* for example) were emancipated from Customs censorship.

The issue of constitutional protection for those charged with publishing or selling obscene literature reached the United States Supreme Court for the first time in *Doubleday & Co. v. New York* (1948). The book up for burning was Edmund Wilson's *Memoirs of Hecate County.* Doubleday argued that fiction and nonfiction treating sex problems could be suppressed only when the publication created a "clear and present danger" to some substantial interest of the state. This basic constitutional issue remained unresolved when the Court divided equally and the ban on *Hecate County* was sustained. But starting in 1957 a series of Supreme Court decisions established that court as one of the bulwarks against censorship in America. In *Butler v. Michigan* (1957) the Court ruled a Michigan statute based on the Hicklin rule unconstitutional, stating that the statute reduced the Michigan adult population to reading only what is fit for children. And Michigan adults were thereby allowed to read John Howard Griffin's *The Devil Rides Outside.* In *Roth v. United States* (1957) the Hicklin rule was officially dismissed, along with the "clear and present danger" test developed in other decisions. For the first time the Supreme Court decided officially that obscenity was not within the area of speech protected by the First Amendment. Censorship was justified when "to the average person, applying contemporary community standards, the dominant theme of the material taken as a whole appeals to the prurient interest," but all writings with the slightest redeeming social importance were protected. The Roth definition of obscenity was further delineated in an ensuing series of *per curiam* decisions which suggested that only true pornography—that which is utterly without redeeming social importance—should be left for the censor. In *Smith v. California* (1959) the Court further restricted the censor by declaring that an essential element to the crime of selling obscenity was *scienter:* the person must know the contents of the publication before he can be prosecuted. In *Manual Enterprises v. Day* (1962) the Court held that proof of another element must be present before an obscenity conviction—that of "patent offensiveness."

But the censors seized upon the Roth definition of obscenity as being paramount, and misinterpreted it to their own advantage. Such lawyers as Gertz and Rembar stressed that *Roth* necessarily exempted material of social value from obscenity prosecution. "But the decision was written in such a way as to make the censors believe that if material were obscene, then, by definition, it had no social value and could be the subject of prosecution," Gertz says. Censorship struggles have revolved around this basic point ever since that decision.[18]

Anticensorship forces received a momentary setback in *Times Film Corporation v. Chicago* (1961), when a sharply divided court upheld the right of Chicago and any other locality to preview and license films and to withhold them from the public. Not *all* prior restraints of expression were necessarily unconstitutional.[19]

Despite this decision, when Grove Press decided to publish *Tropic of Cancer* in 1961, it appeared that it would be favored with an enlightened Supreme Court. Whether the rest of the United States would be equally enlightened remained to be seen.

4
THE TRIALS AND TRIBULATIONS OF CANCER—

What happened to *Tropic of Cancer* had broader significance, of course, than the impact upon Grove Press or Henry Miller. With the American publication of *Cancer,* a new and critical phase in the continuing struggle over freedom of expression in literature began.

From the very beginning, in Paris in the 1930's, *Cancer* was in trouble. When Obelisk publisher Jack Kahane first read the manuscript at his country home in France, he was deeply stirred. This Englishman, publisher of salacious novels as well as books of noted authors, said this of *Cancer*: "At last! . . . I had read the most terrible, the most sordid, the most magnificent manuscript that had ever fallen into my hands; nothing I had yet received was comparable to it for the splendour of its writing, the fathomless depth of its despair, the savour of its portraiture, the boisterousness of its humour. . . . I was exalted by the triumphant sensation of all explorers who have at last fallen upon the object of their years of search. I had in my hands a work of genius and it had been offered to me for publication." After this emotional outburst, however, and after signing a contract with Miller, Kahane waited two years before he published the book, in English, in Paris. Then he had to have a guarantee against financial loss from Anaïs Nin.

Kahane took every precaution to keep *Cancer's* publication shrouded in secrecy. He placed an almost prohibitive price of fifty francs on the novel. An instructive leaflet to Paris bookstores cautioned, *Ce volume ne doit pas etré exposé en vitrine.* ("This volume must not be displayed in the window.") But soon after publication stray copies reached England and the United States—and *Cancer* was promptly banned in both countries. Almost by word-of-mouth recommendations alone, *Cancer* went into its fifth Paris edition before World War II and was translated into three languages. Unscrupulous publishers brought out pirated editions in such places as Vienna, Budapest, Amsterdam, and Shanghai. Miller never received any royalties on these sales.

Through the years, Europeans were amazed at the number of Americans unaware of Miller and his prose, and the impact of his books on their country and the world. But the literati knew and read Miller's works. And American GI's in Paris bought the book and surreptitiously brought it through customs when they came home.

In 1948, Ernest J. Besig thought the book-legging had gone far enough. He tried importing the two *Tropics* into the United States openly through San Francisco customs and was stopped. Federal Judge Louis E. Godman, upholding the ban, said that he was protecting "the dignity of the human person and the stability of the family unit, which are the cornerstone of our system of society." Ten years later a critic commented that one of the intellectual disgraces of the English-speaking world was the fact that *Cancer* still could not circulate legally in the United States and England.[1] But, as the Supreme Court decisions through these years suggest, times were changing, and the social milieu by 1961 seemed open enough for the publication of *Cancer*.

For example, in 1960 *Publishers' Weekly* reported that the hard-core pornography line

enunciated a number of times by the U.S. courts and especially by the U.S. Supreme Court in the past several years . . . now seems to be filtering down through the hierarchy of government and finding a certain acceptance among jurists and legislators at state and municipal levels.[2]

The free circulation of *Lady Chatterley's Lover,* banned in the United States since 1928, was symptomatic of a new pro-freedom-to-read atmosphere. Critics such as Alfred Kazin and Malcolm Cowley were struck by the literary trends and the public's acceptance of them. Observers of the sexual mores of the country, with the backing of the Kinsey reports (circulating freely in the country as best-sellers), were speaking of the American sexual revolution.[3] Writing in 1954, Lockhart and McClure observed that it was common knowledge that in recent years there had been wide distribution and sale of books and other publications dealing with many aspects of sex "from a great many points of view—psychology, sociology, anthropology, education, birth control, marital relations, sex instruction, and sex techniques." [4]

One measure of what was happening is given by the success of *Playboy* magazine, with its formula of racy jokes and foldout nude pictures. *Playboy* editor Hugh Hefner solicited only prestige advertisers and printed quality fiction and non-fiction along with the risqué, so that his audience included a sizable number of serious and sophisticated readers. Starting in 1953 with an initial press run of 70,000, *Playboy* circulation jumped to 175,000 in 1954 and to 350,000 in 1955. By August 1964 it had reached 2,489,000, and by March 1965 it had attained three million circulation. Playboy Key Clubs sprang up all over the nation, so that persons could do in private what the advertising and entertainment industries and the Miss America pageants were doing in public—pay tribute to the female body.

A girl who had posed nude for calendar pictures became the American sex symbol, and the calendars that Marilyn Monroe had graced became collectors' items. Even during the three-year censorship uproar caused by the publication of *Cancer,* another kind of woman became something of a symbol of sexual freedom. Offering such advice as, I consider it "complete lunacy" not to have "slept with the man you're going to marry," Helen Gurley Brown's *Sex and the Single Girl* not only was not banned, it became a best-seller and was made into a movie.

Such free-wheeling sex thinking was not unopposed, naturally, and other developments too brought out censorship forces that did not augur well for Grove Press's latest publishing venture.

Four congressional committees investigated "dirty" literature in the 1950's. During one of these investigations Senator Estes Kefauver reported 50,000 complaints of solicitations for pornography mailed to juveniles in 1958. In 1959 this figure increased to 700,000. In the year of *Cancer's* publication, New York Postmaster Robert K. Christenberry reported that the mailing of pornographic films, magazines, books and circulars had increased nationally 300 to 600 per cent in 1960.

Simultaneously with the growing freedom-to-read, a discernible trend in book censorship had also been developing since World War II:

> The unsettled state of the world, the rise in juvenile delinquency, and a general feeling that moral standards have been relaxed, led to a search for a cause for the current state of anxiety. Many felt that so-called "bad books," particularly those read by young people, were the reason for social upset.
>
> Book censorship occurred before World War II. But the distinguishing difference is that while the major pressures in the pre-World War II period came from government attempts to ban books and other printed matter, during the last twenty years the heaviest pressure has come from private censorship bodies. These groups have by economic pressures or other intimidatory action sought to remove what they regard as offensive books from circulation.[5]

Publishers' Weekly also commented on the American scene that *Cancer* was to disrupt so soon, and what that authoritative journal reported was disquieting:

> In 1960, trade books on retail sale generally enjoyed a greater freedom from official censorship than at any other time in recent years. But while official censorship attitudes and practices were liberalized on the whole, extra-legal censorship pressures in-

creased. And while publishers and their retail and wholesale distributors bore less of the direct brunt of censorship than in some previous years, the pressures of book censorship were intensified on the schools.[6]

For five consecutive years starting with 1958, textbooks in the schools were banned and burned, stripped of many passages that would have enlightened students, and assailed again and again as subversive documents undermining our children's faith in their nation. Textbooks came under fire in nearly a third of the state legislatures from New England to California and from Wisconsin to Texas.[7]

Although one major citizen's censorship group was waning by 1960—the National Organization for Decent Literature with its lists of proscribed publications—the Citizens for Decent Literature had stepped into the vacuum. A sharp increase in the practice of abruptly prosecuting news dealers on criminal charges without forewarning resulted. CDL

> carefully avoids the much-criticized practices of the NODL. CDL counsels against telling any dealer what not to sell. Instead, CDL stirs up public agitation against magazines thought to be obscene, and encourages and assists law enforcement officials in the prosecution of obscenity cases.[8]

The founder of the CDL, Clarence Keating, in May 1960 wrote in these intemperate terms:

> The case for the substantial majority of the American people . . . is seldom heard *due to the control of most areas of mass communication* by a vociferous minority whose position is not only opposed to the basic Judeo-Christian morality of the Nation . . . but actually seems to violently advocate its overthrow.[9]

Stating the censorship forces' case in another way, while still assaulting the press, a more astute procensorship scholar, Terence J. Murphy, notes:

> Only in recent years has public opposition to legislative proposals to control obscenity appeared. *The new critics are, for the most part, spokesmen of the communication industries,* and the Ameri-

can Civil Liberties Union and its followers. These same groups, unsuccessful in the legislative chambers, have frequently transferred the conflict from the legislative to the judicial arena. They have generally been more successful with the courts than with the lawmakers. Thus the line has come to be drawn with the legislatures and *civic groups* on one side and the courts with the American Civil Liberties Union, other libertarians, and the *communication industries* on the other side.[10]

Into this arena of libertarians versus censors, *Tropic of Cancer* plunged. The publication was not happenstance, but a venture long planned by a book publisher who was also an opponent of censorship. American book-publishing history reveals that these two roles are seldom combined.

Our dark era in book publishing came in 1870 and lasted to 1915. Most book publishing is centered in New York, and during this period manuscripts were submitted to Anthony Comstock or the New York Society for the Suppression of Vice for their approval. Publishers began fighting this kind of censorship in 1915, but in the late thirties they once again grew timid, preferring the background to the battleground. As they do today. What results from such an approach? Timidity naturally encourages the censorious. Morris Ernst and Alan Schwartz write:

> More important, it helps produce unconsidered laws on censorship. A street-corner newsstand owner does not make enough profit on the sale of any magazine to warrant the expense of a court defense. It is cheaper to plead guilty. . . . No wonder vice hunters and police usually level their guns, not at the wealthier publisher who selects the manuscript (and who is usually responsible for its publication), but at relatively impecunious retailers who order a few copies, often as samples, and usually on consignment.
>
> In historic terms, perhaps these publishers do not deserve the richness of our freedom of the press. Perhaps freedom of speech and press should belong only to those who dig their heels into the ground and say: "This is my own imprint. I and I alone shall defend it. I do not choose to hide behind the bookseller or the newsstand dealer." [11]

"Publishers," ACLU's Reitman adds, "are not always the most courageous people, particularly when their economic interests are concerned." [12]

But it *is* expensive to defend all lawsuits on a book and fight a case all the way to the Supreme Court, and publishers today cannot be utterly condemned for personally evasive actions. As Ernst and Schwartz point out, however,

> we can at least deplore the failure of those interested in the free dissemination of all literature (perhaps subject only to *judicial* censorship) from establishing a climate of opinion strong enough to counterbalance the activity of the censorious private pressure groups. True, there have been some, but they are too few and their voices weak. [13]

Jason Epstein, a vice-president of Random House, recently chided his publishing colleagues for not seeking out obscure polemicists with radical proposals to make, for not establishing that "climate of opinion" Ernst and Schwartz mentioned. Publishers, he said, are not bold spirits.

> Indeed, they have been so remiss in this respect as to have helped create the impression that such writers should expect as a matter of course not to see their work in print at all—at least not for quite a while. *Over the years the cumulative effect of this attitude may conceivably have been to discourage almost everyone but the genuinely insane from trying to say what he may in his heart have wanted to say,* and to turn whatever his talents and virtues may have been to silence or into the kind of product with which publishers are accustomed to deal. [14]

Not only has the effect been upon writers, Epstein suggests:

> I notice these days a certain despair among my colleagues in the publishing business, more conscious in the wiser ones, but still enough to trouble those who are not so sensitive to their predicament. The joy seems to have gone out of their work and, while the industry thrives and everyone seems to be making money, almost everyone sooner or later gets around to the drudgery and boredom of it all. Everywhere I seem to hear (and it is not just my own echo) that it is not what it used to be in the book business; that everything has grown too complicated;

that the simple pleasure one once could take in publishing a worthwhile book comes less often now and is soon engulfed in all the effort one spends just to keep the business going.

I wonder if the reason for this may not be that . . . we all know . . . what we should be doing—because we are still free to do it—but that none of us is really doing it at all. Perhaps we have even become at last like our cousins on the big magazines or on television or in the universities—frozen in the system and powerless, like them, to do anything about it.[15]

There was one book publisher that Jason Epstein surely was *not* referring to—Barney Rosset of Grove Press, publisher of *Cancer*.

Rosset acquired Grove Press for $3,000 in 1952. From the then expiring company's inventory of three titles he built Grove Press into a thriving, reputable avant-garde publishing house. He introduced the American public to such authors as Samuel Beckett, Jean Genet, Brendan Behan, Shelagh Delaney, Eugène Ionesco, Alain Robbe-Grillet and William Burroughs. Older, established authors' works were also published by Grove Press —books by Herman Melville, Mark Twain, and Henry James. Steadily increasing the number of titles published (fifty in 1958; sixty-one in 1959; ninety-four in 1960), Rosset and Grove Press by 1961—the year of the publication of *Cancer*— had published approximately five hundred books. Grove's best-sellers in 1961 were all plays which appeared on and off Broadway in the fall: *The Apple,* by Jack Gelber, *The Caretaker,* by Harold Pinter, and *Happy Days,* by Beckett. Grove Press titles included fiction and nonfiction, hardcover and softcover —novels, poetry, plays, and works on science, history, criticism, art, and music. Original titles were published in quality paperbacks. And in 1957 Rosset founded the avant-garde literary magazine, *Evergreen Review*—1967 circulation, well over 100,-000.[16]

Perhaps Grove's and Rosset's most significant contribution to the publishing world and the American literary scene, however, is their contribution to freedom of expression. As Henry Heifetz pointed out in 1964:

The last five years have seen immense changes in the criteria of both legality and respectability applied to writing which handles sex. Grove Press, which swept into the big time on the first waves of the Beat Generation, and its lawyer, Ephraim London, have played an important role—through the *Lady Chatterley's Lover* and *Tropic of Cancer* court fights—in turning the legal tide against censorship.[17]

"Rosset is a remarkable man," wrote Chicago lawyer Elmer Gertz. "He has made more contributions to the cause of literary freedom than any other publisher of our day." [18] ACLU believes Grove Press serves an important civil liberties function by challenging efforts to censor the books they publish.[19] Perhaps the greatest tribute comes from the book industry itself, in an article in the March 1962 issue of *Paperback Trade News,* "Grove Press: Little Giant of Publishing." [20]

Barney Rosset's goal as a publisher, the article points out, is: "To do things which stimulate people, to help them see new things, to broaden and irritate them, to give them pleasure and always to keep probing." There is only one way to be a publisher, Rosset declares: "If you feel a book has literary merit you publish it. If you get arrested in the process you fight it." In a free society, there is nothing that an adult should not see. To withhold questionable material from adults is dangerous. And as for censorship, Rosset believes the ultimate responsibility lies with the parent.

Rosset believes that American publishers have not distinguished themselves by their daring in the twentieth century. "It is inexplicable to me," he wrote, "why *Lady Chatterley's Lover* was not published many years before we published it in this country. And the same holds true for *Tropic of Cancer*."

Rosset's reasons for publishing *Lady Chatterley's Lover* and *Tropic of Cancer* are quite simple. In a letter to M. Henri Filipacchi, a French publishing figure, he wrote: "I am personally anxious to publish the books [*Cancer* and *Capricorn*], both because I have always admired them, and because I have started with *Lady Chatterley* a battle against censorship which

I would like to carry on." [21] But Rosset's commitment to *Cancer* should be commented upon. One author writing about why a book sells said:

> Nearly every best-seller, classic or claptrap, shares one quality —it has called forth commitment from those interested in its publication. Commitment, by the author, the publisher, or a third agency (the early readers, perhaps, or someone else passionately devoted to its cause), is what sells most books.
>
> Commitment somehow manages to make itself felt, to give a book an aura. Commitment can enhance an author's reputation or transcend his talent. It can overcome all ordinary resistance —terrible reviews, the house's previous bad luck with similar titles, or the timing, or the competition. [22]

Grove publisher Barney Rosset had just such a commitment for *Tropic of Cancer*. He had become interested in the novel when, as an undergraduate at Swarthmore, he wrote a paper on Henry Miller for an American literature course. (Entitled "Henry Miller Versus 'Our Way of Life,'" it received a B-minus.) His belief in the book as a literary masterpiece, and his basic antipathy to censorship, led to Rosset's first attempts to publish it after winning the *Lady Chatterley* case. But Henry Miller was surprisingly reluctant to agree to the publishing venture. It took three years of persistent wooing before Miller capitulated.

A key figure in the whole affair was Maurice Girodias, then publisher of Olympia Press in Paris. Rosset describes Girodias' role:

> Maurice Girodias' part in the publication by Grove Press of Henry Miller's *Tropics* was very important. He personally introduced me to Mr. Miller; he argued on my behalf with Mr. Miller to allow me to be the publisher of the books; and in various ways he was a vital force in the whole project. All of this recent assistance was, as you know, of course, preceded by the long history of Maurice Girodias and his father [Jack Kahane] having published Henry Miller's work. This naturally put Mr. Girodias in a key position to be an influence upon Mr. Miller's arrival at a decision about American publication. [23]

Girodias first wrote to Rosset from Paris in March 1959. Girodias told Rosset he was writing because of a letter he had received from Henry Miller. *Cancer* had been allowed through Customs for serious study by a professor. What a pity, Miller wrote, that Girodias no longer had the rights to *Cancer*. Girodias then told Rosset how he had lost the rights of *Cancer* to the Parisian publishing house of Hachette through what he referred to as sharp business practices, and outlined the strategy Rosset should follow to obtain *Cancer* publication rights— down to dealing with M. Henri Filipacchi's vanity: treat Filipacchi "just as if he were the top man at Hachette's," even though he isn't. Girodias assured Rosset that Filipacchi was "awfully vain," and that the "rights" decision rested essentially with him. Writing "to him directly (which the other publishers won't think of doing) will give you an initial advantage." Girodias warned Rosset not to mention him to Filipacchi because "he hates me." Rosset was also directed to write Henry Miller and his agent, Michael Hoffman. "The deal will probably have to go through Hoffman as well, and Miller will consult him in any case." The Customs incident, Girodias remarked, "shows that there is an emphatic change in the situation." In only a few years or months, he predicted, there would probably be publication possibilities for *Cancer* in America. More detailed instructions then followed:

It must be an impressive offer; if I were you, I would offer a $10,000 advance, payable half upon signature, half upon publication or at latest one year after the contract has been signed. If you think you can offer more, all the better: you will not lose money on that in any case. The royalty could be 10, 12½ and 15 per cent for the first 10,000, the next 10,000, and above, respectively (they may ask for more, but it gives you bargaining possibilities; and they will be more impressed by the size of the advance than by the actual rate of royalties).

Up to now, Miller has been firmly opposed to expurgation. But . . . explain to him that you want to follow that procedure in order to ward off trouble during the transitional period.

Rosset was to tell Miller that the unexpurgated edition would follow later—Miller no doubt would agree to this.

None of this scheme, however, was to be mentioned to Fili-pacchi. Tell him, Girodias urged, that you'll risk immediate publication, which no other publisher will do. Insist on the United States and open market rights for other countries, except the United Kingdom. "Thus I will be able to distribute for you in France, and symbolically recover my lost property."

Rosset must have written to Miller immediately, because on April 3, 1959, Miller replied to him from Big Sur. "Whether you or New Directions do *Cancer,*" Miller wrote Rosset, "one thing is certain. I will never agree to any cuts or modifications of the text. Not if I were offered ten times as much. For America I will never make any concessions." And the very next day Miller added:

> I think any attempt to publish these books [*Tropics*] here is still premature, but I shall see what my agent, Dr. Hoffman, has to say . . . [but] even if the Treasury Department were to lift the ban on these books of mine, which they have not done! the question of publication and circulation here in America is another matter entirely. Before any move here is made, it would be important to know what might be the attitude of our Postmaster General.

By contract, Miller wrote, New Directions Publishing Corporation had first chance to publish the books.

Rosset assured Miller that there had been no trouble with *Lady Chatterley's Lover,* and that

> The publication of *Lolita* was another big step forward and I think that the time may well have arrived when we can publish another great book, namely *Tropic of Cancer.*
> We would most strongly advise against attempting to get any opinion from the Postmaster General or any local authorities. We have found that that can only create problems where perhaps none exist. We believe that we are as competent as anybody to act in this field. I believe that our legal advice is of the highest quality and the most aggressive in *fighting for freedom of the Press.* I assure you that if we decide to go ahead with *Tropic*

of Cancer—with your permission—we will endeavor to do it in a highly competent and organized manner.[24]

The publishing of *Lady Chatterley,* Miller retorted,

> is, of course, a big step forward. But how slowly everything proceeds. The *Cancer* will be 25 years old this September. Soon I will be dead. I've lived so long without my rightful earnings I'm used to it now. One has to die first, if you notice, before the ball gets rolling. . . .
>
> My own view is that it may take another fifty to a hundred years before these banned books of mine can circulate freely in this country. But I may be wrong.[25]

Relenting on his nonexpurgation vow, Miller added:

> What I sometimes think is that the way to start the ball rolling is to bring out *Cancer,* let's say, with all the censorable words, phrases, sentences, paragraphs deleted. That's what Girodias did with the French version of *Sexus.*

The unexpurgated editions of *Sexus,* Miller added, were given to the reviewers. Rosset said that it might be wise to do some censoring but that he would really rather consider that matter at the last moment. Actually, he was strongly against any expurgation at all.

Warning Miller of possible piracy in America, Rosset said:

> The *Tropics* are susceptible to piracy and I think a contract with me—or New Directions, or somebody else—for American publication, would strengthen your grip on your own work.[26]

But Miller, for his own personal reasons, balked:

> Wait and see what happens with *Chatterley.* If the prospects (later) seem favorable [we'll go ahead].
>
> Frankly, I am beginning to doubt that I ever want to see an American edition of these banned books. *The notoriety, the unpleasantness involved, seem hardly worth the price.* I have always felt deep down that no great change can be expected in America—either on the part of our legislators or our judges. As for the public—it is indifferent, it seems to me. The vast majority, I mean. I am in no hurry to make myself a scapegoat for what seems like a lost cause.[27]

Again Rosset tried to reassure Miller:

> I must say that I very much disagree with your idea that there would be notoriety and unpleasantness involved . . . all has been extremely pleasant thus far. *Perhaps if the United States Post Office had not banned Lady Chatterley from the mails, we would not have known how strongly in our favor the press of the United States is.* Literally, tens of editorials have appeared day by day in papers of cities and towns in the north, south, east and west. In addition to that, we have been deluged with favorable letters from throughout the country. Thus, *I cannot say that the public is indifferent—quite to the contrary, it seems extremely involved in the matter of censorship.* I am absolutely convinced that you would not in any way be made a scapegoat. I also feel quite positive that no lost cause is involved.[28]

Rosset's estimation of the country's censorship climate is interesting. No doubt he was sincere in his assurances to Miller that not much furor would be raised with the *Cancer* publication.

Rosset urged Miller not to "wait and see" what happens to *Lady Chatterley* as James Laughlin of New Directions had earlier advised. "That," said Rosset, "does not strike me as being a particularly courageous" attitude. Rosset offered Miller $2,500 as an immediate advance against future royalties of the *Tropics.* The stipulation was that if the two books were published in the country during the next four years, Grove Press would be the company to do it. If Miller did not grant permission to publish in the next four years, he could still keep the $2,500. If he *did* grant permission, a total advance of $10,000 would be paid against royalties to be earned by the *Tropics.*

Miller answered one month later refusing permission to publish *Cancer:* "I am still of the opinion that the *Chatterley* decision, like the *Ulysses,* is an exceptional one, and would have no bearing on the treatment accorded my works." [29] Rosset replied:

> I definitely do not agree with you in your feeling that the *Lady Chatterley* decision was an exceptional one. I think that it will set future standards, just as the *Ulysses* decision did. We

believe that the *Ulysses* decision directly led to the *Lady Chatterley* decision.

I therefore think that your books could be published here and that any court fight which came up would be won by the publisher.[30]

Rosset, having been "outbid or outmaneuvered" on another best-seller earlier (*Lolita*), was working on all fronts to corral the *Tropics* for Grove Press. He wrote to Hachette's Filipacchi on August 29, 1959, discussing his problems. Miller was holding back, Rosset felt, for these reasons:

> a) He says he is not very much interested in profit he may derive from the publication of his books in America. b) He says he does not like the idea of the publicity which will follow the publication of the *Tropics*. c) He says that he has a moral obligation towards New Directions to give them preference (but New Directions never offered to publish the *Tropics,* and may never do so). d) Finally, I feel that he has gotten accustomed to his status of "literary outcast" *and has some difficulty adjusting himself to the idea of becoming an entirely legitimate "great American writer."* [31]

Miller's reluctance to sign the contract, Rosset wrote, might also stem from his agent's feeling that Hachette's share on the American rights was too high. Rosset advised getting together with Hachette and Miller so that he could modify his proposal.

Rosset kept on with the job of convincing Miller. He visited him in Big Sur, with no success. He wrote once again about the piracy possibilities (having just been pirated himself on *Lady Chatterley*). Just as *Ulysses* had been pirated, *Cancer,* he wrote, could also be. He suggested $10,000 for an option on the *Tropics* with a guarantee of $50,000. "I believe," he wrote, that while

> it is impossible to prevent pirated editions to be published on the strength of the existing copyright laws, I could attempt to prevent publication on the grounds of unfair competition if I could prove that I had a substantial interest in the matter; having paid $10,000 for an option on the publication rights would probably

be considered as a sufficient interest to justify the court ruling in our favor.[32]

In the agreement would be a stipulation that if one of the books were pirated, Grove Press would immediately be able to publish. The contract meanwhile would be signed when Miller decided that the books should appear, "whether it be in six months or ten years."

Two days later, Miller, weakening, dramatically inquired: "There are drastic changes in my life which I'd like to make right now. Travel is only one of them. I'm assuming that if you offer fifty thousand as a guarantee it implies earnings running much higher, no?" [33]

The next month Miller notified Rosset that New Directions had released the rights to the *Tropics*. When I asked Rosset why New Directions had released the *Tropics* instead of publishing them themselves, he was unable to tell me: "They had ample opportunity to do so. I even offered to be their partner. In the end, they released all rights to the books in a most gentlemanly fashion." Years earlier, however, Miller had publicly condemned James Laughlin of New Directions for refusing to publish his banned books. In "Another Open Letter" he bitterly wrote:

> About 1938 or '39 James Laughlin IV of New Directions began to make it known that he would bring out in unexpurgated form an American edition of the books published by the Obelisk Press, Paris. To date nothing of the kind has happened. A great many people think him to be my champion and benefactor. Nothing could be further from the truth.[34]

In the same letter informing Rosset of New Directions' release of the book rights, Miller asked him to write his friend Huntington Cairns, director of the National Gallery of Art, for an opinion. Rosset asked Cairns, who is often consulted by the Customs Bureau on questions of obscenity, to give a *private* opinion on the chances of winning a case if *Cancer* should go to court:

We have been pestering Henry Miller to make a contract with us for publication of *Tropic of Cancer* in this country. Naturally he is worried about possible censorship problems and, although I feel that problem is basically ours, I am writing you as per his request.[35]

Cairns' reply came two weeks later. "I would like to oblige Henry," Cairns wrote, "but I feel that in view of my official connection with the Government I should not venture an opinion." [36]

That was a strange answer for Cairns to give Rosset, for five years later, on January 25, 1965, he wrote to me:

When the *Tropic of Cancer* was first submitted to me I advised the Bureau that as the law then stood it was a prohibited importation within the meaning of Section 305 of the Tariff Act of 1930. After the *Roth* and related cases I advised the Bureau that in my opinion the book was no longer prohibited.

Certainly he could have told Rosset what he freely told me.

When I asked Rosset about Cairns' reticence, he offered this acid explanation:

Cairns is very elusive. It seems (and "seems" is all I can say) to me that he sort of clung to censorship where the "people" were concerned but felt it all right for him and a few others to read books like those of Miller—and even to be friendly with such authors. Maybe this explains why he could not advise us.[37]

Rosset continued writing persuasively to Miller:

As far as censorship problems are concerned—of course there can be some legal mishmash. We are ready to cope with it, that's all. Nobody can be *sure* of what might eventuate, but I am not worried about it and the trouble will fall on us—when and if it develops. It is perfectly possible to have local irritations—there's always some ladies' club to cry out.[38]

Although there is little more in the Grove Press files about the signing of the *Tropics* contract, other sources contribute further information on the subject. Miller left for Europe in April 1960, and in May he told one British journalist:

There's no chance that these books will ever come out in America, or in England. I have had offers from publishers who think they can now get away with it and who want to bring out the books unexpurgated, but I've turned all their offers down.

I'm a marked man: they would seize on me. In England the men who matter are solidly against me. They think I'm a sort of idiot or freak.

So what do I live on? I live on money. At the age of 68 I'm finally getting some royalties, the bulk of it from Europe.[39]

Then, while Miller was visiting a friend in Germany, his agent Michael Hoffman wrote to Rosset a few months later to say that Miller had changed his mind. Rosset discusses this in a taped interview:

What finally made Henry Miller change his mind about publishing *Cancer*? I don't know. All I know is that I tried my best over a period of time to get Miller to allow me to do *Tropic of Cancer*. It's very complex. He actually was in Hamburg, Germany, when he made the decision. He was there with a very close friend, Henry Ledig-Rowohlt, a distinguished German publisher who had published Miller books over a period of many years, and who may well have been the crucial influence in Miller's decision to permit publication.

I flew to Hamburg, where Henry signed the contract.

In a press release of April 25, 1961, Grove Press announced the signing of a $50,000-minimum contract with Henry Miller for the publication of *Tropic of Capricorn* and *Tropic of Cancer*.

5
GROVE PRESS PREPARATIONS

To help induce favorable rulings for *Tropic of Cancer* in future court actions, Grove Press planned its publication very carefully. First of all the announcement of the signing was in good taste, and all news releases emanating from the company thereafter were of the same character. On May 15, 1961, Grove Press released for the mass media a biographical sketch which stressed Henry Miller's greatness as a writer:

> Mr. Miller himself has long been acclaimed here and abroad as one of the most outstanding American writers of our time whose work has had a profound influence on the literature of this century. In 1958 he was elected to membership in the American Academy of Arts and Letters with a citation which hailed him as a writer whose "boldness of approach and intense curiosity concerning man and nature are unequaled in the prose literature of our time." [1]

A statement by the publisher followed the next day. It began in this manner:

> Announcing the forthcoming publication of *Tropic of Cancer*, Mr. Barney Rosset, publisher of Grove Press, Inc., said today: "We are proud that Henry Miller has chosen Grove Press to be the American publisher of his first and perhaps greatest novel—a work we believe to be one of the great literary accomplishments

of our time. It has taken *Tropic of Cancer* twenty-seven years to reach the shores of Mr. Miller's own country; but we take satisfaction in the fact that the maturity and intelligence of the American public now make possible here what readers abroad have been able to do for so many years—to encounter first-hand the singular genius of a great writer whose place in American and world literature is assured for all time." [2]

Although *Cancer* had been first published in English, no copyright was available because of a technicality in the United States copyright law requiring certain works to be printed in the United States within five years after publication abroad. Though the novel was now in public domain, Grove Press had taken the honorable course and signed a handsome contract with the author. The contract not only pointed up the fact that this publishing venture was a serious one in all ways, it was also designed to give weight to Grove Press's legal arguments in case of piracy.

The covers of both the hard-bound and soft-bound editions of *Cancer* were decorous. No appeal was made to sensationalism. An introduction by the poet Karl Shapiro and a preface by Anaïs Nin were included in the hardcover edition. According to Shapiro, Rosset asked him for permission to reprint his previously published essay "because he thought it would help in the trials which would come up." [3] The hardcover edition carried the relatively high price of $7.50.[4] Ten weeks had elapsed from the signing of the contract on April 15.

Advertising for *Cancer* was prepared by the firm of Sussman & Sugar, Inc., whose clients include such publishers as Random House, Harvard University Press, Simon & Schuster and Cambridge University Press. For a book of this prominence, according to Rosset, the advertising was extremely limited. It appeared only in highly reputable newspapers and magazines read by those interested in serious literature, and it emphasized the literary significance of the book. A typical advertisement is reproduced on page 252.[5]

Grove Press itself, by virtue of its total publishing list, had the necessary literary credentials to qualify as a publisher of quality books. As a serious avant-garde publisher, Rosset would be the logical person to bring out such a book as *Cancer*.

The publication date for *Cancer* was announced on June 12, 1961:

> Henry Miller's *Tropic of Cancer* will be published by Grove Press on June 24, twenty-seven years after the book was first brought out in Paris. Leading critics and writers, among them T. S. Eliot, Lawrence Durrell, John Ciardi, and Edmund Wilson, have publicly characterized the book as a modern American classic. Grove has released 40,000 copies of the book to bookstores throughout the country, and has advertised the forthcoming publication widely.[6]

Before the actual publication, as Rosset said, "legal preparations were quite thorough." First of all, the well-known attorney Ephraim London, of Brennan, London, and Buttenwieser, was retained as counsel. Second, the degree of responsibility that Grove's suppliers and distributors would bear received much thought on both sides.

The Grove Press paperback edition of *Cancer* was printed by Western Printing Company. On October 9, 1961, the day before the paperback edition was published, Mark Morse of Western sent a warranty letter to Grove, for Rosset's signature:

> Grove Press agrees to indemnify and hold Western harmless against any and all claims, demands, suits, actions, proceedings or judgments arising from Western's printing of the Grove Press Edition of *Tropic of Cancer*.

Dell Distributing, Inc., then the distributor for Grove Press paperbacks, may have thought about the coming storm somewhat earlier. On May 17, 1961, the executive vice president, William F. Callahan, Jr., wrote Rosset:

> We are exercising our prerogative of refusing to handle any title of Grove Press we deem advisable.
>
> Accordingly, we hereby disclaim any responsibility for the sale or distribution of the Grove Press edition of . . . *Cancer*.

Rosset says that Dell stopped distribution for reasons other than censorship worries, although "I guess Dell was afraid of legal costs on *Tropic of Cancer.*" As a mass market distributor, Rosset wrote, Dell has "shown more courage vis-à-vis censorship than most. Later they distributed *Fanny Hill* and *Candy* for Putnam, and *Tropic of Capricorn* for us." Macfadden Publications, Inc., took over the distribution of the paperback edition of *Cancer* under a contract which included the following clause:

> If any suit is brought, or prosecution instituted, against you or one of your officers, for selling or distributing *Tropic of Cancer* by Henry Miller, published by us, on the ground that the book is obscene, we shall undertake the defense at our own cost, provided we shall have the right to designate the attorney and provided that the books shall have been paid for. If copies of the book are seized and confiscated by government authority because the book is alleged to be obscene, you will be credited with the price paid by you or charged to you for such copies seized and confiscated.

Booksellers were reassured by special releases to them from time to time, starting before publication and continuing through the censorship ban phase of *Cancer*. But as Rosset said,

> We did more than reassure booksellers. We indemnified them against legal costs. And that is how we wandered into our enormous legal expenses. We paid for legal counsel in many, many places where a bookseller had been arrested.

Most of the legal burden was borne by Grove Press in the fighting of official and unofficial bans. Even in some cases of informal police pressure, Grove paid for legal assistance. Grove Press had already made an anticensorship name for itself by publishing and successfully defending *Lady Chatterley's Lover* two years before. Now it embarked upon a campaign which was to leave it wearing the undisputed anticensorship crown of the publishing world.

6
ON THE BATTLEGROUND

For more than a quarter of a century *Cancer* had been on the U.S. Customs Bureau's proscribed list. As we have noted, the government can ban books through Customs (300 ports of entry) and through the Post Office (more than 40,000 offices in the country). The Customs ruling on *Cancer* was challenged by Dorothy Upham, a painter, in October 1960. Having notified Customs officials in advance that she planned to bring the novel into America from Europe, Mrs. Upham was met at Idlewild Airport by Customs men, who promptly confiscated her book.

"We had planned to provoke a Customs case," Rosset told me, "but the case was provided for accidentally by Mrs. Upham."

At Grove's expense, Ephraim London was retained as attorney for Dorothy Upham. Co-attorney was ACLU's Melvin Wulf. A preliminary hearing was set for May 9, 1961. Grove announced that the outcome of the case could affect the publishing schedule for *Cancer,* but it also announced that if the trial took too long, it would not wait to publish the novel.

Grove Press revealed in an April 25, 1961, news release that London had

asked the Court not only to declare *Tropic of Cancer* not obscene, but had also asked for a judgment affirming that the
seizing of books by the Customs Authorities "is unconstitutional
and void in that it contravenes the freedom of the press." [1]

Another release of the same date disclosed that

The Motion Picture Association of America and The Independent Film Importers and Distributors of America, Inc., whose
members together represent almost all films shown in the United
States, have announced that they intend to file briefs as *amicus
curiae* supporting Mrs. Upham's position and opposing the
claimed right of the Customs Authority to censor all material
coming into the United States.

This ready-made test-case plan aborted, however. Rosset
says:

We were quite ready for it except for one unfortunate occur-
rence. The judge took many weeks to render a decision, and the
decision was that we had gone to the wrong Federal District. The
book had been seized at Idlewild Airport and we had gone into the
adjoining district. The judge said that if he had made a decision
he would have found the book not guilty, although he thought
it a terrible work.

A Grove Press newsletter to booksellers informed them:

On the legal front, Federal Judge Thomas F. Murphy refused
this week to rule on a complaint filed against the Collector of
Customs concerning the seizure of an imported copy of the
book, but did comment that, in his personal opinion, it was
"not obscene." He continued: "That is only our opinion, however; we cannot say so as a matter of law." He said the questions
of the case—obscenity and constitutionality of seizure—would
have to be judged in Brooklyn Federal Court . . .
Ephraim London, attorney for Mrs. Dorothy Upham . . .
announced . . . that he was appealing Judge Murphy's decision
to a higher court, and that he had filed an appeal with the U.S.
District Court for the Southern District of New York.

While the Upham case was on appeal, the Post Office Department seized the Grove Press hardcover edition. Three copies

were confiscated on June 12. Grove Press told the story in this release:

The United States Post Office notified Grove Press, Inc., today it had seized copies of Henry Miller's *Tropic of Cancer* pending a hearing by the department which would rule on whether the book is mailable.

Richard S. Farr, Assistant General Counsel of the Post Office Department's Fraud and Mailability Division, said that "approximately three copies" of the book are being withheld from the mails at a New York Post Office, charging that Miller's novel was "obscene, lewd, lascivious, indecent and filthy in content." [2]

In the same release, Grove fought back:

We assume that the Post Office, having once made a serious error which the courts corrected, will not make the same mistake again. The assumption seems particularly justifiable in view of the fact that the Post Office decision in the *Lady Chatterley* case was the work of one man—the former Postmaster General. We trust that the present Postmaster General is fully aware of the fact that serious and respected works of literature cannot constitutionally be excluded from the mails.

The release announced that London would represent them at the Washington and New York hearings:

Mr. London said he would oppose the Post Office seizure on the basis that Mr. Miller's book, far from being obscene, is one of the landmarks of modern American literature, and that a ban would therefore be unconstitutional. He said he would present leading writers and critics at the hearing to oppose the Post Office charge of obscenity.

How was Henry Miller taking all this? He wrote Rosset May 1 from Lausanne-Ouchy, Switzerland. No matter how dark it looks when court proceedings start, Miller said, remember that, according to three of his astrologer friends, the *Tropics* would be a howling triumph. A United Press International story with a Lisbon, Portugal, May 24, dateline quoted Miller: The decision to publish *Cancer* in the United States, he said, marked the turning point "in a too puritanical atmosphere" in that country.

> The lifting of the taboo . . . may be helpful to other writers in the future, the author said in an interview.
> "It will help them to express themselves freely."

But as brave and as cogent as these remarks for the press were, Miller was beginning to have second thoughts about the coming publications. A week later he refused Rosset's request to give *Newsweek* an interview to help the sale of *Cancer*. The reason he was refusing, he cabled from Biarritz, was that he was on the edge of a nervous breakdown.

On June 3 he wrote Rosset about *Capricorn,* which he was preparing for its new publication. He was concerned about the episode in which he reported killing a boy with a rock:

> We never did kill that boy, as you may suspect. But we *thought* we did. A malicious reviewer could make a nasty fuss over the incident—brand me as a cold-blooded murderer, even as a child. Could do us more damage perhaps than anything said about the sexual episodes.

Miller wondered how to alter it and asked for ideas. "Don't print it as it now stands!" he wrote. (Rosset later convinced him to leave it alone.) Miller complained about his "present state of nerves," and added:

> I don't know when I've been in such a state. I had to wire Eve to cancel the children's trip abroad, knowing I couldn't manage them—and not having found a suitable place to spend their vacation. I'm heartbroken. Feel utterly lost and a complete failure. Worst of all is I don't know what to do or where to go next. Each place drives me to the point of despair. I'm becoming a sort of wandering Jew.
> . . . I tell you because I feel guilty in not always being able to do as you request.
> You haven't mentioned any threat of prosecution over *Cancer* yet. It can't be that they are going to let it slide through, can it?
> If I were to return suddenly to the States, do you suppose I would run into a lot of trouble? On top of everything else I am going through that would just about finish me.[3]

Rosset cabled Miller in Paris on June 13, 1961, that the government wanted him to testify at the Post Office hearing June 26 in New York, "AND GUARANTEES NO PROSECUTION AGAINST YOU STOP EXPECT YOU WILL SAY NO BUT WOULD LOVE TO HAVE YOU."

However, Rosset was not to need Miller at any hearings. Four days after confiscating the book the Post Office released it, giving no immediate reason for the action. Later the *Washington Post* revealed that Justice Department lawyers had found that

> many people found Miller's writings, which also include *Tropic of Capricorn* and *Quiet Days at Clichy,* disgusting and shocking but not sexually exciting. For this and other reasons, there was remarkable agreement that the Government could not win if it charged that Miller's work is obscene.[4]

Rosset immediately wrote Miller: "We're astounded by the newest turn of affairs. On the face of it, it seems good. Enclosed is an article from today's *N.Y. Times,* with a strong affirmative headline." The clipping Rosset sent to Miller as encouragement tells what happened:

"TROPIC OF CANCER"
SCORES A VICTORY
Special to the New York Times

WASHINGTON, June 13—The Post Office abandoned its move today to bar Henry Miller's "Tropic of Cancer" from the mails as obscene.

Officials termed this a tactical step. They explained that suits testing whether the novel was obscene by legal definition were pending, and that it would be wise to await their outcome.

However, it was learned that the Justice Department had advised the Post Office to drop the case for another reason—that it was likely to lose in the courts.

Justice Department lawyers warned that the novel, however explicit it was about sexual matters, was recognized by many critics as having literary merit. That fact, they said, would make it difficult to sustain any postal ban in the courts.

Two suits are in New York. They arose from an attempt by Mrs. Dorothy Upham, a New York artist, to import a Paris edition of the book.[5]

The Customs case, however, was still not decided. Years before, Judge Bok in *Commonwealth v. Gordon* (1949) had reported

> a curious but complete confusion between the post office and the customs over what constitutes obscenity. No unanimity of opinion unites these two governmental services in a common standard. Books have cleared the port only to find the mails closed to them: others, printed here, have circulated freely while foreign copies were stopped at the ports. One would expect greater uniformity than this if obscenity could be unmistakably detected.

Time had not changed things. From June 13 until August 10, 1961, when Customs dropped the Upham case, a person could have had his copy of *Cancer* seized at the port of entry, then walked into the terminal and picked up an American edition at the bookstore there. This ludicrous and embarrassing situation was eliminated on August 10 when the government announced that the Customs ban which had kept Miller's novel out of the United States for twenty-seven years had been lifted. Also cleared for importation at that time were *Tropic of Capricorn* and *Plexus*. When the ban was lifted, 130,000 copies of the Grove *Cancer* were in print. Grove Press said in a release that the decision "represents a great setback to censorship in general." [6]

The Bureau of Customs had acted, also, upon the recommendation of the Department of Justice.

Pointing out that Judge Murphy agreed with the Customs and Post Office decisions, as did the Attorney General of New Jersey and law enforcement offices in several other large communities, Elmer Gertz said:

> Normally, this would have meant the end of all efforts to ban the book . . .
> So far as I recall the history of book banning in the United States, when one upper court (particularly a Federal court), or the Post Office, or Customs, clears a book, then that is the end of the matter; no local luminaries superimpose their lowlier views. But in connection with *Tropic of Cancer*, it was a fight every inch

of the way, with over sixty suits of various kinds and results. New York City, San Francisco and Washington, D.C., might permit the book, but not Syracuse, Los Angeles, and Boston—until the upper courts began the process of setting aside the edicts of the tiny tyrants.[7]

The events following these favorable federal anticensorship precedents in the *Tropic* case illustrate that despite all these high-level decisions, a book can be effectively banned in large portions of the country.

The lifting of the bans, said Grove Press lawyer Charles Rembar, was less a blessing than it might seem. Had there been a case pending in the federal courts, some of the local prosecutors might have sat back and waited for the outcome. Now, instead of one case in the federal courts (as with *Lady Chatterley's Lover*) there were scores in the state courts. Dean William Lockhart, commenting on the situation, declared that the only thing that could stop local prosecutions was a federal adjudication and Grove Press did not have this. "A judgment by an administrative agency is not going to stop state prosecutors. Political factors enter into whether to prosecute or not to prosecute. Those fellows want to be elected. They're getting pressure from local groups. And they can't point to a federal decision that says they can't prosecute." [8]

Nearly everyone in the book publishing industry feels that word-of-mouth is one of the most important factors in the sale of a book.[9] A long time ago, Darwin's reply to Samuel Butler's question, "What sells a book?" was, "Being talked about is what sells a book." A year before the publication of *Cancer,* Ian Ballantine, head of Ballantine Books, remarked, "If for some peculiar reason a law were passed that forbade people to talk about books they read, reading would be cut 90 per cent." By the time the two *Cancer* decisions had been rendered by the Post Office and the Customs Bureau, *Tropic of Cancer* was "being talked about." The decisions and the publication date of *Cancer* combined to give Grove Press the proper timing, another important element in best-sellerdom. On June 22, Rosset sent this letter to booksellers throughout the country:

Dear Bookseller:

It gives me great pleasure to be able to share with you the exciting details of the number one success story in publishing today—Henry Miller's *Tropic of Cancer*.

Here are the cheerful statistics:

    1st   printing: 30,000—sold out
    2nd   printing: 20,000—sold out
    3rd   printing: 20,000—sold out
    4th   printing: 30,000—now ready and selling fast
    5th   printing: 30,000—on order

                .   .   .   .   .   .

If you were one of the many who had to wait for your books, please forgive us. Although we did our best, we were out of stock on two different occasions. By the end of this month, and only one week after publication date, we will have 130,000 copies in print. This means that we will be able to fill your order promptly.

Our discount schedule for *Tropic of Cancer* remains the same for all bookstores—regardless of size—a base of 40%, plus our sliding scale up to 46%. All books, of course, are fully returnable.

A week later the booksellers got still more comforting news:

One week after its publication date, Henry Miller's *Tropic of Cancer* has sold over 68,000 copies. Its third printing is on sale in stores all over the U.S. and *The New York Times* and the *New York Herald Tribune* joined numerous other newspapers all over the country this week in adding the book to their best-seller lists.

Cancer was not only being "talked about" because of the banning decisions, but "word-of-mouth" from one reader to another was operating.

Now public demand for a book is nurtured by the sale of copies at the time the demand is strongest, and initially Grove Press was getting the novel into the bookstores to fill the demand. (Weak distribution, of course, can be disastrous.) In the life of a best-seller, the initial flow of books into the hands of the customers must not be interrupted for any reason whatsoever, otherwise the demand for the book which has begun to build up may collapse very quickly. And if a sale is lost because the book is not available in the retail store, then, in at least 95 per cent of the cases, the sale is lost forever.

Rosset, of course, knew of the early dangers of a best-seller. "If you lose a sale to one person," he wrote me, "you've lost a sale to another he would've talked into buying it. You've lost two. There is no doubt about it, if a book is selling and it goes off sale you never recover what you might have had at that moment." [10]

The first few months of *Cancer* sales put it on best-seller lists. The Bookstore Best Sellers (nonpaperback) for 1961, according to *Publishers' Weekly,* listed *Cancer* in sixth place at 100,-000 sales, right behind *The Carpetbaggers* by Harold Robbins. (Number one was Irving Stone's *The Agony and the Ecstasy.*)

But nobody thought that *Cancer's* troubles were over. The executive vice president of Brentano's, a prominent chain of bookstores in New York City, had written to Sussman & Sugar a month before publication: "Our counsel has very strong feelings about the inherent danger in the sale of this book and continues to advise us against it. . . .

"I am very unhappy about this situation and want you to know it." [11]

Another prominent bookstore chain was also refusing to sell *Cancer.* On June 15 Rosset wrote this to John T. Sargent:

It is truly incredible that Doubleday stores still refuse to carry *Tropic of Cancer*—even after the government has officially withdrawn its complaint. I consider this a sad and ominous portent for the future of creative book publishing in this country.

The *Chicago Tribune,* on August 20, announced that it would no longer list "filthy" books on its best-seller list. The action was prompted by the presence of *Cancer* on that list.

Writing in July to Belle Rosenbaum of the *New York Herald Tribune* book review staff, Rosset said:

I am most happy that you are interested in our rather unique problem. I can't recall such a situation in the history of publishing.

We have contacted many of the stores on your list of 43 best-sellers reporting for your best-sellers' list, "What People Are Reading" of last week (July 9) and found some astounding and, I might add, disheartening facts: *at least 11 of these 43 are not even selling Tropic of Cancer*. Another six are selling it under the counter. I'm sure you can see what this does to the accuracy of the best-seller lists.

You know about the refusal of the Doubleday Stores, Scribner's and Macy's in New York to sell the book. Some other stores throughout the country feel the same. For example, Lamson's in Toledo is selling it on "special order" only. The buyer, Miss Helen Tiffany, says, "I don't believe in the book and wouldn't report it on the best-seller list." I wonder if she is selling *The Carpetbaggers* like so many other stores which refuse to handle *Tropic of Cancer*.

An interesting sidelight to the whole problem is that, although the above figures show that 26 per cent of the bookstores reporting to you do not carry *Tropic of Cancer,* our sales reports indicate that nationally only 10 per cent are not. This apparently means that the "little" stores are handling the book. Why this is true, I don't know. Unfortunately, the small stores, where the book is selling marvelously, don't report to the best-seller lists and consequently don't help to solve this inequitable situation.

By July, of course, the book review returns were in. Most reviewers treated the book as a serious work, finding much that was repulsive in parts, but still holding that *Cancer* was not obscene. Many reviewers were "inclined to be sympathetic, partly because of the censorship issue involved." [12] But *Time* called *Cancer* "a very dirty book indeed," while *Life* gave this word to its 6,726,796 readers:

> *Tropic* will be defended by critics as an explosive corrosive Whitmanesque masterpiece (which it is) and attacked as an unbridled obscenity (which it is). It will probably sell a million. On *Tropic*'s literary merit? Guess again.[13]

Grove Press had other things to worry about, however, besides totting up favorable and unfavorable book reviews. That ancient citadel of book banning, Massachusetts, was about to engage in its favorite pastime—and theoretically insure *Cancer*'s best-selling status. This Grove release tells the story:

NEW YORK, N.Y., July 14—The Attorney General of Massachusetts yesterday asked that state's Obscene Literature Control Commission for a recommendation on the book *Tropic of Cancer.* He described the book, which is on leading best-seller lists throughout the country, as "filthy" and "rotten," and said he is prepared to proceed against its distribution in Massachusetts if the Commission decides it is in violation of the Commonwealth "dirty book" law.

Attorney General Edward McCormack called the book "positively repulsive" and "an affront to human decency." He said, "I have never in my life read anything that was so degrading and demoralizing and so brazenly animalistic."

Barney Rosset . . . said of the . . . proceeding, "It seems obvious that Mr. Sontag, acting in the dual capacity of assistant to Mr. McCormack and also as consultant to the Obscene Literature Control Commission, will obtain from the Commission the 'obscene' verdict that Mr. McCormack desires. It appears that Massachusetts, with the one-track mind of the rhinoceros, is again about to assault the Constitution and its amendments which the forefathers of her citizens fought so hard to obtain. If the Commission supports the Attorney General, we are prepared to fight the case in court with all our resources."

The Commission voted unanimously on July 20 to recommend that the Attorney General take court action to ban *Cancer* in Massachusetts. For the first time in its three-year history, the Commission had recommended the banning of a book considered pornographic.

In Dallas, Texas, *Cancer* was banned on August 15 under the state's new obscenity law. Bookstores were warned by detectives. The chief of police himself condemned the book for its "crude, vile, indecent language."

All these actions were auguries that the barometric pressure was going down, but Grove Press could scarcely foresee what a nadir would be reached with the publication on October 10 of the paperback edition of *Cancer*.

Rosset had not wanted to put out a paperback edition this

soon because the hardcover edition was still on the best-seller lists, and a paperback distribution could very well put an end to hardcover sales. He was forced into it because another American publisher was planning to print a large paperback edition. The piracy that Rosset had feared was about to happen. In a letter to Filipacchi of Hachette's in 1959, he had described how he had obtained rights to *Lady Chatterley's Lover* from Lawrence's widow in Mexico, only to have three or four publishers announce various cheap paperback editions.[14] The *Tropics,* Rosset pointed out, were even more vulnerable:

> The two *Tropics* are universally considered in America as works of considerable importance; the fact that they are more "modern" than *Lady Chatterley,* plus the story of their long suppression by the Anglo-Saxon censorship, *gives them a potential "selling value" which it would be a great mistake to ignore* . . . On the other hand, they are in a very unfortunate copyright position—their only advantage over *Lady Chatterley* is that their author is a citizen of the U.S.A., and that he is alive; although this has no absolute legal value, it would make a legal defense of Miller's rights much more convincing in an American court. Of course, this defense against eventual piratic publishers would be impossible if an authorized edition had not first been published. One idea is that such a defense should be based on the commercial damage caused by the pirated edition (here called unfair competition) to the authorized edition—which implies that the authorized edition should appear first of all.
>
> The danger is very real, first of all because the case of *Lady Chatterley* will have changed all the rules prevailing up to now; and also because the authorities have recently modified their attitude with regard to the *Tropics.* . . . [He here relates the incident of *Cancer's* being allowed into the country because a professor needed it for serious purposes.] This creates a precedent of considerable importance, as it means that the responsible federal authorities do not any longer judge the two books as pornographic novels—which was their attitude until recently.[15]

Rosset's fears were realized in the middle of September, when he found out that a paperback edition of *Cancer* was being prepared at Hall Printing Company in Chicago for the

Universal Publishing and Distributing Corporation of New York City. Universal intended to publish it in its Envoy paperback line, with copies available the first week in October, priced tentatively at seventy-five cents.

Rosset describes Grove's moves to forestall this pirating attempt:

> We had, of course, long investigated the possibility of proving that *Tropic of Cancer* was *in* copyright, by contending that although the book was first published in Paris without *ad interim* protection in this country the novel still should not be thrown into the public domain because it was impossible at this time to obtain *ad interim* protection for it. We were never able to establish that to the satisfaction of the United States Copyright Office, which, incidentally, tells us that the law is wrong and should be changed. But in the meantime the book cannot be copyrighted.
>
> The book had already been printed by the time we began to negotiate with the Universal Publishing and Distributing Corporation. We took every legal action we could think of including various types of threats against the Hall Printing Company and against Universal itself. But whether any of that would have succeeded, we shall never know.

Among those legal actions was this telegram to Universal on September 21, 1961:

> On August 24 and again on September 13 you stated to our counsel that you had no plans and no intentions to publish Henry Miller's . . . *Cancer* which as you were informed we are publishing under a contract with the proprietor of the work which gives us exclusive publication rights. It now appears that you are publishing the work and at a date so early as to make your statements an obvious misrepresentation. This is to inform you that we intend to hold you liable for this misrepresentation and for any infringement of our rights.

Similar threatening telegrams were sent to the Hall Printing Company and to a distributor, the Kable News Company.

Grove also prepared letters for wholesalers and booksellers. This was the letter sent in September to booksellers:

Dear Bookseller:

Word has just reached us of a turn of events that must fill all responsible members of the book trade with a sense of outrage: In defiance of the specific protests of Henry Miller, an unauthorized paperback edition of *Tropic of Cancer* is at this moment being prepared by another publisher for distribution.

Henry Miller has informed all parties concerned that Grove Press is the *only* authorized publisher of *Tropic of Cancer*. Yet despite this warning, preparations for the unlicensed edition are going ahead.

Naturally, we would have preferred to continue with the sale of the hardcover edition. But the turn of events has left us no choice. We are rushing through our own AUTHORIZED paperback edition of *Tropic of Cancer,* and we will get it into your hands as quickly as possible. . . . This edition will be:

1. The ONLY paperback edition authorized by Henry Miller;
2. The ONLY paperback edition on which Henry Miller is being paid royalties (the advance and royalties have been substantial);
3. The ONLY paperback reprint of the famous hardcover edition which has risked prosecution and costly legal battles to fight for the admission of . . . *Cancer* in the United States;
4. The ONLY paperback reprint of the famous Grove Press edition which, as a result of substantial sums spent in advertising and promotion, has become one of the nation's leading best-sellers.

Any unlicensed and unauthorized edition is evidently trying to hitch a free ride on the coat-tails of Grove Press and the efforts we have made on behalf of *Tropic of Cancer*. An unauthorized edition also exploits the courage of booksellers throughout the country without whose help the fight for admission of the book could never have been won.

This turn of events is reminiscent of that of two years ago when a number of publishers sought to take advantage of your and our efforts for *Lady Chatterley's Lover*. We appealed for your help then, and you responded magnificently. We are asking for your help again now. You can help by ordering and displaying prominently the AUTHORIZED paperback edition of *Tropic of Cancer*.   Cordially,

(Signed) Barney Rosset

The outcome of this piratic attempt is told by Rosset:

> In the course of angry and protracted negotiations, protracted in the sense that there was a great deal of conversation but limited to short periods, actually a short number of days, we reached an agreement . . . under which we gave them $30,000 in cash and purchased 400,000 copies of the book printed in Chicago, for printing costs.
>
> By discarding the covers and reprinting the first thirty-two pages of the book we were able to salvage partially the investment in the book. Universal signed an agreement with us stating that they believed the book to be in copyright and that they would make no further attempts to pirate the book.
>
> Since that time, at least to our knowledge, nobody has made an attempt to pirate the book in the United States, although a photographic offset was printed in India.[16] We have received a copy of that edition and it is almost identical to our own. The book is in copyright in India, but we do not hold the rights in India and we have had little success in finding what the situation is and what to do about it.
>
> In view of what happened to *Candy* . . . one pirated edition on the market, and two more will be in a short time, in view of this, our success in keeping pirate editions of *Cancer* off the market is remarkable.
>
> The contemporary pirating problem started with our publication of *Lady Chatterley's Lover*. After publication and successfully fighting it through the Post Office and the Federal Courts . . . Pocket Books came out with their own edition . . . in paper, and then, of course, we also. Then New American Library, Pyramid and still another company . . . Since that time I think there has been a much greater tendency for more or less reputable publishers to seize any opportunity to pirate valuable out-of-copyright works. *Fanny Hill* and *Kama Sutra* are recent examples.

The legal aspects of the pirating problems were handled by the firm of Rembar & Zolotar of New York. Charles Rembar had replaced Ephraim London as lawyer for Grove Press after the Massachusetts case. This letter to London from Rosset on September 25, 1961, regarding the Massachusetts case explains in part why London was replaced:

Dear Ephraim,

Unfortunately, a misunderstanding seems to have arisen as to how the Miller case should be conducted. Perhaps it would be a good idea if I briefly outlined the Grove Press position.

The Supreme Court has now said that the protection of the First Amendment extends to works that have "the slightest redeeming social importance." A work fitting that description cannot constitutionally be considered obscene and is not subject to suppression or censorship. Obviously, a serious work of literature comes within the Constitutional protection. It has been and is the position of Grove Press that the law permits it to publish any such book.

Under the law as it now stands, inquiries as to whether a book is "erotic" or "lustful" or whether it has a "tendency to corrupt" in this context were never really meaningful—or in any case are no longer relevant. The question is whether Henry Miller wrote as a serious artist and produced in *Tropic of Cancer* a work which has some literary merit.

The answer is that it is a good book—the author is a good writer. We think so, his peers think so. The book has literary merit and makes a contribution of literary value.

If the above is proven there is ample legal precedence to support the hopes for victory in this case, even if it must first go to a higher court or courts.

Grove does not wish to be associated with any other type of defense and especially does not want to be a party to defending the book on the basis that it could not excite anyone to lascivious thoughts or actions [the Justice Department's feelings]. We will not hide behind a hypocritical position, one which will not fail to react unfavorably to us in the future. The line of defense we wish to pursue allows the lawyer ample scope to prove his own abilities, to exercise his own creativity. We are not attempting to tell him how to exploit that proper line of defense.

Since this is our position, if a lawyer has a different point of view we do not wish to impose upon him ours, neither can we accept his views as representing the Grove Press position.

I hope that you can see your way to representing our position, but if you cannot we should find another way to proceed.

Although London, Rosset wrote me, is an extraordinarily fine lawyer, he was less flexible than Rosset wished.

With the pirating attempt disposed of, Rembar was able to turn his full attention to defending the numerous *Cancer* lawsuits developing throughout the country. Explaining the legal preparations made for Grove Press, Rembar wrote to me in 1964:

> I had tried the *Lady Chatterley* case for Grove, but the number of *Tropic of Cancer* actions [approximately sixty] made it impossible for me to act as trial lawyer. I prepared a general brief, which, with some adaptation for local conditions, was used by the attorneys in the various states. My direct participation was limited to the arguing of two appeals.

Generally, "I attempted to oversee this welter of litigation and to supply the basic legal defense."

The general brief began with this statement:

> The case before the court involves the resolution of an issue of constitutional law. The First Amendment to the United States Constitution, with its guaranties of freedom of speech and press, protects the publication and sale of Henry Miller's *Tropic of Cancer* unless the book can be shown to be utterly worthless trash that lies outside the protection of the First Amendment. *Roth v. United States,* 354 U.S. 276. This is true whether action by federal government officials or action by state government officials is involved. *Alberts v. California,* 354 U.S. 476. By virtue of the Fourteenth Amendment, state statutes as well as federal are subject to the guaranties of the First Amendment. *Butler v. Michigan,* 352 U.S. 380.
>
> It is submitted that this book, being a recognized work of literature, cannot be found to be worthless, and that therefore its publication and sale may not, under the Constitution, be suppressed or impeded.

Then followed a historical survey of the law of obscenity which noted the Hicklin, Kennerley, *Ulysses,* Besig, Butler, Roth-Alberts, Sunshine Book, One, Inc., and Mounce cases. After reviewing the Roth-Alberts decision and the *per curiam* cases after it, the general brief concluded that it would seem to be an inescapable inference that only hard-core pornography may now be condemned, and that the majority opinion in the Roth case was "imposing stringent limits on the operation of the anti-obscenity statutes." Obscenity statutes, Rembar argued, cannot extend to works of literary value. For when those works are involved, the Supreme Court's declaration that the First Amendment protects speech or writing of the "slightest redeeming social importance" is sufficient to dispose of the case. Rembar also pointed out that the *per curiam* decisions emphasized that the question of obscenity is a constitutional question which must be decided in the first instance by the courts.

There was little legal precedent to guide the court in dealing directly with *Tropic of Cancer,* the brief said. The Besig case could no longer be considered, and the Department of Justice which had fought *Lady Chatterley's Lover* so vigorously had determined *Cancer* not obscene. Although Massachusetts had maintained the time-honored tradition of "banned in Boston" in *McCormack v. Tropic of Cancer,* Rembar argued that the decision was on appeal and that it was difficult to see how it could be sustained, especially in view of the court's finding that the book had great literary value. The Attorney General of New Jersey had issued a formal opinion that *Cancer* was not obscene, and Judge Murphy in an *obiter dictum* had held the same view.

Rembar then considered the objectives of anti-obscenity statutes and listed those things which the statutes are supposed to prevent:

1) the causing of antisocial sexual conduct;
2) the advocacy of ideas that depart from current standards of propriety;
3) the sexual thoughts and desires that the reading may stimulate in the reader;
4) the disgust and revulsion that the reader may feel.

The general brief then considered each of these in turn. There was "no demonstrable connection between the reader of material dealing with sex . . . and criminal activity . . . indeed, psychiatric evidence indicates that the contrary may be the case." *Kingsley International Picture Corp. v. Regents* (the

Lady Chatterley's Lover film case, in which adultery was suggested as one solution to a wife's problem) eliminated the second objective as a factor in judicial decision. As for the third and fourth objectives of obscenity statutes, Rembar pointed out that they have solely to do with the effect on the individual, without regard to any effect on conduct:

> it is axiomatic that the law may not attempt to regulate what goes on inside a man's mind. The law does, of course, concern itself with questions of morality. . . . But the law is concerned only with a man's actions in relation to his fellow members of society. It is quite another thing to say that a man's internal reactions, divorced from any possible effect upon others, constitute a fit subject for legislation. Thought control, all free men agree, is an abomination.

The values of a free press outweigh any attempt to legislate against the stimulation of sexual thoughts.

A work of literature, no matter how effective the writing, can hardly add anything to the constant and ubiquitous sexual provocation with which our environment assails us, Rembar added. "Much of our advertising, our motion pictures, our television, and our newspaper stories, is calculated to provoke sexual thoughts and images. We live in a sea of appeal to our sexual interests."

As for the fourth reason why a book might be suppressed —offensiveness—Rembar said that the courts were generally agreed that offensiveness was not a legitimate ground for censorship. "Offensiveness," Rembar wrote, "is hardly the kind of objection that can be intruded through 'the slightest crack necessary' which the Supreme Court will permit in the ramparts protecting freedom of speech and press."

The general brief concluded:

> The fact that none of the objectives of anti-obscenity legislation are applicable to a serious work of literature confirms what is apparent from the Roth opinion itself and from the Supreme Court's *per curiam* reversals that followed it. The law at present is that the Constitution will not permit the application of such

statutes to works of literary value. It is on this evidence that the Court must decide the matter.

Other legal preparations made by Grove Press and Rembar included the Grove Press legal "packet," which was widely distributed. The packet is introduced with this letter from Rembar:

Dear Sir:

You may be in an area where efforts have been made to censor and suppress Henry Miller's *Tropic of Cancer*. There has been what amounts to a campaign to intimidate wholesalers and booksellers. It is a campaign which is bound to fail, and meanwhile Grove Press (publisher of Black Cat Books) is doing everything possible to protect you and your booksellers.

Whether or not you are in such an area, we think that you will be interested in the enclosed material. It consists of an affidavit that is being used in court proceedings, together with exhibits supporting the statements in the affidavit, including newspaper editorials, book reviews and other evidence that put the situation in its true light.

Tropic of Cancer is, in the opinion of all sober, conscientious critics and scholars, a work of literature. It is clearly *not*—as the self-appointed censors (many of whom have admitted that they have not read the book) are trying to say—an example of commercial pornography. The trouble that has been created is not the result of any court holding that the book is obscene. The courts will undoubtedly ultimately hold (as the United States Department of Justice already has concluded) that the book is not obscene and that its publication cannot be censored.

We also hope to have judicial rulings to the effect that the activities of the police and certain prosecuting attorneys in trying to suppress the book by threats, seizures and arrests, are illegal activities. If we can accomplish this, we feel that we will have done a great service to publishing and bookselling generally, apart from anything relating to *Tropic of Cancer* specifically.

Similar material is being sent to the editors of many newspapers. You may be interested in discussing the problem with those in your locality. In addition, you may wish to show the material to civic groups, government authorities and other people who may be interested in the situation.

>   Sincerely
>   (Signed) Charles Rembar, Counsel
>   Grove Press

An affidavit by Barney Rosset led off the packet materials. The affidavit, dated November 1961, spoke of the literary triumphs of Grove Press, and the adoption of its books by colleges and universities—naming some forty-odd influential institutions. It extolled the prestige of Grove Press and named the authors it published. Critics citing Miller's achievements were mentioned, and there was a brief treatise on *Cancer*'s litigations. The events connected with the publication of *Cancer* and those immediately following (pirating attempt, advertising, etc.) were related. The Roth decision was discussed, with the "hard-core pornography only" reasoning stressed. Rosset cited *Butler v. Michigan* to dismiss the effect-of-a-book-on-children argument brought up by censors; he went on to say, "The reading habits of children are the responsibility of their parents, not of the law." The affidavit ended with:

> I respectfully submit that the book itself, read as a whole, and all the surrounding circumstances, as set forth in this affidavit and the annexed exhibits, demonstrate
>
> (a) that Henry Miller's *Tropic of Cancer* is a serious and important work of literature, and not an attempt at commercial pornography;
>
> (b) that as such it is entitled to the protection of the First Amendment and cannot be deemed obscenity within the meaning of *Roth v. United States,* and, consequently,
>
> (c) that the publication and sale of *Tropic of Cancer* cannot be a violation of any federal or state statute.
>
>   (Signed) Barney Rosset

"Exhibit A" included statements about *Cancer* from John Ciardi, Norman Cousins, Lawrence Durrell, T. S. Eliot, Wallace Fowlie, Horace Gregory, Aldous Huxley, George Orwell, Sir Herbert Read, Karl Shapiro, Osbert Sitwell and William Carlos Williams. "Exhibit B" was a copy of the advertisement presented earlier. "Exhibit C" was composed of reprints of reviews of *Cancer* by Dorothy Parker, Maurice Dolbier (*New York Herald Tribune*), Ben Ray Redman, Harry T. Moore (*New York Times*), Lester Gorn (*San Francisco Examiner*), John Barkham (Tucson *Daily Citizen*), Eric Moon (*Library Journal*), Gerald Walker (*New York Post*), John K. Sherman (*Minneapolis Sunday Tribune*), and Leslie Cross (*Milwaukee Journal*). A collection of editorials and cartoons from newspapers across the country was "Exhibit D"—from the *Minneapolis Star,* the *Providence Journal,* the *Washington Post,* the *Dallas News,* the *Chicago Sun-Times,* and the *Long Beach* (California) *Press-Telegram.* "Exhibit E" was a reprint of the *New York Times* news story about the dropping of the *Cancer* ban by the Post Office. The last exhibit of the packet, "Exhibit F," was a reproduction of the court order dismissing the Customs ban on *Cancer, Capricorn,* and *Plexus* in the Upham case.

Extensive as these preparations were, they were not enough to stem the number of legal and extralegal actions against *Tropic of Cancer.* So serious and widespread was the movement against the novel that *Publishers' Weekly* wrote:

> The year 1961 saw a reversal—perhaps only temporary—of the trend toward freedom from censorship for serious works of literature. It had seemed, in the late 1950's, that this trend was becoming well established—through Federal court decisions which, it appeared, were filtering down the hierarchy of government to state and local levels. In particular, the U.S. Supreme Court's 1957 pronouncement that censorship may be practiced very narrowly—i.e., only on "hard-core" pornography—seemed to be gaining acceptance by courts of lesser magnitude and by some officials charged with enforcing anti-obscenity laws.
>
> This happy state of affairs went out the window in the case of the book which made 1961's biggest censorship news, . . . *Cancer.* And while this news was, in a narrow sense, limited to one book, its implications were much broader, representing a complete flouting of the "filter-down" theory on which proponents of the freedom to read had relied . . . *despite favorable anticensorship precedents at the Federal level, a book can be banned effectively in large portions of the United States.*[17]

7

PAPERBACKS ARE FOR BURNING

Despite the old saying, "You can't tell a book by its cover," censorious members of the American public made a distinction between the hardcover and softcover editions of *Cancer*. The paperback edition of *Cancer* brought most of the trouble to Grove Press. But this was something which Grove could and no doubt did anticipate.

Paperback books in one form or another have been with the American book-publishing industry almost since its inception, but the current paperback thrust came in June 1939, when Pocket Books, Inc., under the leadership of Robert F. DeGraff published ten titles at 25 cents each.[1] DeGraff published twenty-four more titles that year and sold 1,508,000 copies. So began the first of two paperback revolutions. The Armed Services Editions of books published during the war was actually the forerunner of the big American paperback industry. Shipped overseas to GI's, pocket books were handy to carry around. The GI's kept the paperback habit when they were discharged back in America, and the cheap books appealed to the general public.

Initially, bookstores were not even included in the paperback publishers' distribution plans. They relied instead upon newsstands, cigar stores, and drug stores. In 1951, some 950 new titles were published and 230,000,000 copies sold. By 1953 there were twenty principal paperback publishers in the field and bookstores were stocking softcover books.

The second revolution, the higher-priced paperback revolution, came in April 1953, when Jason Epstein published higher quality books with covers frequently of modernistic and often abstract design in Doubleday's Anchor Books line. In 1955 Cornell University Press became the first university publisher in the field. On the eve of the publication of *Cancer,* there were seventy-nine trade publishers and university presses in the paperback field and the two revolutions had merged into one.

Americans in 1960 bought 1,000,000 paperbacks a day at the more than 95,000 newsstands, cigar stores, supermarkets, drug stores, bookstores, and college and school bookstores. These paperbacks brought a new prosperity to the American book industry. Their prices had risen from 25 and 35 cents to 95 cents and as much as three dollars. Their sales were a "godsend to the men who tend the newsstands in a period when magazine sales were sagging," Raymond Walters, Jr., wrote in 1960. He added:

> There are some indications that they may slowly be changing the Americans' reading tastes. Reprints of recent fiction best-sellers and books designed simply to entertain continue to sell well. But mass-market firms, like publishers of the higher-priced lines, report that in the last year the greatest gains have been made in the field of serious non-fiction.[2]

Censors rose up like dragons when the first paperbacks were displayed in neighborhood stores. Before the paperback revolution, censors had only some 1500 bookstores scattered lightly across the country and the slightly more than one per cent of the adult population regularly patronizing those bookstores to worry about. This widening of the book distribution channels to 95,000 outlets brought anguish to brooding censors who vividly imagined day-by-day corruption of children in their neighborhood haunts.

The reasons for the nationwide efforts to censor paperbacks have been neatly summarized by Lockhart and McClure:

> The volume of their sales, the manner of their distribution, their modest price and ready accessibility to the public, the provocative nature of some of their jackets and blurbs, and the existence of a national organization that had already sharpened its teeth on comic books and magazines [the National Organization for Decent Literature]—all these contributed to the outbreak of censorship aimed at literature in this form.[3]

Of these paper-bound books, some 70 per cent are reprints of hardcover books which receive little censorship attention. As Larrabee puts it, "the implication is that an adult who can afford to pay three dollars and fifty cents for obscenity can take care of himself." [4] Those who suppress paperbacks are reluctant to use normal and traditional legal procedures—a judicial proceeding is not conducive to secret mass suppression.[5] And lest we think that suppression of paperbacks is of little moment, one critic reminds us that "the inexpensive book, more than other modern instruments of mass communication, is today an outpost of freedom in our democratic culture." [6]

In July 1962, Rosset wrote Miller that the hardcover sales were finished. Some 100,000 at $7.50 each had been sold. But he added that because of the censorship and litigation that *Tropic of Cancer* had encountered, Grove Press would have suffered a disastrous loss without the ninety-five-cent paperback edition.

When the paperback edition of *Cancer* was published on October 10, 1961, it was one of 13,900 paperback titles which had been brought out in the United States to that time. (Some eighteen months before, the titles had numbered 6500.) It picked up where the hardcover left off in sales. The paperback *Cancer* helped launch Grove Press's Black Cat mass market line (along with Robert Lindner's *Rebel Without a Cause*). Throughout 1962 and 1963, in spite of the most massive censorship assault ever mounted against a book, *Cancer* remained on the best-seller paperback list, in ninth place. Although some

750,000 copies were returned to Grove Press by bookstores and distributors because of censorship fears, more than two million copies were sold.

Legal actions against allegedly obscene books can be taken at the local, state, or federal level. Cities and counties have hundreds of ordinances providing for the arrest and trial of sellers and distributors of such books. Almost all states have anti-obscenity laws. Before *Cancer* had run its course more litigation had been launched because of it, more extralegal pressures had been exerted against it, than for any other book in modern publishing history.[7] As early as December 7, 1961, Fred Jordan, a senior editor of Grove Press, wrote this about *Cancer's* troubles to Russell Lynes of *Harper's:*

Dear Mr. Lynes:
  As I told you on the phone today, we here at Grove think we are sitting on the story of what is undoubtedly the biggest single case of literary censorship in modern American history—yet nothing has been said or written anywhere to indicate the scope and extent of the current battle.
  I am, of course, referring to our troubles over Henry Miller's *Tropic of Cancer.* In the past few weeks police intimidation, whether through threats or actual arrests, has resulted in *Tropic of Cancer* being taken off sale in a major part of the United States.
  Cities such as Philadelphia, Cleveland, Chicago, Los Angeles, Dallas, Seattle, just to name a few of the larger ones, have no copies, or almost none, on sale. Entire states, including Massachusetts, Rhode Island, most, or all, of New Jersey and New Hampshire, have seen fit to ban the book.
  If all this had been accomplished by orderly legal procedure, it would have been bad enough, especially in view of the fact that the Department of Justice cleared the book and officially allowed it to go through customs and the mails. But we have seen very little semblance of orderly procedure.
  In Amarillo, Texas, the sheriff seized several thousand copies from an interstate carrier after the thoroughly terrorized wholesalers had returned (or were returning) the books. The local paper there states the sheriff wants to burn the books. Perhaps he has.

In New Jersey the Attorney General of the state said the book could not be legally prosecuted. The day after his statement three of his county prosecutors secured a number of criminal indictments and books were seized all over the state. *Also, a Jersey paper in an editorial demanded the Attorney General's removal from office.*

In suburban Chicago some eleven communities confiscated books through police action and with no due process of law whatsoever. We can point out many, many other such instances.

To our knowledge there have been over fifty arrests. In Chicago itself a detective went into the Greyhound Bus Terminal and asked if the book was on sale. He was told no, but that the store would like to sell it if the detective did not object. He said he had no objection. A clerk sold a copy, the detective arrested him, and the clerk not only is now awaiting trial, but has also been ejected from the YMCA where he lived because the arrest made him undesirable.

Of course, we are defending him and the others. As of now we have some fourteen court actions pending. In most instances we have been hiring legal firms in each area and putting them to work. In three cases (Chicago, Cleveland, and New Jersey) we ourselves have started actions against the police. Of course, when we decided to publish *Tropic of Cancer,* we anticipated trouble, and were prepared to meet it. Our case on a Federal level was disposed of with a victory on our part. Then we were banned in Massachusetts. After the trial the judge pondered for six weeks to produce a negative decision which charged the book with being indecent and impure and, moreover, with not having a plot.

Since then the roof has fallen in. One police chief after another joined the parade. One of the suburban officials said that there had been no intimidation in his town; they had merely pointed out to local booksellers that they *had* the book—after which observation the book disappeared from sale. Hoke Norris of the *Chicago Sun-Times* says that he believes police intimidation is the biggest literary story of our times.

We have been told by more than one informant that at a recent convention of police chiefs held, I believe, in Montreal, the book was discussed and two pages (5 and 91) were specifically pointed out as a guide for those chiefs who did not have enough spare time for reading.

As black as the picture looks, it has not been all black. Some booksellers have refused to be intimidated with the result that a few of them have been arrested so that the matter may be tested in court. In Rhode Island, Brown University brought action against the state's Attorney General. In Cleveland, a group has been formed to fight police censorship there and a law firm has volunteered to fight the battle; in Minneapolis, a two-day ban imposed by the police chief was lifted when the press aroused the citizenry and the mayor to the steps to curb the police.[8]

"The current censorship drive against *Cancer* is being conducted entirely at the state and local level," reported the ACLU *Weekly Bulletin* of November 27, 1961. "The pattern was brush-fire censorship, most of it taken in hasty disregard for the due process but most of it highly effective," *Publishers' Weekly* noted in January 1962. Said Charles Rembar, "It's like being in the middle of a battle. We know we're being shot at, but we're not always sure about the direction the shots are coming from."

The rapidity and breadth of the attacks, reported *Publishers' Weekly,* were nationwide:

> The paperback edition of Henry Miller's *Tropic of Cancer* is being banned locally on such a wide geographical front that even the publisher . . . remains uncertain as to the number of American communities where the book has run afoul of official or semi-official censorship. . . .
>
> Spot-censorship has been the pattern in the local-level campaign . . . The book has run into trouble, e.g., in suburban Silver Spring, Md., but not in the District of Columbia; in Montgomery County, Pa., but not in neighboring Philadelphia.[9]

"Tropic of Cancer," Melvin L. Wulf, assistant legal director of the ACLU, wrote to Wilbur Goodhue on January 11, 1962, "is being attacked from coast to coast." (Goodhue was an interested party—affiliated with Dartmouth Bookstore, he was about to go on trial for selling a copy of *Cancer.*) From Wilmington, Ohio, as early as October 25, 1961, came this letter

from distributor J. C. Bevan to E. P. Thompson of Macfadden Publications, Inc.:

> As per your letter of the 16th in regard to *Tropic of Cancer* I believe it best that we do not distribute it as dealer after dealer are asking that we do not send them any and *from the local papers each night another city near us is banning it.*
>
> We have been able to keep down most censorship in our territory but I believe this one would just about start it as there is much talk about it now.
>
> We have 300 copies ready for reshipment at once.

Anthony Lewis reported in the *New York Times* in January 1962:

> *Tropic of Cancer* has run into more massive opposition from censors across the United States than any other serious publishing venture in memory. Though 2,500,000 copies are in print, it is impossible to buy the book in most parts of the country.
>
> It is not on sale in Massachusetts, Rhode Island and these among many cities: Los Angeles, Chicago, Philadelphia, Cleveland, Atlanta, Miami, Dallas, Houston, Seattle, Hartford, Wilmington (Del.), Indianapolis, Des Moines, St. Louis, Trenton, Buffalo, Phoenix, Oklahoma City, Birmingham.
>
> Grove Press, which is the authority for that list, finds it easier to keep track of the places where the book is sold. The press says that sales in quantity have come chiefly in New York, Washington, San Francisco and Minneapolis—*the last after a strong editorial attack by the* Minneapolis Star and Tribune *chased the censors.*[10]

Two months earlier Grove Press had reported that *Cancer* was banned in at least fifty-seven cities and two states (Nebraska and Massachusetts), because of arrests or threats of arrest. By March 1962 Rosset claimed that only in four cities—New York, Minneapolis, Washington, D.C., and San Francisco—was *Cancer* being sold openly. Grove Press estimated that 75 per cent of the nation's dealers either never accepted copies or returned them after shipment because of local police action, actual or threatened. All in all, this was pretty rough treatment in the first few crucial selling months for an industry that has built itself on the principle that a product has to be readily accessible to its purchaser.

The leading American bookstores are concentrated in twenty cities. Some 950 bookstores of the 1500 reported in this country are located in these twenty cities. Of these twenty leading book cities, only four sold *Cancer* openly. Some 330 bookstores are located in New York, and this is one of the four book cities which at first sold *Cancer* openly. Later, arrests were made in Brooklyn and other places in New York State. Rosset wrote this to me of the situation:

> If the pirated edition of *Cancer* had been successful, Grove Press would have suffered perhaps disastrous financial losses. However, we have sold over two million of the 95-cent edition and there is rather a good profit margin on the paperback. Much better than that on the hardcover edition, and the profits from the paperback edition have paid for the legal fees and all the various assorted side costs.
>
> To show how lucky we were, we sold probably over half a million copies in the neighborhood of our publishing company. Mainly Manhattan. After this an arrest was made in Brooklyn and it was illegal to sell *Tropic of Cancer* in the State of New York and that included Manhattan. If this had happened before we sold the half million copies we probably would not have survived to make the battle to have this book made once again legal.

Once an action was brought against *Cancer* in a community, most book dealers refused to handle the book until a higher court said it was all right. And in San Diego a bookseller, acquitted in a trial with Grove Press legal counsel acting on his behalf, *still* refused to handle the novel because of fear. Booksellers were arrested in the first few months alone in New Jersey; Maryland; Hawaii; Los Angeles and La Jolla, California; Chicago; Cincinnati; Atlanta; Fort Lauderdale; Hanover, New Hampshire; and Hartford. These cases were awaiting trial at the end of 1961.

In the suppression of *Tropic of Cancer,* wrote Elmer Gertz, "There was evidence everywhere of police state methods, wholly alien to our American philosophy of freedom and due process." [11] Informal police and prosecutor suggestions were reported in the local press in many instances:

"A voluntary ban has been placed on . . . *Cancer* by Roanoke news dealers at the suggestion of the police department," . . . *The Roanoke* (Va.) *Times* said.

The *Pasadena* (Calif.) *Star-News* reported that the local police had called the book obscene, "and bookstore owners consequently banned the book voluntarily." In Stockton, Calif., reported *The Sacramento Bee*, the distributor stopped handling *Tropic* although he thought the courts would find it not obscene. He explained: "I don't want to be involved in any mess. We have been living here too long."

"Censorship through intimidation" was what *The Cleveland Plain Dealer* called a prosecutor's threat of criminal action that succeeded in driving the book out of that city. In Rhode Island the State Attorney General, J. Joseph Nugent, made similar threats and announced that the book was "banned from sale in the State of Rhode Island." It effectively was.[12]

The ACLU, active throughout the *Cancer* campaign, reported helping to defend a Minnesota bookseller who had been arrested by a police morals squad. The ACLU also supported a North Platte, Nebraska, editor protesting a police banning, and a San Diego bookseller arrested for violation of a local obscenity ordinance. It protested a ban in South Bend, Indiana; police threats of prosecution against distributors in Buffalo, New York; police practices of "literary blackmail" in New Jersey; a Philadelphia District Attorney's attempt to restrain a major distributor from filling *Cancer* orders; and Louisville and Cincinnati police activities in obstructing the sale of the novel.

The *Cancer* censorship campaign flowed across American borders; even the Royal Canadian Mounted Police of Vancouver, Canada, were involved in the activities when a Vancouver columnist remarked that it was too bad the book was banned in Canada. Excerpts of *Cancer* were broadcast in NATO military code, and monitored by NATO stations throughout Western Europe, when a twenty-year-old Danish soldier thought it "would be fun to see what happened." He was sentenced to twenty days in the guardhouse.

From Olympia, Washington, Mrs. Alison M. Mathews wrote to ACLU's John Pemberton, Jr.:

> I would like to add the name of Olympia's Police Chief Roy Kelly to your list of unauthorized censors. Kelly removed *Tropic of Cancer* in paperback from local bookstores in December, while *leaving the expensive hardcover edition.* There has been no City Commission or other official action on this, merely Kelly's own dictatorial action.[13]

And so it went on the prosecution front. In December 1961, Rosset wrote to the *New York Post*'s James A. Wechsler:

> I personally am appalled by this book lynching and I feel immensely frustrated when one well-informed person after another congratulates me on our "victory" with the book, and then says, well, a little banning will help sales. There has been no victory, and the sales have been mainly confined to New York City, Washington, D.C., Minneapolis, and San Francisco.

Some benefits in isolated instances accrued from the banning. In Rhode Island, Attorney General J. Joseph Nugent declared on October 1, 1961, that he believed *Tropic of Cancer* was the "foulest, most obscene work" he had ever read. He indicated he would start a campaign for voluntary withdrawal of the book by news dealers but that, for the time being, he would not seek court action under the state's obscenity statute. The *Library Journal* recounts what happened next in Rhode Island and neighboring Massachusetts:

> President Barnaby C. Keeney of Boston University announced that the University would not sell the book for the time being, and would try to seek a determination from the Superior Court as to whether the novel was legally obscene.
> Public demand for the book began to rise following these announcements. One bookseller received twenty calls in one day; it was reported that a copy of the book has been offered for $20 downtown; the public library reserve list increased to thirty-five; and an out-of-town radio station reported that people were waiting "thirty-five deep" for the book in Providence![14]

Henry Steele Commager has said that the "most effective censorship is not, in fact, legal; in a democracy it is . . . public opinion." [15] Nine days before the publication of *Cancer,* Robert B. Downs commented upon some groups which are dominant in forming public opinion:

> We are witnessing today the frightening spectacle of innumerable veterans organizations, religious bodies, White Citizens Councils, superpatriotic societies, Congressional committees, and other misguided pressure groups working around the clock to place restrictions and limitations on what we may read, or see, or hear. Not realizing or caring that they are seeking to destroy the basic concept upon which America was founded, the voices calling for conformity, for unanimity of opinion, for eliminating all ideas with which they happen to disagree grow more strident, intolerant and uncompromising. Their opponents are discredited by such epithets as Communists, subversives, fellow travelers, sex perverts, nigger lovers, egg heads, or as Mr. Kilpatrick contemptuously refers to them, the "literati." [16]

"Press freedom," Nieman Foundation Curator Louis M. Lyons agrees, "is endangered far more by private group pressures than by government." [17] In the case of *Tropic of Cancer,* wrote Alan Reitman, "many influential groups in these communities are mounting campaigns to drive such books from newsstands." [18]

By the middle of 1962 the most widely circulated list of "disapproved" books was still the one issued by the National Office for Decent Literature,[19] even though its authority had been "considerably reduced because of the many cases in the past half-dozen years in which the illegal use of the list has been opposed and struck down." [20] An organization founded in Cincinnati in 1958, the Citizens for Decent Literature, by 1961 was also extremely influential. Lockhart and McClure, who reported on the Citizens for Decent Literature groups in 1960, said at that time:

> Perhaps as a result of the encouragement given to them by Citizens for Decent Literature groups, law enforcement officials all over the country increasingly resorted to swift police raids,

followed by arrest and criminal prosecution for selling obscene publications.[21]

By the time of its second national conference in February 1960, the CDL had two hundred affiliated committees, and interested inquiries from three hundred additional communities. By 1965 the CDL had about some three hundred twenty-five branches. A member of the Board of Directors of the Milwaukee branch wrote of CDL's activities:

> CDL counteracts the propaganda of the Pornographer by educating the public to the malice and extent of the problem and by providing legal consultants to aid and abet the Prosecuting Attorney's staff in this specialized field. Through Citizens for Decent Literature, other interested parties and groups are advised of proper legal processes to effectively channel their efforts toward arrest and convictions.
>
> Our function in educating the public, explains what steps they can take to encourage more enforcement of existing laws, more letter-writing to Mayors, public officials and supreme court justices, to show the Community standards.[22]

As one procensorship writer said, this "is the sort of pressure that distributors, druggists, newsstand dealers, and police officials can feel." [23]

The CDL was active in the *Cancer* bannings across the country. In Chicago, when a court decided *Cancer* was not obscene, the CDL mailed thousands of printed letters with twenty passages from *Tropic of Cancer* reprinted out of context. Carefully chosen for their shock value, they were used to besmirch the court's opinion that the book as a whole did not violate obscenity statutes.

When confronted with a *fait accompli* of censors prevailing in the open marketplace, the concerned citizen likes to believe that the public library, at least, will make the books in question available to the public. But such was not always the case with *Cancer*—or with other questionable books during the *Cancer* campaign. The American Library Association's Everett T. Moore noted in October 1961 that "there was evidence that many public librarians were moving cautiously, not wanting to be in a position of having purchased a book that might be declared obscene by the courts." [24]

In Massachusetts, the director of the Springfield Public Library, John A. Humphry, appeared to be reducing adult reading to that of juveniles. He told the *Springfield News* that he doubted if he would purchase *Cancer* even if there were a demand for it, because of young readers.

The director of the Syracuse University libraries, Wayne Yenawine, told the *Post-Standard* that the university libraries had no special interest in the book—that he might buy it *if* a faculty member recommended it for course reading. Yet the Syracuse University libraries *were* interested in getting Grove Press's records—which are now on file there—including the news clipping that registers the library director's lack of interest in *Cancer*.

Up in northern New York, a St. Lawrence University man wrote to the ACLU of the legal tragicomedy playing there:

The District Attorney of St. Lawrence County, Mr. Charles E. Bowers, recently notified the Ogdensburg Public Library and the North County Library System in Watertown, that he would arrest the librarian of any public library in St. Lawrence County which offers to circulate *Tropic of Cancer*.

When the Faculty and Theological Students questioned Attorney Bowers on his reasons for banning the book, he replied that he spent "twenty minutes looking it over," and was upset when he found passages containing obscene, four-letter words.[25]

Esther Featherer tells what happened in New Hampshire:

[*Tropic of Cancer*] was judged obscene by New Hampshire courts in 1961, but the sale of the book was still permitted. Yet . . . it is statutorily illegal to possess and sell obscene things unless "they are intended for the advancement of art, literature education, etc." And, it has never been established whether . . . a library in the state is safe in circulating the book, but, it does not seem to matter because simply the existence of the court case has inhibited most of the New Hampshire libraries from buying the book . . .

This . . . shows how pressure can transcend a singular case

and instead become part of, or create, a climate of opinion which has its roots in censorship.[26]

The *Library Journal* conducted a survey among libraries on "Problem Fiction" in 1961 and reported these results: Of 151 libraries asked by *L.J.* if they had purchased twenty controversial books, 113 answered the questionnaire. Most of the libraries were medium-sized or large and were located in every state in the Union. Fifty-eight, or 51.3 per cent, said that they had bought *Tropic of Cancer*. One library bought *Cancer* and didn't catalogue it or reveal that it was available. And 41 per cent kept *Cancer* under cover. The Los Angeles and Philadelphia public libraries withdrew and canceled orders. Concluded *L.J.*, "Readers in the Northeast can expect the widest range of controversial novels would be available on the shelves of their public libraries." The Western and Southern states are similar, with approximately 9.1 controversial titles per library. "The area where selection is most rigid (restrictive) is the Midwest, which averages only 7.5 titles per library." [27] That, of course, is for those readers who have access to a library. Twenty per cent of Americans have *no* direct access to a local public library.

In an article entitled "Who Reads *Tropic?* Or, What Happens When You Leave It Alone," Richard J. Neuman described what happened in Salina, Kansas, when *Cancer* was placed on the open shelves in the adult reading room without fanfare:

> There has been no local controversy about the book, so readers with prior knowledge of the book would have obtained such information from national coverage. . . .
> Perhaps the only real conclusion which may be made from the survey is that, if no local controversy becomes involved, a book such as *Tropic* will have pretty much the same pattern of circulation as that of any other widely read book.[28]

The irrational and unconstitutional local *Tropic* bans placed a tremendous burden of defense on Grove Press. *Publishers' Weekly* in January 1962 warned:

> If the *Tropic* censorship pattern continued—and at the end of 1961 it *was* continuing—a publisher with a book as "contro-

versial" as *Tropic* might in the future decline to issue it, rather than run the innumerable local police gantlets. (Among such books could be other Henry Miller titles not yet published in the U.S.)[29]

The censorship pattern did continue, and when Grove Press published *Tropic of Capricorn* in September 1962, Rosset issued a statement that Grove could not defend it on behalf of the booksellers. Intoned Ernst and Schwartz, "Governmental and private pressures have taken their toll." [30] But *Capricorn* caused little excitement and no new lawsuits—even though 25,000 hardcover copies were sold in the first three months and the book itself is more erotic than *Cancer*.

"Some publishers probably *were* deterred by *Tropic of Cancer* litigations," Rosset said, "but the same publishers were deterred from publishing anything with possible danger before *Cancer*." By 1963 the many obscenity convictions (*Eros, Tropic of Cancer, Fanny Hill*) had further shaken some book publishers, and several controversial titles due for fall publication were canceled. When Putnam published *Candy,* the bestseller by Terry Southern and Mason Hoffenberg, it was with the agreement that the authors would be responsible for defending it.[31]

More than sixty cases in twenty-one states were inspired by the publication of *Cancer,* according to the ACLU's Annual Report for 1961–1962. Rosset reports that there were well over seventy cases eventually, while Rembar speaks of sixty.[32] Assisting Grove Press in legal work was the ACLU. Reitman writes:

> There is no precise way of judging exactly how much legal work has gone into cases involving *Tropic.* Except for items mentioned in our annual reports' financial section, we do not maintain such a detailed breakdown of legal expenditures. We do know that our Illinois Division, Greater Philadelphia Branch, Southern California affiliate, and Connecticut Civil Liberties Union were heavily involved in cases challenging the censorship of *Tropic* in their areas. Over all I would assume that at least 15

lawyers were concerned with developing such cases or friend of the courts briefs.[33]

" 'Comstockery' is reincarnate," exclaimed the *Bulletin* of the American Book Publishers Council in the fall of 1963.[34]

Each *Cancer* case took about four weeks to settle. The verdicts were as varied as the judges and juries in the cases—from quite liberal through strait-laced. Most juries rejected *Cancer* as obscene. But as *Publishers' Weekly* commented March 5, 1962, "The most censored book in American publishing history has neither been universally exonerated by the law nor universally condemned." [35]

Miller wrote Rosset March 13, 1962, from California:

> I imagine you must be eager to have *Cancer* come up before the Supreme Court as soon as possible. That would settle the issue, wouldn't it? From another standpoint—what matter if certain cities or states do ban the book? Isn't there a big enough market outside? I wonder sometimes what sense there is in trying to get a clean bill of health all around. There are only a few big market areas in the whole god-damned country, isn't that so?

Rosset answered:

> The problem is in *getting* to the Supreme Court.
> Also, not a problem of "certain" big cities. Most of them are refusing sale, e.g. Boston, Los Angeles, Philadelphia, etc.
> We are not trying to get a clean bill of health all around, but we are forced into defending where there is criminal prosecution.

A few months afterward Miller became a wanted man in his old home town of Brooklyn. In October a Brooklyn grand jury accused Miller, Grove Press, and Rosset of "conspiring" to produce an obscene book. Although Rosset was a child when Miller was writing *Cancer,* and Grove Press was many years from being founded, Kings County District Attorney Edward Silver's informations—equivalent to indictments—stated flatly, "It was the plan of the said conspiracy that the said book . . . was to be prepared and authored by the defendant Henry

Miller." Failing to appear in Brooklyn Criminal Court, Miller caused a warrant to be issued for his arrest. Rosset and three Brooklyn distributors of *Cancer* did appear, pleaded not guilty, and were released on parole. Some two years later, on October 2, 1964, the same Criminal Court granted a motion by the Kings County District Attorney to dismiss the informations against the defendants.

In addition to the criminal prosecutions of persons there were some half-dozen civil actions, *in rem,* against the book itself. Among the communities taking these actions were Philadelphia, Miami, West Palm Beach, and Milwaukee. But three long censorship-filled years would pass before *Cancer* finally reached the Supreme Court.

In the meantime Grove Press filed two injunction suits in Illinois and one in New Jersey. In Cleveland, Grove sought $4,800,000 in damages from local law-enforcement officers. As for the outcome of those and other suits, Rosset remarked, "We did not realize any damages on *Cancer*. We filed one suit, in Chicago, against the police. It was dropped in return for favorable court maneuvering." As early as January 1962, Grove Press had retained twenty-one local counsel for fifty-three legal actions. Several of the attorneys were handling more than one case involving the book. One attorney in New Jersey was handling twenty-six criminal and one federal action. Sixteen actions were being handled by Elmer Gertz in Illinois. This number included cases against some young actors connected with the Great Books groups who gave a private reading of portions of *Cancer.*

The cases in the various jurisdictions reached the highest court of the state in five instances—Massachusetts, New York, California, Illinois, and Wisconsin. For Grove Press there were three victories and two defeats.[36]

In the Massachusetts decision, the first, the vote was four to three in favor of Grove Press. Reading that decision one discovers that in *Cancer*'s 318 hard-bound pages, "there are sex episodes on 85 pages, some of which are described on two or more pages, and all of which are described with precise physical

detail and four-letter words." But in the opinion by Justice
Cutter the court concluded

> as in effect the New York Court did in the Richmond County
> News case, that, with respect to material designed for general
> circulation, only predominantly "hard-core" pornography, with-
> out redeeming social significance, is obscene in the constitutional
> sense.[37]

The California Supreme Court also found that their laws
against obscene material were applicable only to hard-core
pornography, and on July 2, 1963, unanimously found that
Cancer was a work of social importance and so protected by
the First Amendment.[38] In light of this decision the United
States Supreme Court sent back to a Los Angeles appellate
court for reconsideration an appeal from the verdict of a California Superior Court jury which had convicted a bookseller,
Bradley Reed Smith, for possessing and distributing *Cancer,*
which the jury found to be obscene.[39] The U.S. Supreme Court
thus "foreshadowed its later reversal . . . of the Florida ban
against *Tropic of Cancer*." [40]

The national tide of judicial opinion was running in the direction of tolerance, if not approval, of Henry Miller's *Cancer.* The
Wisconsin Supreme Court had voted four to three May 20,
1963, that the book was not obscene. Then, to the surprise of
many, the New York Court of Appeals voted four to three on
July 10, 1963, that *Cancer* was not within the area of constitutional protection because the dominant theme of the novel
appealed to the prurient interest of the average person in the
community and as such constituted hard-core pornography.[41]

And after that, the Supreme Court of Illinois, citing the New
York Fritch case freely, voted unanimously that *Cancer* was
obscene:

> Tested by the applicable tests of the *Roth* and *Manual Enter-
> prises* cases, this court is . . . compelled to conclude from the
> testimony presented and the book itself that *Tropic of Cancer*
> is obscene, is patently offensive and is not entitled to any pro-
> tection under the Federal or State constitutions.[42]

Gertz and Rembar, the Grove Press attorneys, welcomed the Illinois ruling as the best case for a test in the U.S. Supreme Court. They conferred with Rosset almost constantly about a petition for certiorari.

Through it all, Grove Press sought a U.S. Supreme Court decision on *Cancer*. Rembar describes Grove's difficulties:

> Where we won in the top court, the opposition was either unable (for procedural reasons) or not inclined (for various reasons) to go to the Supreme Court. In New York there was no final judgment, because the court sent the matter back for further trial on the issue of *scienter*. The Illinois decision was very recent. Accordingly, we were left without a Supreme Court case, except for a very slim hope in Florida.
>
> The Florida case had not gone to the top Florida court; it had reached final judgment at an intermediate level. (And was thus ripe for the United States Supreme Court, if the necessary jurisdictional basis was present.) The difficulty was that the Florida lawyers who had been handling the case for Grove Press had apparently *waived all constitutional issues*.
>
> The only basis on which the United States Supreme Court can consider one of these cases coming from a state court is on the ground that the state statute is unconstitutional or that in some other way the party has been deprived of a federal constitutional right. Nevertheless the attempt was made to get the Florida case into the Supreme Court by petition for certiorari.[43]

What eventually happened to this petition for certiorari will be discussed later. Some comments about the performance of the press on the national level should be presented now.

8

THE NATIONAL PRESS AND CANCER

Newspapers have always believed in freedom from government censorship. But when government officials restrict the printed word with obscenity charges, even the mighty daily newspapers sometimes refuse to do battle in the name of freedom of the press—or any other freedom. The press fails to realize, as the president of T. Y. Crowell Publishing Company, Robert L. Crowell, realizes:

> An attempt to besmirch a reputable work of scholarship represents a serious threat to the free press, i.e., freedom to read. . . . If a few individuals can, in violation of the rights of authors and publishers, misrepresent and abuse a respectable work and pervert selected portions of it to their own ends, then the guarantees of the First Amendment mean very little indeed.[1]

Seventy-five per cent of American editors some years ago, for example, believed that their readers had a right to read a rough summary of the second Kinsey report. What was the stand of *Editor & Publisher,* that trade journal of the newspaper industry, on this? Too much of the material was "offensive to womanhood and harmful to the morals of youth." Said *E&P,* "Our hearty congratulations *to the twenty-five per cent* of the nation's press which ignored the report and refused to publish

its lurid details." [2] The *New York Times* reviewed the first
Kinsey report but refused to advertise it in 1948. Five years
later, however, the *Times* accepted advertising for the second
report even though it was more shocking than the first to most
Americans. Of fourteen Kansas editors who were queried about
their state's new obscenity law in 1961, eight did not view it as
a threat to freedom of the press.[3] Newspaper publishers forget,
apparently, that what appears in their news columns and advertisements in the way of lurid sex crimes and cheesecake and
movie advertisements differs little from "questionable book"
material.

Newspapers' attitudes in regard to unofficial censorship of the
CDL type, for example, have not been particularly laudable.
Publisher Peter Jennison says:

> The public has, for the most part, acquiesced in these erosions
> of its freedom to read, apparently regarding the sporadic in-
> cursions into bookstores, libraries, and newsstands with bemused
> tolerance, if not approval. *Press reaction has been somewhat
> ambiguous.* With rare exceptions, newspapers across the coun-
> try have taken vigorous editorial stands against forms of federal
> censorship, but *they have not always been as alert to the
> dangers of unofficial censorship or as concerned as they might be
> over some of the extreme measures adopted in state legislatures.*
> . . . *News coverage of censorship incidents by much of the
> press has too often been shocking.* Old "yellow press" words
> and headlines crop up in far too many instances: "smut" is
> clearly an exploitable word that titillates a large number of
> newspaper readers.[4]

The press needs to realize that it and other mass media,
to reduce censorship activities, should help create an artistic
climate for a work.[5] In the climactic years of the *Cancer* banning campaign, for instance, the *Saturday Evening Post* failed
in its responsibility by running an article entitled "Paperback
Pornography" by Cleveland Amory in April of 1963. The article
noted:

> It is no secret these days that in the field of paperback books
> the big best-sellers are the Erskine Caldwells, Henry Millers,

Harold Robbinses, Irving Wallaces, Grace Metaliouses, *et al.* Compared to the real hardcore paperback pornography which has followed in their wake, however, these are boy scout manuals.[6]

The article provided impetus for police action, evidently, for *Kansas City Star* newspaperman Thorpe Menn wrote Rosset asking him if he had seen the Amory article. He added:

A few days later, the police made their more-or-less annual raid on a trashy paperback store here, picked up samples of the girlie and boyie magazines, and ignored the big table display of the really awful paperbacks . . . I discovered this too late to add a sentence to my column this week on "censorship."

Rosset answered Menn on April 24, 1963, telling him that he had seen the Amory article on "let's stamp out paperback obscenity" in the *Post.* "I was very upset by it. I predicted trouble, and I was right. Within three days, thirty-nine booksellers, from twenty-two stores in the Times Square area, were arrested, and large quantities of books were confiscated. I hope that Mr. Amory feels uplifted."

The *New York Times* occasionally clouds the artistic climate by refusing advertising to books it deems "improper." "We have had a great deal of trouble placing advertising in the *New York Times,*" Rosset wrote me, "and this began with *Lady Chatterley's Lover,* which was refused space in the *Times* and the *New Yorker.*" (*Candy* was also refused advertising space in the *Times.*) "No other paper or magazine refused *Lady* space that I can remember," Rosset added. However, the *Times did* accept *Cancer* advertising.

Certainly *Tropic of Cancer*'s publication presented the United States with a severe test of its principles of freedom of expression. How did the press respond? The widely read *Time, Life,* and *Newsweek* reviews with their flip treatments—"*Cancer* is a very dirty book indeed"; "an unbridled obscenity"; "*Cancer* is a bedroom travelogue"—did little to indicate that the book should be taken seriously. The reviews in the various newspapers and in other magazines seemed on the whole to be sympathetic to *Cancer.* Kenneth Rexroth, reporting on newspaper reviews across the country, said that reviewers minded the bad words less than "Miller's windy generalizations and empty profundities." [7] One general criticism of the newspaper reviews is that they did not try to create that particular "artistic climate" in which *Cancer* might be purchased as well as read. The newspapers failed, perhaps, to anticipate the censorship activities the novel would encounter in their communities and prepare for them. That such activities were a distinct possibility had been indicated by various citizen censorship group activities as early as 1960, before the Grove edition of *Cancer* was published.

During the embattled years of *Cancer* many members of the press stand guilty of not fighting its censorship, but no easy generalizations can be made here. Rosset, queried about press performance, wrote:

In some areas the press was wonderful, including such places as Minneapolis, Dallas. . . . However, this was not true everywhere. The worst perhaps was Chicago where the Chicago *Tribune* conducted a violent campaign and then finally banned all mention of the book whatsoever. Which was sort of spiting itself because when a trial came on in Chicago the *Tribune* could not mention the name of the book. It could only say that there was a book on trial in Chicago.

I would say that where the newspapers were procensorship we had a tendency to lose the court cases. This was true in such large cities as Los Angeles, where the Los Angeles *Times* was procensorship and very much against us. (Its fine book critic, however, was pro-*Cancer.*)

ACLU's Reitman notes:

The reason for lack of support in other media in opposing book censorship, *and especially Tropic of Cancer,* is due to the fact that many communities have seized on so-called dirty books as the final answer to the problem of present-day juvenile delinquency, and many influential groups in these communities are mounting campaigns to drive such books from the newsstands.

My private opinion is that *most newspapers,* even though

they recognize the danger of censorship, *do not have the courage to oppose what appears to be majority community sentiment.* Editorial courage is not a common thing, especially where the welfare of children is concerned. This is not to say that the picture is entirely black. There have been a few newspapers that have stood up and opposed censorship of the Miller book.[8]

And in a later letter Reitman added:

Our experience is that many newspapers have been wary about editorializing against *Tropic of Cancer,* recognizing that once the gates of censorship are open it could affect newspapers, too. However, there has not been 100 per cent agreement, and undoubtedly newspapers, looking for dragons to slay, have inveighed against *Tropic.*[9]

Time faithfully reported to its readers what the *Chicago Tribune* had to say editorially about its best-seller list, two months after the publication of *Cancer*:

Recently and tardily, we have become aware that some of the bestsellers that have appeared on our lists were sewer-written by dirty-fingered authors for dirty-minded readers. We aren't going to further this game by giving publicity to such authors and their titles.[10]

And then *Time* added, "This week the *Trib* printed a revised list of bestsellers from which two titles had been scrubbed. The missing works: . . . *Cancer,* Henry Miller's steamy *bedroom-and-gutter account* of his expatriate years in France; and *The Carpetbaggers.*" [11]

When the CDL mailed its thousands of letters containing twenty abstracts from *Cancer* to protest Judge Samuel B. Epstein's finding that *Cancer* was not obscene in Illinois' Cook County Superior Court, columnist Jack Mabley of the *Chicago American* wrote a column supporting CDL's campaign. Mabley had distinguished himself earlier by saying in his column that *Cancer* "deals heavily with carnal experiences, with perversion, with human filth and excrement." In the Chicago *Cancer* trial he admitted that when he wrote that column he had read only part of the novel! [12]

Other newspapers sensationalized their stories. The Boston papers, for instance, played up the titillating aspects of local *Cancer* litigation. The *Herald* ran such headlines as: TROPIC OF CANCER SEX DIDOES DEFENDED. The papers apparently under-played other aspects, however. David Littlejohn, a member of the English faculty at Harvard, wrote Rosset that there would be a public forum on the Massachusetts decision as soon as possible "after the word is out." Inviting Rosset to join Perry Miller, Harry Levin, and another in the forum, with himself as moderator, Littlejohn wrote, "*The proceedings have been stifled by the Boston press,* and you would be assured an interested, intelligent, and (I trust) generally sympathetic audience." [13]

Some papers made editorial statements like that of the *Stamford* (Connecticut) *Advocate: Cancer* is a "masterpiece of filth." [14] Others carried veiled comments by such syndicated columnists as Inez Robb, who wrote on July 19, 1963:

> The historic trend of the 20th century is against censorship in any and all forms.
> The line between liberty and license has become invisible. The result is that there is no longer any license only liberty. And liberty is indivisible, and not subject to attack.

Movie columnist Sheilah Graham reported that Henry Miller's "unfilmable" *Tropic of Cancer,* a "sex-ridden story," was "the number one best-seller in England." [15] Other papers were as apathetic as the *Newark Star Ledger,* which seemed uncon-cerned about the problem. The reading public, in the end, the *Ledger* believed,

> is protected by the literary quality of a novel. If it's trashy and salacious, it's generally short-lived. If it's a serious novel of quality and esteem, it usually is around for a much longer time. The reader becomes, in effect, a self-censor.[16]

The *Star Ledger* evidently did not feel that thirty years was too long to wait for *Cancer*.

Then there was the case of Norman Cousins, editor of a magazine that used to be known as the *Saturday Review of Literature*. In a letter dated March 17, 1961, Cousins had given

Rosset a statement to use in connection with the publication of *Cancer*. It read, in part:

> My congratulations on the courage and good taste which have led you to plan an American edition of Henry Miller's *Tropic of Cancer*. Henry Miller is both condiment and nutriment. With the passing of the years his fare is much less exotically remote than it once seemed. It may be that we are growing up to him. In any case, we can celebrate our return to the feast. *Tropic of Cancer* is one of the noteworthy books of this century, as Miller is one of the adornments of modern American literature.

Seven months later, in the midst of the battle, Cousins requested that Rosset not quote the comment again. Henry Seidel Canby had pointed out to him, Cousins remarked, that the quote

> might or might not conflict with the regular reviewer's opinions and that it was bound to be confusing. . . . What happened proved that Henry was right. I must have had to answer two dozen phone calls plus letters and questions at the end of lectures. . . . Please do not use the comment any further.[17]

What happened was *not* that Cousins' comment conflicted with the remarks of the *SR* reviewer, who was Ben Ray Redman. In fact, Redman praised the novel, as did *SR*'s poetry critic John Ciardi, in the magazine. Cousins no longer wanted to be placed in the position of defending his statements about the novel.

Sigma Delta Chi, the distinguished professional journalism fraternity, might have been expected to have an opinion on the issue, and the editor of its magazine, *The Quill,* did have one. Asked if he would like an article on the banning situation in Milwaukee, editor Clarence O. Schlaver replied to me, in part, on May 29, 1962:

> Frankly, I believe that an article now would be rather superfluous, considering that the legal cases are pending. I can not personally see how the freedom of the press issue can be stretched to protect book sellers from peddling filth which is not literature and which is being placed in every drug store at reduced rates primarily to attract the teen agers. Henry Miller's

book is available in libraries and in hard-bound cover at a higher price for adult readers. But the Grove Press wanted to flood the country with this pornography and in fact incited test cases to give the book publicity.

By way of contrast, what happened in the literary community when Judge Epstein delivered his *Cancer* opinion should also be recorded here. Finding the novel not obscene, Judge Epstein observed that "taste in literature is a matter of education. Those who object to the book are free to condemn and even to urge others to reject it." But

> voluntary discrimination is a far cry from censorship established by law whereby all readers are geared to the taste of the relatively few. . . . Let the parents control the reading matter of their children; let the tastes of the readers determine what they may or may not read; let each reader be his own censor; but let not the government or the courts dictate the reading matter of a free people. The constitutional right to freedom of speech and press should be jealously guarded by the courts.

When this decision was reported, a hundred and ninety-eight leading American writers and critics and sixty-four publishing companies signed a statement supporting Judge Epstein's decision and calling for an end to the widespread censorship of Miller's novel. Grove distributed the statement and its signatures to news media, along with a press release. It also placed them as an advertisement in newspapers in Chicago and Los Angeles, where the book was being attacked.

Ironically, the Illinois Supreme Court reversed Epstein's decision, but the aftermath of the Illinois trial, even with the Chicago CDL's actions, was as nothing compared to what happened in liberal neighboring Wisconsin.

9

A FOCUS ON
CANCER IN WISCONSIN

Some harsh revelations of censorship activities in Wisconsin will appear in the next few chapters of this study. Because of this I should reiterate that I do not believe Wisconsin to be a peculiar state where censors run rampant. Although Milwaukee may have a more streamlined censorship program than most other major cities in this country, as a counterbalance Madison, the capital, is certainly one of the liberal cities in America. Despite its heavy Catholic population in comparison to the rest of the country,[1] despite its spawning of McCarthyism, Wisconsin probably has a more liberal social and political outlook than most of the United States.

Wisconsin is the birthplace of Theodore Schroeder. A pioneer champion of freedom of expression, Schroeder was secretary of the Free Speech League and its principal fighter. Wisconsin is the birthplace of Robert LaFollette and the Progressive Party. A great university helps that state nurture its liberal tradition. Wisconsin is also one of the few states to have in its statutes a declaratory judgment act that helps combat extralegal censorship.

In fact, an important reason why Wisconsin was selected as a focus for this book is that it is in many ways more liberal than most states and so appeared to be an ideal stage for a presentation of the detailed story of the damage that unbridled censorship can do in our society.

The basic law on undesirable literature in Wisconsin goes back to 1849, when a statute was enacted prohibiting the importation, publication, sale, or distribution of anything containing obscene language or pictures manifestly tending to corrupt the morals of youth. Apparently modeled after a Massachusetts statute, parts of it are identical to the earlier Massachusetts law.[2] In 1901, the first major addition to the 1849 law made it illegal to distribute or possess any printed matter devoted primarily to publication of crime news, police reports, or accounts of criminal deeds, or pictures and stories of the deeds of bloodshed, lust, and crime. This probably unconstitutional provision was struck down in 1955, as was a 1941 provision barring any publisher from distributing for a period of two years a publication in which obscene material had appeared.

Reflecting the growing concern in Wisconsin over obscene literature are the numerous newspaper stories and editorials appearing from 1938 on, and the fact that between 1939 and 1959, some twenty bills relating to the problem were proposed in the legislature. Four became law.

As early as 1926, Wisconsinites were being assured by a state treasurer, Solomon Levitan, that they needed "a housecleaning," that sex magazine influence "cannot but sap the moral fiber of our youth." Community clubs throughout Wisconsin were urged to "purge through combat." [3] Catholics, who have many times been in the vanguard when it comes to censorship matters in this country, were being asked in 1938 in Wisconsin to help suppress obscene literature. One news story reads:

Suppression of obscene and indecent literature was demanded throughout the archdiocese Sunday as Catholic priests led the attack on objectionable publications.

In scores of churches parishioners repeated after their spiritual leaders the Legion of Decency pledge.

Committees were appointed in many parish societies to canvass their districts, searching drug stores, newsstands, cigar stores and filling stations, and asking cooperation of the proprietors in the campaign. . . .

If magazine dealers fail to cooperate in the campaign, their names will be handed to parish priests and posted in church bulletins. Parishioners will be expected to boycott the stores thereafter.[4]

Concern about objectionable literature brought about that probably unconstitutional 1941 law, the Doyne bill. In the early months of that year a group of a hundred men met in Sheboygan to determine what should be done to rid the county of salacious literature. Significantly, the meeting brought in Milwaukeeans to tell about Holy Name Union activities in their area. The *Sheboygan Press* on February 3, 1941, called for action—the result was unconstitutional action.

Activity in the Wisconsin questionable-literature arena virtually ceased during World War II, but it picked up in 1949 with renewed vigor. A surge of proposed bills hit the legislature. Wisconsinites were worried, as many other Americans were, about juvenile delinquency and antisocial behavior and the concomitant increase in comic books and paperbacks. As did most censors throughout the nation, Wisconsin censors linked the two. And more and more, groups within groups were organized to fight the flood of questionable literature.

Marquette University, through some of its faculty, has for many years played an influential role in censorship in the Milwaukee area. Writing in the *Marquette Law Review* of 1951 (just after a three-semester editorial reign on the *Review* by student Howard H. Boyle, Jr., who grew up to become prominent in the Wisconsin *Cancer* campaign), James E. Harpster decried the flood of obscene literature in newsstands and bookstores. Although it was debatable whether "this deluge of indecent literature is the cause or the effect of America's moral disorganization," Harpster cited J. Edgar Hoover and his frequently quoted statement on the subject: "The increase in the number of sex crimes is due precisely to sex literature madly presented in certain magazines. Filthy literature is the great moral wrecker. It is creating criminals faster than jails can be built." [5]

In the same year, 1951, the *Milwaukee Sentinel* (a Hearst paper at this time) conducted a survey of "peeper type magazines" in Milwaukee that stirred the District Attorney to action.[6] The *Milwaukee Journal* joined the chorus. In an editorial entitled "Filth on the Newsstands," it said:

> There's a strong and growing public demand for reasonable, generally acceptable standards of decency for the cheap pulp publications. With that to back them up, the publishers, individually and through their organizations, could certainly reduce the flood of plain filth on the newsstands.[7]

The Wisconsin Pharmaceutical Association (a potent censorship force) told the legislature in 1953 that the druggists were concerned about the literature on the stands.[8] During this same year Mrs. E. Harold Hallows, head of the Decent Literature Committee of the Milwaukee Archdiocesan Confraternity of Christian Mothers, related how most proprietors "co-operated excellently" when her committee members took book lists of the National Office for Decent Literature to them and asked them to remove the listed publications from their shelves.[9] (Mrs. Hallows is also the wife of one of the Wisconsin Supreme Court Justices who were later to rule on *Cancer*.)

Several people among those working for tighter obscenity laws in Wisconsin belonged to national organizations such as the PTA, which were conducting nation-wide campaigns against questionable literature. Congressional committee hearings on the topic in the fifties also indicated that Wisconsin's concern at this time was not atypical. And because of pressure from civic and religious groups, thirty state legislatures in 1955 considered "bills broadening the definition of obscenity to cover crime and horror comics." [10]

One of the most common means of restraining obscenity is by prosecuting dealers on criminal charges. Wisconsin's adoption of a new criminal code in 1955 (Chapter 696) broadened and modernized its obscenity statutes. More distribution methods and different materials, such as films, recordings, etc., were brought under its jurisdiction. Booksellers and distributors in

Wisconsin now operate under these provisions of the criminal code:

944.21 LEWD, OBSCENE OR INDECENT MATTER, PICTURES AND PERFORMANCES.
(1) Whoever intentionally does any of the following may be fined not more than $5,000 or imprisoned not more than 5 years or both:
  (a) Imports, prints, advertises, sells, has in his possession for sale, or publishes, exhibits, or transfers commercially any lewd, obscene or indecent written matter, picture, sound recording, or film; or
  (b) Has in his possession any lewd, obscene or indecent sound recording or motion picture film; or
  (c) Has in his possession, with intent to transfer or exhibit to a person under the age of 18 years, any matter prohibited by this section; or
  (d) Advertises, produces or performs in any lewd, obscene or indecent performance.
(2) Whoever requires, as a condition to the purchase of periodicals, that a retailer accept material known by the distributor to be lewd, obscene or indecent may be fined not more than $5,000 or imprisoned not more than 5 years or both.

944.22 POSSESSION OF LEWD, OBSCENE OR INDECENT MATTER. Whoever knowingly has in his possession any lewd, obscene or indecent written matter or a lewd, obscene or indecent picture may be fined not more than $1,000 or imprisoned in the county jail not more than one year or both.

944.23 MAKING LEWD, OBSCENE OR INDECENT DRAWINGS. Whoever makes any lewd, obscene or indecent drawing or writing in any public place may be fined not more than $100 or imprisoned not more than 60 days or both.

Two other pertinent sections of the statute provide for search warrants and give officials the right to keep and, on court order, to destroy obscene material.

The criminal code was passed after extensive public hearings at which responsible representatives of school, church, civic, and veterans' organizations explained the need for adequate protection. A law relating to the distribution of crime comics to minors was passed in 1957.

Another important law supplementing Wisconsin's criminal statutes in the obscenity area was passed in 1957. It climaxed nearly "a decade of public agitation for more stringent censorship within the state." [11] This is a civil statute (Wis. Stat. 269.565 [1957]), which is also patterned on a Massachusetts law and which provides for

> a procedure for judicial determination as to whether a particular writing, picture, sound recording or film complained against is actually obscene. The process is begun when the district attorney files a complaint in the circuit court against allegedly obscene material. The court then examines such material to determine if there is reasonable cause that such matter is obscene. If so the court then issues an order against persons interested in the publication, production or distribution of the material to show cause why such material should not be judged obscene. If no person answers the court order, the court may make judgment that the matter is obscene. Otherwise, the defendant may request a jury trial and is entitled to a speedy hearing subject to the ordinary rules of evidence in civil actions.

At such a "speedy hearing" the court receives the testimony of experts and evidence as to the literary, cultural, or educational character of such matter. The court also hears *testimony on the manner and form or its production, publication, advertisement, distribution and exhibition.*[12] The dominant effect of the whole of such material shall determine whether that material is obscene. The findings of the court can then be used as evidence in prosecution under the state's criminal code. Under this civil law *Cancer* was prosecuted in Wisconsin.

A declaratory judgment act accomplishes a number of things. Under a criminal action there is usually some delay between the time obscene material is offered for sale, an action is started against it, and a court judgment is rendered. During this time the material continues to be sold. The Wisconsin declaratory judgment act provides for an injunction to *prevent* sales until a judgment is rendered. (A thirty-day leeway in this matter was circumvented in December 1961 by an amendment to the act which provided for *immediate* stoppage of sales.) Under the criminal code, prosecution rests upon a "beyond reasonable doubt" clause. Under the Wisconsin declaratory judgment act, that bothersome (to prosecutors) clause is eliminated. A big hurdle in criminal cases is proving that the seller is aware that the material he was selling is obscene—the *scienter* issue. The declaratory judgment act takes care of this obstacle since the seller is notified of the action taken by the court. Once notified, of course, few sellers continue selling that objectionable material.

But the primary purpose of the declaratory judgment act is to enable a bookseller to prevent a possible prosecution against himself by presenting a book for a judgment. Prior to 1957 in Wisconsin, there was a trial without evidence, by a judge alone. Under the declaratory judgment act the publisher, author, distributor, and bookseller are called to defend, and literary evidence can be offered in support of a defense. Under the criminal law, the bookseller suffered an economic loss even with ultimate acquittal, or taint in case of criminal conviction, which would effect an economic loss also.

Various authorities have attested to the value of such declaratory judgment acts.[13] Wisconsin's act, prior to the amendment, had features even more attractive than Massachusetts'. A court's findings were *not* to be "conclusive evidence" in a criminal prosecution, as is the case with the Massachusetts law.

State Senator Kirby Hendee (R-Milwaukee) gave as the reason for Wisconsin's adoption of the statute the idea that a "jury is more apt to convict a book than a man," a reason which seemed to be borne out later in the trial and appeal of *Cancer*. He introduced the measure at the request of the Milwaukee Junior Bar Association.

Massachusetts had given as *its* reasons for adoption:

(1) Alleviation of the power of private pressure groups, especially in Boston and their imposition on the community of absurd standards of morality; (2) alleviation of the entrapment of booksellers and their clerks by district attorneys influenced

to take action by private pressure groups; (3) protection of the innocent bookseller and his clerk who often could not know they were violating the law; and (4) prevention of the attraction of nation-wide attention to a book because it was "banned in Boston." [14]

The real reasons for the passage of Wisconsin's declaratory judgment act lie within those given by Massachusetts, and this became clear as the *Cancer* case developed.

These were the laws, then, which were at the state's disposal in the treatment of questionable literature at the time *Cancer* arrived. None contained a definition, really, for obscenity. What was the social censorship scene like in Wisconsin by 1961?

As far as public libraries in the state were concerned, the fact that Wisconsin is in the Midwest indicated, according to the *Library Journal*'s 1961 survey, that most questionable literature would not be found on their shelves. When the *L.J.* found that only 7.5 titles of 20 listed questionable books, including *Cancer,* were purchased by Midwest libraries, it also noted one Wisconsin librarian's reply to its questionnaire. She wrote that she

felt that the patron needed to be protected both from his own ignorance and from the evils of advertising and best-seller lists. Among her comments were: "Often, almost always, patron does not know content of book he is requesting and is embarrassed by it. . . . Best-seller lists and prolific advertising create a false demand for these titles. I wish that more book reviewing media would have the courage of the *Chicago Tribune* which is not listing these so-called "problem" titles with their best-seller listing. *More power to them.*" [15]

There was much self-censorship in school libraries too, by librarians and administrators. In an article called "The Pressure of Censorship on Wisconsin Public Schools," Lee A. Burress, Jr., revealed this along with other findings of an extensive survey sponsored by the Wisconsin Council of Teachers of English.[16] Some 1640 questionnaires were mailed to administrators and teachers. The returns revealed that in a two-and-a-half-year period covering roughly 1961–1963, some eighty books and seventeen periodicals came under fire. They included such books as the Bible, *The Scarlet Letter, Brave New World,* and J. Edgar Hoover's *Masters of Deceit.* Burress found that the better books were more likely to be attacked than the poorer ones. News stories about censorship troubles over a certain book at one school would bring inquiries at other schools about the same book. "Any book questioned by anyone becomes 'controversial,' no matter what its merits," Burress wrote. Stating that this was a national problem, that such incidents were just as plentiful in other states, Burress concluded that "the pressure of censorship is a prominent part of school life in Wisconsin." [17]

A year before the publication of *Cancer,* the *Green Bay Press-Gazette* opposed editorially Senator Alexander Wiley's speech advocating that more authority be given to the Post Office Department to keep obscene literature from the mails. We must suspect, the *Press-Gazette* said, that there are two primary reasons for Wiley's actions. One is the rise of and emphasis on juvenile crime. The other is political in nature.[18] In 1961, the *Press-Gazette* warned again, "There has been an alarming tendency in recent years for more regulation and restriction that borders upon violations of the Bill of Rights . . . usually from extremist groups." [19]

Through the years up to and including the years of the *Cancer* banning campaign, Wisconsin groups opposing obscene literature grew in number and in vociferous protest.[20] The Wisconsin Federation of Women's Clubs, for example, a prominent organization on the Wisconsin censorship scene, alone numbers some 20,000 members. Throughout all these years, the Wisconsin Civil Liberties Union seems to have been the only organization to oppose group pressures.

The Citizens for Decent Literature had entrenched itself in Wisconsin by 1960. CDL chapters were reported at Milwaukee, Winona, Sheboygan, Racine, Kenosha, Beloit, and Antigo. In March 1960 fifty organizations sent representatives to a meeting to sound out public opinion on forming a CDL chapter in LaCrosse. (Waukesha was forming one in 1964.)[21]

In 1956 the Wisconsin Pharmaceutical Association, a con-

stant and effective censorship power in Wisconsin, had sent its
1000 druggist members kits with decals and signs for window
display, showing druggist participation against obscene literature. The signs invited customers to call attention to objectionable books and magazines. The Wisconsin Pharmaceutical
Association was also reported at that time to be working with
distributors and civic organizations.[22] Druggists in Wisconsin
now use a list in screening their books. Grocery stores reportedly
use an Independent Grocers Alliance list.[23]

Censorship bodies acting with official sanction in 1960 were
the Milwaukee Motion Picture Commission and the Milwaukee
County Literary Commission. Similar organizations existed in
Racine and Kenosha, while Green Bay had the Committee on
Movies, Books and Television (COMBAT).

During the *Cancer* campaign such things as these happened
in Wisconsin: The American Legion Post in Eagle River demanded that the *New York Times Book Review* and the *Saturday Review* be removed from the high school library because
they were subtly putting forth "sex, filth and dirt." [24] In Ashland, a librarian allowed a Catholic priest to check out Nikos
Kazantzakis' *The Last Temptation of Christ.* Librarian William
Sloggy said that the book would be put back when the "borrower" returned it. The permanent borrower, the Reverend
Conrad Schneider, had previously protested in vain that the
book was "blasphemous." [25] In Edgerton some five hundred
people attended a public hearing in January 1963, after a telephone campaign by about twenty-five parents protesting the
fact that high school seniors were allowed to read *Catcher in
the Rye, The Ugly American, 1984, Brave New World,* and
Crime and Punishment. Mrs. Edwin Thalacker of Edgerton
called the books "filth." *Catcher in the Rye* was taken off the
reading list. In 1964, *1984* was removed.[26] In Oshkosh, peti-
tions with 160 signatures were presented in February 1963 for
the removal from the public library of such books as *Peyton
Place, The Carpetbaggers,* and *Strangers When We Meet.*[27] The
American Legion State Convention in July 1964 pledged support in the fight against pornography. The proposal was started

by the Plymouth Post, and the Sheboygan County Council of the American Legion adopted it. The *Sheboygan Press* editorially supported the move, quoting Keating of the CDL.[28]

Not everything that actually happened in Wisconsin when *Cancer* was placed on the bookshelves and the newsstands will ever be known, of course. Few cases of literary suppression by public officials ever reach the courts for a formal trial. Usually these matters are settled quietly at the level of complaint, warning, and withdrawal. This is true, for example, of practically all suppressions of comic books in recent years, and nearly all the suppressions of paperbacks. No newspaper accounts are given of these "minor" legal suppressions. Extralegal censorship receives even less newspaper attention, and this kind of censorship is more efficacious, cheaper, and more successful than legal censorship. The censor would rather have it this way to keep down sales of books under fire, and the bookseller does not generally want the taint of "dirty books" hovering around his shelves.

By 1961, when *Cancer* loomed over this horizon, we can safely assume that libraries and booksellers in the major Wisconsin cities were engaged in "unofficial collaboration" with law-enforcement officials. All that can be done here is to report the scattered instances that came to light in various parts of the state, and then concentrate in more detail on what happened to Miller's novel in that most liberal of all Wisconsin cities, Madison. Then the Milwaukee banning will be studied.

From the library reports just cited, we can surmise what happened to the hardcover edition in most Wisconsin libraries. Knowing how druggists and grocers censor themselves, we can also assume that very few copies of the paperback could be bought in drug stores and supermarkets. From various sources it was learned that the distributor in Richmond Center was not selling the paperback edition as early as October 26, 1961, so Macfadden Distributors reported. Two days earlier, in Racine, "Tex" Reynolds in his front-page "Between Lines" column noted that *Cancer* was being sold there even though there was a banning attempt in Milwaukee. "I've heard no agitation against it here," he wrote. There was a fine line between what's obscene and what isn't, Tex allowed, but if *Cancer* wasn't obscene, "the word may as well be taken out of the dictionary." [29] Racine's District Attorney must have noted the column, because within two weeks this was reported by UPI:

> RACINE (UPI)—Dist. Atty. John Peyton, citing complaints about the content of . . . *Cancer* said Thursday he is considering prosecution under state obscenity statutes of Racine county dealers who sell the book.
>
> Peyton said he has been examining the book himself and would notify dealers to withdraw it or face legal action before starting prosecution. [30]

Tex Reynolds in his November 4 column told more of the Racine story. He said Peyton read *part* of *Cancer*.

> Mr. Peyton agrees that circulation of the book can't contribute anything but an unwholesome effect on public morals. So he wishes, in lieu of possible prosecution, dealers here would voluntarily quit selling it. And maybe they will. One bookseller tells me: "I've been sold out for weeks, and I'm not ordering more copies. The trouble I might get in isn't worth it." [31]

In liberal Madison—kept liberal by, among other things, the omnipresence of the University and of that progressive newspaper, *The Capital Times,* this is what happened:

First of all, the public and school libraries of Madison were included in the two reports cited earlier and it is doubtful whether the liberal influence in the city affected them much. The University of Wisconsin Library, for example, had a copy of *Cancer,* but it was still, as late as 1965, in a "locked case." A special trip has to be made for "locked case" books by UW librarians, and students must read these books in the library. Even faculty must get special permission to take them home. Among other "locked case" books at that time: *Plexus, Candy,* and most of Burroughs' books. *Memoirs of Hecate County* was "released" a year or so ago. With the acquisition of *Sexus,* I assume that *Plexus* and *Cancer* will also soon be placed on the open bookshelves, because in comparison they are pretty tame fare, though there is no certainty they will be. The UW librarians say that experience has taught them that "certain books" come back mutilated. Hence the locked case. But here is what Margaret Culkin Banning has written about the "restricted shelf" so dear to many librarians:

> Sometimes it means a locked bookcase. Or it may be a row of books which stands in the backroom of a library, a row composed of volumes that are not admitted to the open shelves nor even listed in the usual catalogues. Sometimes it is only an informal place under the librarian's desk, where books which are never put into general circulation must wait until borrowers ask for them. Sometimes they wear out quickly and sometimes they gather dust. To borrow these books you must make a definite request, and although they would not be denied to any respectable adult, since permission is involved, so is censorship. The device of restriction may be one thing or another, but the interesting fact is that the administrators of most public libraries still think it is wise, or at least expedient, to have a hideaway for some of the books which they buy.[32]

The common interpretation of the locked case is that the library has the book, "but you have to have the nerve to ask for it." (Speaking from empirical evidence, it takes nerve.) On occasion too, the UW Library has bowed to police and other pressures.[33]

When the paperback *Cancer* came to Madison in the fall of 1961, it had to run a gantlet. A Madison distributor told me, "I don't like people who try to pressure me or tell me what my business is and what I can or cannot distribute."

"If the DA called you now," I asked, folding the Grove Press legal packet he had given me, "and told you to take the Miller book from the stands, would you do it?"

"You damn right I would!" he replied.

This distributor fears the criminal code. The declaratory judgment act was nice, he admitted, but what "they" would hit him with was the "other law"—the criminal code. The distributor was also afraid of what other children would say to his children if they found out he was distributing "dirty" books.[34] Lockhart and McClure envision just such a situation:

Criminal prosecutions have an enormous impact upon retail and wholesale news dealers—reputable businessmen in their communities. The embarrassment and shame of being charged with the crime of selling obscene literature, added to the trouble and expense of defending against criminal actions, are enough to terrify dealers in any community in which the practice of criminal prosecution without forewarning has been employed.[35]

"Frankly," the distributor said, "*Tropic of Cancer* doesn't bother me in the least. It's been made available to a class of people who are discriminating." Which means that such questionable books get to the "University area only, and selected reputable newsstands." Use nothing which will cause controversy, is his motto.

"We held off on distribution of *Tropic of Cancer* a while," said Arthur Sweet, manager of the distribution agency. "Then the publisher recommended we 'high spot' it—make it available only in a limited number of stores—which we did, after checking with the DA's office." [36]

The druggists and supermarkets in Madison, then, generally did not get *Cancer*. If it had been distributed to them, it probably would not have gotten onto the shelves anyway. Madison druggists, of course, belong to the Wisconsin Pharmaceutical Association. During the *Cancer* banning, Albert J. Niebauer, purchasing agent for the large local chain of Rennebohm Drug Stores, said that if he or a store supervisor sees a magazine that is objectionable, he will take it off the rack and send it back. Occasionally, he said, church groups will call him and object to a particular book. He checks it and removes it if he agrees that it is objectionable. So far, he emphasized, he has never disagreed with any complaint.[37]

Those Madison newsstands which did receive copies of *Cancer* soon removed them. Describing their activities to a special legislative investigation committee, Elery Johnson, owner of Otto's News Stand, and Carroll E. Boyd, co-owner of Snappy's Place, said that the newsstands "made some efforts to police themselves in the materials they carried on their newsstands and were always willing and eager to *cooperate* with local authorities." [38] The Madison District Attorney's Office, Johnson said, had asked him to take *Cancer* off the stands.[39]

What happened at the District Attorney's Office, and how it all came about, was pieced together from news stories and interviews. Police Inspector Herman Thomas, in a letter to the Madison *Capital Times* publisher, William Evjue, said that he obtained a copy of *Cancer*, read three pages and then showed it to Police Chief Wilbur Emery. Emery sent it with a note to District Attorney William Byrne for evaluation.[40] The note said in effect, I do not have to read any farther than page 9 to know that this is a filthy disgusting book which should be removed from the bookshelves of Madison.[41] The District Attorney's office decided to "request" the local magazine and book vendors not to sell the book until the Milwaukee case had been adjudicated. *"All vendors complied."* [42]

Inspector Thomas showed a *Capital Times* reporter a copy of "Who Is Tampering with the Soul of America?," an article printed and distributed by Madison's conservative *Wisconsin State Journal* (some 290,000 copies of it have been distributed, the *Journal* proudly proclaims). Thomas remarked that his thinking paralleled that of the article's author, Jenkin Lloyd Jones. The *Capital Times* called the article a "puritanical outburst" from the "reactionary *Tulsa Tribune*," of which Jones is the editor. In Jones's article, *Tropic of Cancer* is described as a "collection of inscriptions taken from privy walls." Published by the *Wisconsin State Journal* during the critical phase of *Cancer,* on October 29, 1961, the article has other forceful, if not intelligent, statements: "Let's quit being bulldozed and bedazzled by self-appointed longhairs. Let's have the guts to say that a book is dirt if that's what we think of it, or that a painting may well be a daub if you can't figure out which way to hang it." Russian literature, said Jones, "may be corny but it is clean." [43]

There was no police ban on *Tropic of Cancer*'s sale, Police Chief Emery protested, according to the *Journal*. "We simply asked the vendors not to stock them." [44]

Captain Frank E. Forster of the Madison Police Department

said that obscene literature in the city is prohibited by Madison City Ordinance 26.04, but that there are few objectionable books on sale in Madison. Everyone "cooperates." (There is evidence, too, of police censorship of movies in Madison.) [45]

Edward Nager, Assistant District Attorney at that time, within whose province obscene literature fell, remarked to me in an interview in December that the police always work this way. He quoted Emery as saying that part of the police's duty is to prevent crime, and this is part of the prevention. The new District Attorney, he added later, "may, probably will, tell the police off, when the chips are down." [46] If police want to "nudge" merchants on their own, Nager said, they can. "If I were the merchants," he added, "I would be upset." Booksellers, however, were told by the Madison District Attorney to "undertable" *Cancer* pending the appeal of the Milwaukee trial result. At the instigation of the Madison CLU the DA admitted this was poor advice and said that it would be withdrawn. [47] But even prior to the trial result, of course, in the first days of *Cancer,* Madison had unofficial banning:

"I called the Coop [the University bookstore]," Nager said, "and asked them how they were fixed on *Cancer.* They said they had about a dozen copies on the shelves. I told them to reserve one for me because I was pretty sure they'd get a request from the police to remove them. But they never heard from the police. The police don't bother the University too much."

All this took place in the first days after publication, and without the knowledge of the local ACLU unit.

Assistant District Attorney Nager allowed me to go through copious notes of major obscenity cases which had been taken down in preparation for prosecution against *Cancer.*

"When," I asked, "will prosecution begin?"

"As soon as Milwaukee decides the case," he replied.

"Are all the other district attorneys in Wisconsin also waiting for Milwaukee?"

"Yes," Nager replied. "Most of them are."

When it comes to "obscenity" then, the liberal state of Wisconsin has some illiberal tendencies. Even in Madison, censorship is carried out through police, law-enforcement officers, druggists, and grocers. But what happened in Madison seems minor indeed when compared to what took place some eighty miles away, in one of the most censored cities in this country—Milwaukee.

10
MILWAUKEE—
A PROGRAM OF GUARDIANSHIP

At the start of the *Cancer* campaign, the Milwaukee Assistant District Attorney concerned with obscene literature wrote me about how he dealt with the problem. After describing what he was doing, with the help of the Police Department Vice Squad and the cooperation of Milwaukee businessmen, Richard B. Surges concluded his letter with: "Consequently, we do not consider ours a program of censorship, but rather a program of guardianship." [1] Before reading about that "program of guardianship," and what happened to Miller's novel when it became a pawn in the program, we should glance briefly at Milwaukee's censorship history.

Milwaukee has always led the way on the state's censorship road. At least partly because most instances of bona fide pornography circulation in Wisconsin occur in Milwaukee County, many of the obscene-literature bills in the legislature have been proposed by Milwaukee legislators. What is most noteworthy, however, is that far more pressure groups are engaged in suppressing questionable literature in Milwaukee than in any other city in Wisconsin. In recent years many of these groups have operated from strong bases of Catholic institutions fighting what they consider "bad books." (About 40 per cent of the Milwaukee population is Catholic.) And these citizen groups have been joined by other religiously oriented and secular groups. The *Censorship Bulletin* of the American Book Publishers Council, Inc., reported in September 1956:

> A three-year campaign against indecent literature in the Milwaukee Archdiocese has taken on an interdenominational aspect, it is reported by the *Sentinel* and the *Journal* of that city. At a meeting early in July at the home of a district chairman of the Milwaukee Archdiocesan Confraternity of Christian Mothers, representatives of the Ascension Lutheran Church pledged the support of the United Church Women and the Parent-Teacher Association Council. "We believe we can aid the drive against objectionable literature," the *Journal* quotes the spokesman for the Lutheran group as saying, "by joining forces with the Catholic women not only in the immediate area of our church, but in other parts of the city and county."

Three years later, fifty representatives of civic, veterans', educational, and religious organizations, according to the *Milwaukee Journal,* sent copies of allegedly offensive magazines to law-enforcement agencies.

Periodic pressures are put on drug stores and supermarkets by these citizen groups.[2] In public testimony during the *Cancer* campaign, a Milwaukee distributor told of magazine racks in supermarkets being raided by irate women objecting to (1) pictures of a strapless bathing suit in *Life* magazine; (2) an article on artificial insemination in *McCall's;* and (3) an article on birth control in *Reader's Digest.*[3]

On the eve of *Cancer's* prosecution in Milwaukee, Mrs. Walter Merten, chairman of the Mothers' Decent Literature Committee of the Milwaukee Archdiocesan Confraternity of Christian Mothers, proudly announced that her committee had been in operation for nine years. (Mrs. Merten is the wife of former Assemblyman Walter Merten of Milwaukee who, incidentally, tried to get obscenity bills passed in the 1953 and 1955 sessions of the legislature.) Members of the Committee go out two by two in their parishes and look over newsstands. The Home and School League joined the Confraternity, Mrs. Merten reported, "and now fifty parishes have formed committees to combat the problem within their boundaries." NODL methods and lists were used, Mrs. Merten said, with much success. Still other citizen groups were working on the problem. Mrs. Louis Pagels of the United Church Women testified publicly in 1964 that one-man committees jot down questionable magazine titles and give them to the Milwaukee Police Department, which is ready to help at any time.[4] And in this same year the Rev. John Baumgartner of Capitol Drive Lutheran Church told his congregation that they would be "surprised at what the bookstore of the University of Wisconsin at Milwaukee was selling."[5] The Citizens for Decent Literature of Greater Milwaukee is also a strong force in these clean-up operations.

The CDL, formed in Ohio in 1958, got an early start in Milwaukee. Its first national meeting was attended by Dr. George E. Vander Beke, professor emeritus of education at Marquette University and chairman of the CDL of Greater Milwaukee. At a CDL meeting on March 21, 1962, the *Milwaukee Journal* reported that those attending represented in the main religious organizations, or were teachers. Presiding was Hoover T. Grimsby, pastor of the Ascension Lutheran Church. Vice-chairman was an attorney, Richard Yanisch. The "lip-smacking" and "glittery eyes" at CDL meetings as members hand the latest specimens down row after row, according to one *Journal* newspaperman, are hair-raising. There is "fanaticism there thick enough to cut."[6] The leading fanatic of the Milwaukee CDL, according to newspaperman Donald Olesen, is Father Gene Jakubek. Corroborating this is Morgan Gibson, a faculty member and poet at the University of Wisconsin at Milwaukee. Gibson wrote early in 1964:

> As you probably know, Father Jakubek, of the Marquette University High School [is] the prime mover of the Citizens for Decent Literature. Recently, the CDL has conned the Wisconsin Federation of Women's Clubs into joining in a campaign against smut.[7]

Blanshard has described the struggles which go on with such citizen groups:

Most of today's conflicts about printed obscenity are taking place in a kind of literary underworld where the publishers of the "girlie" magazines and the comics are pitted against reform committees and police censors. This underworld struggle rarely reaches the courtroom because of the appalling potential costs involved in court battles. Very few bookdealers or publishers make enough profit on the sale of any one book or magazine in one community to justify a challenge to a police ban. As a consequence, most bookdealers accept quietly a system of extra-legal censorship imposed unofficially by police, prosecutors and vigilante committees, even when they resent it fiercely and consider it unconstitutional.[8]

Though these groups may be small in comparison to the rest of the community, their power lies in fanaticism. As Lawrence A. Lowell said:

> One man who holds his belief tenaciously counts for as much as several men who hold theirs weakly, because he is more aggressive, and thereby compels and overawes others into apparent agreement with him, or at least into silence and inaction. *This is, perhaps, especially true of moral questions.* It is not improbable that a large part of the accepted moral code is maintained by the earnestness of a minority, while more than half of the community is indifferent or unconvinced.[9]

The pressure applied by the private groups to suppress questionable literature is generally exerted at the retail level, where boycott has its greatest effect. From 1953 to 1958, some 2500 such instances were reported to just one American Book Publishers Council official alone.[10] Milwaukee made the list (1958) compiled by Hempel and Wall, as a community subjected to this extralegal censorship.[11]

One active group in Milwaukee, however, exerts pressure at a higher level. Although the Milwaukee Radio and Television Council has a total of 306 actual members, through a delegate system some twenty thousand persons are represented. Each year MRTC concerns itself with various aspects of programming (it is primarily concerned with television), views the programs, and evaluates them. It distributes cards to all its members. Criticisms are written on them and the cards are mailed to stations. A close associate of the group, a professor, calls it "confused and lacking in direction." Although MRTC has been in operation for eighteen years, it may not have much power. The comments are rarely constructive or even well informed, and two station managers reportedly patronize or ignore MRTC members. One manager calls them "a bunch of do-gooder women" and says he never pays them any attention.[12]

Milwaukee's citizen groups have been criticized for their activities by the city's two newspapers only once, according to my research. That criticism came *after* the *Cancer* campaign and was directed at the CDL. Groups were actually encouraged to participate in censorship activities by a report of the Milwaukee Junior Bar Association in 1956. This important report, the result of an investigation of Milwaukee's Literature and Motion Picture Committees, recommended that private groups be utilized to bring questionable literature to the attention of the Literary Commission. The activities of the private groups were condoned:

> It is the perfect right of any private individual or organization —religious or otherwise—to request the District Attorney to bring prosecutions under the present obscenity laws or under any other law to be enacted. It is also the perfect right of private groups to ask proprietors of drug stores and other distributors of magazines, as well as motion picture theatres, to sell or show only those magazines, books or movies which, to the private group, are unobjectionable. *They may apply any standard— vague or not—which they choose.*[13]

No word appears about abusing that right of request. Nor did the Milwaukee *Journal* or *Sentinel,* in reporting the Junior Bar Association's conclusions, remind these groups that such a thing is possible.

Milwaukee's movie and literary commissions have played important roles in its "program of guardianship." How they were formed and how they work is important to this study because it shows how good social intentions can be thoroughly subverted.

Milwaukee is not the only city to have a Motion Picture Commission. As many as ninety American cities have had them. By 1958, however, the number had dropped to about twenty. The decrease probably came about because of abuses, or because officials realized that such screening is a form of prior restraint—something which Ernst and Schwartz refer to as the most severe method of intellectual suppression known in modern times. They explain the operation this way:

> This form of censorship is in reality a precensorship that occurs before a particular film is shown to the public. Without allowing the theatre owner or producer the meager luxury of showing his film and taking his chances on going to jail if it is later declared to be "obscene," precensorship makes him submit his film to a governmental board in advance of public display. If the board feels the film is not proper for display, the public never gets to see it.[14]

The Milwaukee Motion Picture Commission (the Mayor's Advisory Commission on Motion Pictures) was authorized by state law in 1917. Composed of nine commissioners appointed by the mayor, the commission also has thirteen aides appointed by the commissioners themselves. Commissioners serve without pay for a term of four years. The selection of commission members supposedly results in a representative sampling of the community; however, by 1956 at least three commissioners had served more than three terms. The movie commission supposedly operates in this fashion: Individual commissioners and aides are assigned specific theaters to review motion pictures not shown to the commission as a whole. Reviews and trade publications are scanned to apprise the commission of forthcoming controversial films. These films are then shown by the distributor to the entire commission. When the commission finds a film objectionable in part, it usually recommends deletions of the parts in question. Through the years distributors have generally complied with these recommendations. At other times the distributor has been asked to withdraw the entire film because the commission has found it objectionable. Usually the distributor has complied.[15] The most easily frightened men in America are the theater owners.[16]

In Milwaukee, these movies were among those censored: *Blackboard Jungle* (scenes deleted); *The Moon is Blue* (not shown); *Rebel Without a Cause* (partial concession to the commission's requests); *Diabolique* (another compromise); *The Lovers* (withdrawal); *Garden of Eden* (withdrawal); and, more recently, *Kiss Me, Stupid* (withdrawal).

How the commission actually operates was revealed by the *Milwaukee Journal* in a 1965 news story. Only one of every five films "reviewed" by the Commission in 1964, it seems, was actually seen by a member.

> Judgments on the others—481 of 588—were based on motion picture trade papers and film rating services, according to Valentine J. Wells, executive secretary of the commission. Wells made the statement . . . when he was asked to comment on a complaint from a Chicago film distributor who accused the commission of creating "an extremely disturbing and frustrating situation."
>
> Last year, the commission recommended that 23 movies not be shown here. Deletions were advised on about 20 films; "adult only" labels were suggested on 53, and "mature entertainment" tags on 83. . . .
>
> None of the commission's "suggestions" was defied by theater managers, although the commission has no legal power.
>
> However, the commission has a potent weapon in a city ordinance which gives the common council the power to revoke a license "whenever the good order and welfare of the city will be promoted thereby." [17]

The film in question at the time of the news story was a Cannes Film Festival winner, the Japanese *Woman in the Dunes*. Although Wells seemed willing to follow reviews and trade publications and ratings in judging films, he said this about the Cannes award:

These awards are no indication that a picture is a good one. They give out these awards like Cracker Jack. *It's not our business to determine a picture's excellence.* We judge it on the basis of the standards of decency in the community.[18]

There is a city ordinance, Wells added, that "bans human exposure from the shoulder to the knees in movies." [19]

This is the same movie commission that the *Milwaukee Journal* in 1956 recommended should be kept in its present form and not made official, *since this would mean censorship!* This from one of the top newspapers in America. The occasion was the release of the Milwaukee Junior Bar Association report. Allow me to reiterate. This recommendation came from the *Journal,* even though one of the reasons for the MJBA investigation was that Milwaukee lawyers and the Civil Liberties Union were deeply distressed by the censoring of films and literature that was taking place. This recommendation came from the *Journal* even though these censorship activities were divulged by the report.

One year after the MJBA Report was released, a Junior Bar Report consultant and a Milwaukee CLU member, Leonard S. Zubrensky, explained how movie censorship was enforced in a letter to Madison's CLU president, William G. Rice:

> With regard to movies, the device is to threaten license revocation or to threaten a refusal to renew when the yearly renewal period comes up. This device very often scares motion picture exhibitors from showing "controversial movies." [20]

Something equally reprehensible so far as movie censorship in Milwaukee is concerned, however, was revealed in public testimony in 1964 by the First Assistant District Attorney. Surges said

> he did not feel that movies were a very extensive problem. He explained that *his office has established liaison with the company which purchases the movies for showing in Milwaukee,* and they have been asked to help screen out objectionable ones.[21]

Milwaukeeans are "safeguarded" by a double screening process.

The Milwaukee County Literary Commission's censorship record is not so distinguished. Disagreements among members and many periods of inactivity spot its record. Despite this, the District Attorney's use of it was not impeded. Established by Chapter 25, Ordinances of Milwaukee County, June 1, 1949, the Literary Commission was to be composed of:

A representative of the Milwaukee Public Library Children's Department, a representative of the County Council of Parent-Teacher Associations, a member of the County Board, a representative of a women's club, a member of the faculty of a school, university, or college located in Milwaukee County, a psychiatrist, and a member of the clergy.[22]

These were to be appointed by the chairman of the County Board. The Milwaukee Public Library refused to appoint a member to this Literary Commission, however, so an amendment provided for an alternate member with youth counseling experience. At the time of the writing of the MJBA report, the commission was inactive. Three of the seven appointees had lost interest and failed to attend meetings, and among the four remaining, a stalemate had developed over the policy and application of the ordinance to literary censorship in Milwaukee County. Within six months after its formation, commission members were unable to agree on what reading matter was correlated with juvenile delinquency.

The Literary Commission operated, when it operated, in this fashion:

A request to investigate particular periodicals or books would be received by the Commission from either the District Attorney's office or an interested church or civic committee. The Commission would then proceed to examine the questioned publication, discuss its merits or demerits, and forward its recommendation to the District Attorney. While the Commission has apparently never made a practice of following up its recommendations with the District Attorney, it is believed that the matter has generally been resolved by the District Attorney's forwarding a letter to the distributors of the publication in the Milwaukee area, patently threatening prosecution in the event the publication is not withdrawn from circulation. *The distributors have always complied with the "request."*

To date, no clothbound books have been banned or censored in Milwaukee County. Paperbound pocket books and magazines occupy the principal source for action.[23]

The MJBA Report commented upon the Literary Commission's conspicuous restraint, and said that in 1953 by a five-to-nothing vote the commission agreed to recommend that ten paperback books out of twenty-two examined be removed from distribution.

But the Literary Commission served other purposes. One of its main functions, according to Perry Hill and Donald Olesen of the *Milwaukee Journal,* was to take the pressure off the District Attorney and minimize prosecutions. In 1951, the late District Attorney McCauley, acting as a result of that investigation of peeper-type magazines made by the *Milwaukee Sentinel,* and on the recommendations from the Milwaukee County Literary Commission, told magazine distributing companies to remove eight of the offensive magazines from the stands, and six more from stands near high schools.[24] (The chairman of the Commission was David Host, professor of journalism, Marquette University.[25]) These magazines presumably were those the County Ordinance specified should be suppressed: those which "had a tendency to stimulate juvenile delinquency or corrupt morals, or might become a vehicle for inciting violent and depraved crimes against the person." Max Fenske, of the Milwaukee News Company, told reporters on this occasion that he was "always ready to cooperate with the district attorney." [26] McCauley, for his part,

> noted "previous cooperation" in similar instances, on the part of magazine distributors. But he warned that if he did not receive cooperation this time, "I will be compelled to hold you criminally responsible." [27]

By the end of 1952 the *Milwaukee Journal* reported: " 'Filth' Record of the City Is Good." The story beneath this head recounted the activities of the Literary Commission. Chairman Host reported that there had been about 50 complaints during the year:

> In about half the cases . . . the commission recommended that the particular book or magazine be taken off the stands.
>
> Host and Dist. Atty. William J. McCauley said that newsstand dealers and wholesalers had given "excellent cooperation" since the commission was founded two and a half years ago. *The questionable literature has been withdrawn without invoking the state law. . . .*
>
> Host said the commission asked a number of civic organizations and parent-teacher groups to assist.[28]

The threat of action if "requests" are not met once again is emphasized and reported in the *Journal* without editorial comment. Once again citizen groups are encouraged "to assist."

Among those responding to Professor Host's request for help was the Milwaukee Archdiocesan Confraternity of Christian Mothers. Said Mrs. E. Harold Hallows, chairman of the decent literature committee of that organization, the inspection of newsstands has been delegated to Catholic parish committees in the county.

> "We just got started on this last September," she said. "Our guide is a monthly code list sent out from Chicago [NODL]. We leave a copy of the list with the dealer and ask him to remove the objectionable literature. The dealers have cooperated very well, at least in my parish." [29]

Finally, the *Milwaukee Journal*—whose editorial policies on these matters have wavered from blessing to condemnation— reported on March 8, 1953, that during the past three and a half years few Milwaukeeans had *realized* that their newsstand literature had been censored. (Certainly they had not been alerted by the *Journal*.) Gerald W. Kloss of the *Journal* then outlined the operation of the Literary Commission.

Kloss's charges were reiterated by the *Milwaukee Journal* later that year when District Attorney McCauley, no doubt impatient with the Literary Commission's vacillations on these matters, acted unilaterally and banned *The Naked and the Dead, From Here to Eternity,* and *To Have and Have Not.* The *Journal* thundered:

> Dist. Atty. William J. McCauley is presently imposing his own personal censorship upon the community. This is without warrant in law, follows no authorized procedure for the safeguarding of individual rights, has no standing under any principle of democracy.
>
> He has been engaging in this misuse of his power for several years, to be sure, bolstered by a "literary commission" that the county board created *at his own request* to "advise" him. The current incident merely spotlights this abuse of the district attorney's office.[30]

After so revealing what led to the creation of the commission, and outlining how it operated, the *Journal* concluded: "There should be no more of this high-handed business."

The District Attorney had banned the three books at first not only from the bookstores but also from the public libraries. Under pressure from public opinion and the newspapers, McCauley withdrew bans on all but *The Naked and the Dead.* Then, belatedly, the Literary Commission was called upon to rule on the Norman Mailer novel. By a five-to-one vote it decided that the book could circulate in Milwaukee County.

Presumably deciding that the Literary Commission had outlived its usefulness to him, District Attorney McCauley in early 1956 barred ten magazines from the courthouse newsstand without consulting the commission.

The damage this Literary Commission wrought, combined with the censorship activities of legal officers, led the Milwaukee Junior Bar Association to propose a declaratory judgment act. Zubrensky had this to say about the reasons for this proposal in a letter to Professor Rice:

> You end by asking what is wrong with our present procedure with regard to obscenity laws. I participated with the Junior Bar committee on their fourteen-month study of censorship and the obscenity laws in this state and in . . . Milwaukee. We

found, among other things, that there is a simple device used in Milwaukee to prevent the sale of questionable or controversial literature.

With regard to books, all the district attorney has to do is send a list of special titles to the two distributors in Milwaukee County, and the distributors will immediately cease distributing the books. (This device is used only with regard to paper books.) *I have a list of some 81 titles that are no longer distributed* in Milwaukee. Obviously the distributors do not wish to court the enmity of the district attorney and so they quickly cease distribution.[31]

The 1956 MJBA Report questioned the constitutionality of both commissions' activities, stating that they may fall under the heading of "prior restraint." The report suggested that the commissions be abandoned, and the vacillating *Milwaukee Journal,* at this particular time, applauded the suggestion.[32] As we know, however, movie and literary commission censorship activities in Milwaukee did not end with the suggestion or the applause.

11
GUARDIANS AT WORK

Just before *Tropic of Cancer* directly encountered Milwaukee's "program of guardianship," the *Milwaukee Journal* on May 11, 1960, reported that Assistant District Attorney Surges had told the Citizens for Decent Literature of Greater Milwaukee at the Knights of Columbus Building that he was forming a literary review board (a literary commission) which would seek the "cooperation" of publishers and distributors to keep objectionable material off newsstands. Surges said that this was his private idea and that he would pick members of the review board personally. The members, he said, would be a dealer in books, a distributor, a police officer and a university professor. *Publishers' Weekly* reported on January 16, 1961, that a review board for obscene publications had indeed been created in Milwaukee.

The day before legal action was taken against *Cancer* in Milwaukee, District Attorney McCauley and Professor David R. Host, who once again headed the new Milwaukee County Literary Commission, explained the commission to the *Milwaukee Sentinel*. It was "purely advisory . . . but so far its recommendations to remove certain books . . . have generally been complied with." [1]

From the talk Surges gave to the CDL, one could gather

that he was beginning to get interested in the obscenity side of the District Attorney's Office. Surges came to the District Attorney's Office in 1957, and was promoted to First District Attorney about 1962. By the time *Cancer* was published, he was generally recognized as the obscenity expert in Wisconsin. His "program of guardianship" for Milwaukee was in full swing, and apparently he had relieved McCauley of the worries attending the curbing of obscene literature in Milwaukee. The ardor and the zeal with which Surges embraced his duties make McCauley seem like a patron of the arts. But Surges is probably not atypical of district attorneys or of other official but still somewhat self-appointed censors whose professional occupations are tracking down smut.

Richard Surges is a Catholic. In 1962 he was the father of five children. A fellow lawyer in Milwaukee has described him as "a very ardent crusader entirely dedicated to his Church and to whatever the Church stands for." That he is a zealot in his pursuit of questionable literature there is little doubt.[2] The chairman of the Milwaukee unit of the ACLU wrote me that "our local district attorney's office has . . . been a leader among the censoring groups."[3] (McCauley, also, was a Catholic.) Robert Hess, who defended *Candy* in Milwaukee, wrote that he also felt that the District Attorney's Office stirred up censorship groups.[4] Leonard Zubrensky noted that Surges is very pleased with the censorship situation in Milwaukee. He is reluctant to allow questionable books to be sold, and "any telephone call to him will cause a book to be removed."[5]

Surges outlined the problem in Milwaukee to me, presumably as it existed when he took over in 1957:

> Initially, the citizen groups, in a very emotional manner, were crusading against what each of these groups, and each of the individuals within these groups considered obscene, in an effort to gain permission to take from the stands and bookshelves printed and pictorial matter. Their anger and chagrin was levied against most officials, including the District Attorney's Office, due to their opinion that sufficient action was not being taken

by this or other official groups within this community; at least, not the kind of action which they considered to be within the duties of these people in authority. The primary problem, then, was to temper these citizen groups, and explain to them the nature, quality, intent, and value of the recitation of rights, contained in the United States Constitution, and the Wisconsin Constitution. It was also necessary to instruct these well-meaning people of the danger involved in arbitrary censorship, and book burning. You can well imagine that the initial work in this field was most time consuming, frustrating and painstaking, but eventually rewarding. In the course of this field work, there was developed an unofficial commission, made up of men from the following categories:

1. Druggists (the largest number of book dealers fall within this category).
2. University professors (to insure the protection of art and literature).
3. Book and magazine distributors (the means through which the printed material comes into the community of Milwaukee, and the person who would suffer the most, financially, from the diminution of literature coming into this community).
4. The District Attorney's Office (whose duty it is to prosecute under the obscenity statute).

Because of the balances and counter-balances contained within this group, it was felt that an effective evaluation of questioned literature would be obtained.[6]

This commission turned out to be more unofficial than Surges implied when I began querying the members in connection with *Cancer*.

One of the difficulties with governmental censorship in the area of morality is that the official connected with the job is no better equipped than the butcher and/or the baker to make precise moral judgments. Today's censor is no more discriminating than his predecessors. Lockhart and McClure point out:

The same ignorance or disregard of the literary and other values of a book marks the censor's activities today as it has in the past, and the reasons for this are not hard to find. For the censor is seldom a person who appreciates esthetic values or understands the nature and function of imaginative literature. His interests lie elsewhere. Often an emotionally disturbed person, he sets out to look for smut and consequently finds it almost everywhere, oblivious of the context and the values of the book in which he finds what he seeks. His one-track interest often is reinforced when his smut-snuffling becomes a professional occupation.[7]

In the light of these comments let us examine Surges' thoughts on obscenity and literature and the Supreme Court decisions involving them. Through a letter and an interview, and Surges' public testimony on these matters during the *Cancer* litigation, we are able to glimpse all these things as they seem to appear to him.

This Wisconsin obscenity expert commented freely on the *Ulysses* decision in a letter to me in December 1961. "The noteworthy aspect of the *Ulysses* decision," Surges wrote, "was that the test of obscenity was changed, to substitute the 'average, normal, healthy human being' for the person most susceptible to corruption, as a standard." Surges neglects to mention that portion of the decision treating the dominant effect of the work as a whole, for one reason or another. That it is through ignorance will be apparent from his statements later in connection with the banning of *Cancer*. In a later interview he admitted that he had not read *Ulysses*.[8]

Of erotic realism in literature Surges wrote:

With regard to your question as to whether an author is pandering to prurient interest, when coincidental to his intent to portray realism, and the subject stirs sexual emotions, my spontaneous response would be, an unqualified "no," if I were to answer the question in the form presented. Whether or not the subject matter stirs sexual emotions, is not the question involved in determining whether or not such subject matter is, or is not obscene. Frankly, as you may well know, sexual emotions can be stirred in different individuals by as many things as exist in this world.

Elaborating upon prurient interests, Surges also touches upon "community standards," something he bases his later legal arguments upon in the *Cancer* litigation:

> It is most important to recognize that there exists in each individual, a prurient interest, and this pruriency is somehow intermingled with the individual's animalistic beginnings, and functions. I stated that pruriency exists in every person, and it is controlled or not controlled in varying degrees, depending on the environment, education, culture, and in some instances, the mental capacity of an individual. If, therefore, written or printed or photographic matter appeals to this pruriency which exists in everyone, and in descriptions and representation of these things (sex, nudity, or excretion) goes beyond the customary limits of candor, it is obscene. It must be apparent that within the meaning of the term custom, or customary, there is encompassed, standards of a particular community, and the essence of candor also involves the standards of a community with reference to morals, customs, etc.

Surges will be quoted at length here and elsewhere because it is important for us to know as much as possible about a typically official censor's attitude toward such matters as literature and prurient interest, and because Surges is the key figure in the whole Milwaukee censorship story.

The reasons for Surges' actions against obscenity are outlined in the next paragraph, along with his attitude toward the nature and function of imaginative literature:

> A rather underlying premise involved in legal actions against literature, or against persons, for the sale of literature considered to be obscene, is that we consider that people do not exist for the sake of literature. On the contrary. Literature exists for the sake of people. People do not exist to give an author fame, the publisher wealth, or a book a market. . . . [Literature] exists to increase a man's interest in the world, his joy of living, his sympathy and understanding of all men in all walks of life. It exists to refresh, to console, to please, and enhearten. So that people do not lose their faith and confidence in the written word, it is necessary to protect the manner in which the printed word

is used by persons only interested in commercial or other extremely selfish considerations in its use.

Later, in public testimony, Surges would tell a Wisconsin legislative committee that some of our best-known authors are writers of pornography.

Most persons engaged in the suppression of obscenity strongly assert they are immune to its influence. But Surges does not feel this way. In an interview in his Milwaukee office, Surges declared that you "could be 'hooked' by obscene literature," and that it destroys your control. He admitted to going to confession two or three times a week to help keep him from becoming "addicted." Obscenity, Surges said, is like narcotics.

However, the Wisconsin civil libertarian Theodore Schroeder has said that psychologists have found that "to exhibit great touchiness about obscenity indicates mental inflammation over sex." [9]

Elaborating upon his "addiction" statement, Surges gave an example. If there were a window cut into this wall here, he said, indicating the wall above his office desk, and there were a man and a woman in bed on the other side having sexual intercourse and you and I knew it, we would feel "compelled," drawn to the window, to watch them. [10]

Surges told about a case that involved a man who used pornographic pictures to seduce his small niece and nephew. Then he said, "Let me show you what we've collected." [11] Surges opened his office closet and pulled out a cardboard box full of photographs and girlie magazines. Then came a most startling performance. Holding them close to the red vest he was wearing at the time of the interview, Surges thumbed through the examples, showing them to me. And as he did so, he made small throat-clearing noises. At that time, my business concluded, I quickly ended the interview.

Surges explained how his "program of guardianship" operated, in part, in this paragraph of his letter to me:

Within the Vice Squad of the Milwaukee Police Department, there are several men, who have been trained and instructed in the manner in which to proceed in dealing with questioned magazines, books, records, pictures, etc. I have worked with them for well over a year, and as a result, they are fairly well acquainted with what type of matter will offend the current legislative prohibitions. Even if these men are certain that the material is obscene, according to current definitions, they do not seize the material, but purchase the material, and bring it to the District Attorney's Office for review. In this way, we have taken more than just the necessary precautions in protecting the rights of individuals and the printed word.

This method of procedure, with the help of many druggists and book stores, whose cooperation I am pleased to say we have, has developed into a community-wide interest in advancing the position of good literature, by removing slowly but surely, pornographic literature from the shelves. The awareness of this effort has also had the effect of controlling the amount of "junk" that would normally appear on the newsstands and shelves. Consequently, we do not consider ours a program of censorship, but rather a program of guardianship.

What actually happens when the bookseller is selling questionable material and it is bought by the vice squad members was related by Surges in the interview. The bookseller is asked to appear at Surges' office. He is shown the material, or pages in the book or magazine, and asked if he knew he was selling such material. According to Surges, "Nine out of ten booksellers 'cooperate,' " and remove the objectionable material.

But many of the booksellers never make it to Surges' office to be intimidated by the grandeur of the Milwaukee County Building. Two members of the vice squad, James Donnelley and Robert Gaurke, admitted that they "nudged bookdealers and the distributors," and that 99 per cent of the booksellers took the "nudge," and removed the material.[12] Distributor William Aschmann said police were "continually going through my literature." [13] The vice squad men are self-educated. They have read *Cancer, Lady Chatterley's Lover,* and the Kronhausens' *Pornography and the Law.* They have not read *Ulysses.*[14]

Surges described them later to a legislative committee as men
who

> worked very closely and hard, both during working hours and
> after working hours, on obscene literature, [and they] became
> well known [versed?] in the field of obscene literature because
> of their studies in it.[15]

Everyone acquainted with the obscenity problem in Milwaukee, from legislators to newspapermen, seemed to know
that the policemen and Surges operated as they did.[16] If they
hadn't known it at the time of the *Cancer* trial they could certainly have learned it the following year during the public hearings of a Wisconsin legislative committee investigating smut in
Wisconsin. For with these public hearings the censorship fabric
was fully exposed, with the clear fact that all had existed for a
long time before *Cancer* and, indeed, though the trial was over,
did still exist.

When Cleveland Amory wrote his article, "Paperback Pornography," for the *Saturday Evening Post* in April 1963—that
article which so infuriated Rosset because he felt it would bring
out more censors—Amory reported that the chief publisher of
this paperback pornography was *located in Milwaukee.*[17] The
furor this revelation created can be imagined. State Senator
John Potter (R-Port Edwards) promptly proposed

> a bill which would appropriate $15,000 to establish a legislative
> committee to determine if and how smut is being published or
> distributed in Wisconsin.
>
> "I put this in the same category as dope and narcotics. . . .
> It poisons our youths' minds as drugs would poison their sys-
> tems." [18]

After a series of legislative maneuvers the bill was passed February 12, 1964, over the Governor's veto.

This smut committee revealed a number of things: The
publisher was not in Milwaukee, but had its headquarters at
Amherst, Wisconsin. Surges told the committee that he as-
sumed the Hall Printing Company of Illinois (the same company that had printed the pirated edition of *Cancer*) had

done the printing for Freedom Press.[19] A United States Postal Inspector out of Chicago, James P. Kelley, stated "that information had been received that one of the better-known families in the United States was backing some of this printing. He explained that good financial backing is essential in the business."

Most important for the reader is the committee investigation revelation, in Surges' own words and through his own cross-examination of witnesses, of how his "program of guardianship" worked. Having been called as an expert in the field to assist the legislative committee, he offered his Milwaukee program as a solution to Wisconsin's obscenity problem.

When Surges was present at the meetings of the Wisconsin joint Legislative Obscene Literature Commission, State Senator John Potter deferred to him in such a way that Surges dominated them. Certainly from the public transcripts it appears to be Surges' show.

In another way, too, it was Surges' show, as we are able to see from the testimony that opened with Milwaukee distributor Aschmann. Queried by Assemblyman Adrian J. Manders at the September 23 public hearing, Aschmann admitted that through

> a great amount of effort *we* have eliminated *a tremendous amount of titles.* And I have in front of me—it is not—I won't use this as a rule of thumb, but *we have here an N.O.D.L. list* which I think we distribute approximately 22 per cent of, and included in this are titles such as "Sexology," which has already gone through the courts, or some men's adventure-type merchandise which, I agree, if you asked me, have no basic value except that there are certain elements of people that read it. But if I come down to the girlie titles, we are talking about somewhere in the realm of 10 or 12 titles. I assure you that *Fling* will never get distribution through our area, but that is the only specific way that I can eliminate them if I get some kind of action against them. I am not a censor, and I don't ever and I never will contend to be a censor.[20]

"I only wish," Aschmann told the committee, "Mr. Surges would write me a letter and say 'Don't carry these 12 titles.' "

Throughout Aschmann's testimony, though he may be ungrammatical and ambiguous at times, he rarely forgets to include Surges as a party and a motivating force to what he is doing. Notice the *"we"* in the first line of the preceding quote. When Aschmann declares that *"we* have eliminated a tremendous amount of titles," he is being modest. Two years before in an interview he had told me that 2000 titles are not handled because the "quality is not good." There are no restrictions, he said, "outside of sex." And although some authorities feel NODL has declined as a potent force in the suppression of books and magazines, from the actions of Mrs. Merten, earlier, and now Aschmann, it seems clear that NODL is still influential in Milwaukee.

Despite Aschmann's declarations of not being a censor and not engaging in prior censorship, the following exchange took place. Surges asks the questions:

Q. Mr. Aschmann . . . when you get your shipments in, on many occasions you have conferred with me on the quality of some of the things that you consider questionable; is that correct?
A. We certainly have, and one of which was *Tropic of Cancer,* and I got nothing but trouble on that one, and—
Q. (interrupting) But even on magazines you have done that?
A. Oh, yes. Well, our last occasion was but a few weeks—well, I guess it was last week, and we have eliminated titles and there have been many magazines, one of which I predominantly, I mean, I specifically think of is with the last issue of *Nugget.* You and I sat on that one there for about an hour one morning discussing it.
Q. And you sent a letter then to the publisher?
A. I didn't put it out. [The magazine.]
Q. But, and in addition to that, Mr. Aschmann, you have called to our, the Office of District Attorney, and asked for opinions on titles; is that correct, and magazines, before you circulated them? Is that correct?
A. Absolutely, and I feel that I have every right to. I am a taxpayer and I am asking you for help, too, Dick.
Q. Right.

And so does Surges reassure Aschmann. But to reassure himself, Aschmann continues, "Just the situation is so great that I just don't know which way to turn, but I feel that the direction I'm going in is absolutely correct."

Surges believes the direction Aschmann is taking is correct too. Either unaware that he is engaging in extralegal pressures, or not caring that he is, Surges displays his "program" for the edification of the committee members. Here is a solution to the obscenity problem, says Surges, for the state, and, through Aschmann, for the nation. Aschmann sometimes wavers and questions the whole process, but whenever he does, he is always reassured by Surges.

Aschmann sees a public spiritedness behind the "program," and uses this to rationalize his actions:

A. Milwaukee is a tremendous, tremendously fine reading town, and they deserve to have good merchandise, and I try to get them as many as I can.

Q. [Still by Surges.] Now, after there has been some complaint about particular titles, in what manner do you operate then, Mr. Aschmann?

A. There I use more of an affirmative or a direct approach. Now, I don't know if you recall, Mr. Surges, that during the course of one of our meetings several years ago we thought this title was objectionable. I don't think any legal action was taken against it, but I wrote to the publisher, and since then he has been sending me a copy of the title each and every month, and as yet I have not personally even felt that the thing is capable or within the program which we are trying to talk about, and I would not take it down before Mr. Surges. . . . So this is the format we are running, if that is what you mean.

Q. Then your procedure is that if—if an issue of a particular . . . magazine, has been determined to be beneath the standards of this community, you then ask them to show that they are improving their quality or their format; is that correct?

A. That is correct. And some of them have improved, and then some I have shown you that they have made improvement, and I think you will agree.

Q. I can recall one, as a matter of fact, was *Swank,* is that correct, that had improved their format?

A. Yes, sir.

Q. And another one was *Cavalier*; is that correct?

Aschmann, of course, agreed:

A. . . . they came well within the scope of being of some value. If I recall, *Cavalier* went out and hired some very fine national writers and that improved the scope of the book. There was some merit to the book itself.

Q. In conjunction with your effort and the efforts of our office to exterminate this type of material, you have withheld many titles from distribution in this community?

A. Oh, yes, without even—well, Dick, you are such a busy man, I know what kind of, more or less in the format, and without even second question I have sent back many tons of merchandise that I don't put out.

Q. You refuse to distribute?

A. Yes, sir.

Q. As a matter of fact, you just recently made out a list for me; is that correct?

A. Yes, sir.

That list Surges refers to is not of Aschmann's *own* doing, however. As Aschmann makes clear in the next few sentences:

Q. Would you like to refer to that list?

A. Yes, I could, but these titles are specific titles which *you and I* acted upon in one way or the other.

Referring, once again, to the list, Surges asks:

Q. Specifically you have taken off these titles without the requirement of actual Court action; is that correct?

A. Yes, *and more,* as you say.

When asked to read the list of titles taken off the newsstands, Aschmann is careful, once again, to include Surges as a partner in removing the magazines from the stands:

A. These titles were *quietly* cut off the newsstand distribution *through efforts on your part and my part* after feeling that they had no basis or value to the area of Milwaukee, and they are as follows: *Ace, Bachelor, Bachelor's Best, Black Lace, Bode,*

Caper, Carnival, Casanova, Dare, Debonair, Don Juan, Exposé for Men, Fizeek, both annually and quarterly; *Fling, Follies, Futurama, Fotorama, Frolic, Furry, Gala, Gentleman, Glance, Grecian Guide Pictorial, He, Hi-Life, Jem, Joy, Manorama, Manual,*[21] *Mars, Men's Digest.* The tabloid newspaper *Midnight. Mister, Monsieur, Ogle, Pose, Rascal, Rat Fink, Real Life Guide, Scamp, Scene, She, Sir,* an annual. *Topper, Trim, Vim, Vue,* and *Zest.* And I believe the last one was *Fling.* However, I would like to say this: That this might be a rule and guide which we first worked on with—through Mr. Surges' office, but—and I can go right down our, which I have either withheld or cut off or refused to handle, and if you will notice all these blank spots—I notice you have such a list—and it deals in *many, many hundreds of titles because now we have a format, we have a basis for working* which we, without going through your office, we did not handle or care to handle.

For many years publishers submitted texts to the postal officials, in advance of mailing, for their advice on whether they were mailable. "Postmaster General Frank C. Walker regarded this as censorship . . . and notified publishers this would not be done any more." [22] According to one astute newspaperman, this practice "had every appearance of the kind of prior restraint plainly offensive to the First Amendment." [23] Milwaukee's Aschmann, and other distributors, are carrying on in the manner of the publishers. Surges, meanwhile—unlike some district attorneys in recent years, who in the role of extralegal literary censors have issued blacklists to local dealers of titles of books and magazines never condemned by a court—engages in a different kind of illegal prior restraint. With the prestige and backing of his legal office, he coerces distributors to make out a list *for* him. But actually, as Aschmann time and time again makes plain, Surges is not only consulted, Surges guides the distributor's blue pencil as it crosses off objectionable titles.

Aschmann is a key figure in Surges' "program of guardianship" for Milwaukee. The owner of the Milwaukee News Company at this time was Victor Ottenstein, who lived in Washington, D.C. Ottenstein gave Aschmann permission to take all objectionable material from his warehouse. Distributing 95 per cent of all printed matter in the community, the Milwaukee News Company is in a virtually monopolistic position. How Aschmann came to be so completely under the control of Surges and the District Attorney's Office is not known, but Walter Gellhorn has explained how intolerable pressure can be exerted upon persons in Aschmann's position by law-enforcement officials:

Application of pressure is especially easy in the case of paperbound books. In few cities are they distributed by more than two wholesalers, whose trucks also deliver magazines and comic books to news dealers and other retailers. [Aschmann's delivers paper-bound books and newsstand material.] The police need not attack upon a broad front, but can entirely control the situation by squeezing this narrow bottleneck. Truck operators are usually heavily dependent on police tolerance of brief violations of parking regulations, during unloading operations; wholesalers' warehouses are subject to being especially closely examined by building, fire, and health inspectors. Moreover, the retailers may be municipal licensees. Both wholesalers and retailers (who often combine ignorance of their rights with a disinclination to defend those of which they are aware) are therefore readily influenced by police "suggestions" that particular books be suppressed.[24]

Aschmann no doubt was aware of how unpleasant things could be made for him if he didn't "cooperate." That he was under some emotional strain seems obvious from his sometimes vague, ambiguous, and sometimes just plain incoherent ramblings about the operation he is running. His speech difficulties occur many times in the following extensive testimony when he is discussing the "agreement" that he has entered into with Surges and the District Attorney's Office. He admits to a fear possessing him when he entered into the agreement, he confesses to uncertainties about the program, and then embraces it too wholeheartedly. But listen to the exchange between Surges and Aschmann. Surges has just asked Aschmann why he doesn't carry certain titles which are carried in nearby Madison—titles which Aschmann has just expressed a thorough disapproval of:

A. Because you and I have talked it over, and we felt, through our so-called unofficial committee, that had no basis or value for the—we in general are trying to increase the reading, the betterment of the reading habits in the City of Milwaukee, not through censorship, but we feel we just needed the titles.

Q. Now, "agreement" is a term you mentioned sometime, did you not?

A. Absolutely.

Q. What do you mean by "agreement" and how? I think the members of this committee would be interested in understanding the manner in which you think that this entire problem of the dissemination of smutty literature can best be controlled in this state, and, as a matter of fact, since we don't publish it or print it in this state, *in other* states from whence we get this material.

A. Well, Mr. Surges, I think you have pointed out that monetarily we have come out ahead on this thing since we started it. And I can almost recall when we first made the approach on this matter, and *there were certainly a great amount of qualms on my mind, I did not have the sincerity of purpose, I probably were a little afraid of you, afraid of the District Attorney and afraid of the people I work for, and also afraid of the publishers which I represented.* Now, I base this on the fact that everything they [the publishers] put out is supposed to be legal. I know my position. I work as a professional man. I did not own any part of the business which I represent. And when we had our meeting, and I know Mr. McCauley *specifically* says we have to do something about it, and I know you had preliminary plans on it and we thought it over quite a bit, and *you came up with this cooperative effort, and I hate to call it "self-censorship," but I think I'd like,* for the lack of another word I don't have, but we—you had a writeup where you would get other people to help us and so forth, which you have. [The "paper" committee once again.] *But in general the whole thing is encompassed around you and I and what you do and other than that, I know that you have been putting in a great amount of work on it where other people have helped you.* I am very, very pleased in the way we have proceeded, and the gist of the whole thing is almost as simple as talking to these gentlemen where I continually spot magazines *and Mr. Surges continually spots magazines* and the complaints that I get *and the complaints he gets and the police department,* and we sit down and talk about it. And I remember one evening when you came up to our place of business, I think we stayed about 7:30, I think *we lopped off about 12 titles in the matter of 30 minutes,* and I had my assistants in on the meeting. And in general I think what has happened is we have a spirit of cooperation and accomplishment, and I think *I have in turn tried to spread it on a national level.*

Q. To other distributors?

A. To other distributors, that is correct.

Q. And have you discussed this particular type of program with them to any extent, Mr. Aschmann?

A. Yes, I have. Not only have I discussed it, I advocated it in open forum. In the first place, a wholesaler has no right to force anything on a local level. I think *you* are highly more professional and competent to know what the interest of the local people is concerned, and they don't want it in the city. I have talked it up in open panel and discussions and as late as two days ago we discussed it in New Orleans, and I was very pleased to hear the chairman of the Obscenity Committee of the Bureau for Independent Publishers and Distributors make the statement that it appears that no matter how much faith we do have in our publishers—and he's talking in open forum—that *he advocates the instillment of self-censorship.*

Q. And that would be through the distributor, would it not, Mr. Aschmann?

A. Originally through the distributor, but I have great hopes that it will go all the way down the line into the retailer, and probably where it belongs the most is into the consumer.

Q. You and I discussed that particular proposition with Mr. Kelley, the postal inspector, did we not?

A. Yes, sir, we had occasion.

Q. And he expressed some optimism concerning that possibility; is that correct?

A. Yes, sir.

Aschmann could conceivably have had even more success on the national level because he was president at this time of the Midwest Independent Distributors Association whose territory includes Wisconsin, Illinois, Indiana, and parts of Michigan. Aschmann goes to fifteen conventions a year in every part of the country.[25] (Surges told the committee that as a result of a conference held recently in Chicago great results could be expected through cooperation between states in solving the obscenity problem.) On the state level Aschmann has already had much "success" in his (and Surges') program. Surges gives Aschmann the opportunity to reveal his Wisconsin operations with this disquieting question:

Q. We had hoped to have Mr. Kelley here today, and he said he's going to try to be here, but he's in Detroit so I'm not certain if he would, and I just want to get on the record his own opinions that you heard from him concerning the possibility of such self-governorship of the industry effecting the eventual *complete elimination of trash and smutty literature, and he said that this appeared to be very possible from his contact with distributors;* is that correct?

A. That's correct. Dick, the other way will never work, and I don't know if the gentlemen [the Committee] are convinced, but the only thing I know we have done a tremendous amount of work on this problem, and I know it's—something has been accomplished. I have a tangible proof that it has been accomplished and I will say this: That I feel outside of probably some very, very small towns in Wisconsin that we probably have a greater, much better distribution of certain titles and elimination of this smut in Milwaukee than we do in the State of Wisconsin. To illustrate, we purchased the distributions in the County of Racine and Kenosha and overnight we washed out probably seven distributors and 60 titles within our own, and I don't know how many more of others that came in on direct. Now, this is a tangible proof that something has been done.

Q. That wasn't done before?

A. No, sir. And I don't know if you had occasion to talk with the District Attorneys in those two areas, but I am sure they are cognizant of it.

Q. *Yes, I have.* Now, do you think that *this procedure could be facilitated by individual state committees on that subject, statutory committees?*

And in his answer to this Aschmann indicates that he is aware of the illegality of the whole program.

A. Well, I believe the only state that I know specifically that had something similar to this, but I understand it was abolished recently, was the State of Rhode Island, because of some legal problems. And frankly, I think you will find that wholesalers in general want to sit down with people, want to be told or discuss the problem, want to cut off these titles, but there is always some legal effects coming out of New York City and things like that. I don't know what legally could be done on this, Mr. Surges, but I sure want to do something in that vein because I know that we probably can do better and I know *we will do more* in Milwaukee, but I know what we have done here.

Q. And you think it can be done with other distributors in the entire state and in the country?

A. I think the other distributors in our state, which we are predominantly interested in, would welcome such a system. . . . There is only one realm which we cannot—I can't—such as *Playboy*, where they make an outright commitment that they will go, and *it has to be handled on a legal basis.* I'm talking in general all this multiplicity of trash.

What Aschmann means by *Playboy*'s "outright commitment" keeping him from taking a title from his distributing list is made plain a little later in the meeting:

If Mr. Surges sends me a letter tomorrow to take off *Playboy,* I'd be more than glad to do it. I'm confident that two hours later there will be 15 lawyers in here from *Playboy.* I have within —and probably I have violated the law by going as far as I have on this thing—I know when I took off *Tropic of Cancer,* I had quite a problem because I mandatorily took it off, and I don't— I don't attempt to be a censor. My primary purpose here is to attempt to cooperate 100 per cent with a tremendous problem, and *I think we have done something.*

Aschmann speaks always in terms of "trash"—*that* is what he is eliminating. His ideas of trash, however, do not coincide with what other persons believe it to be. As he explains how much "trash" he distributes, this comes out:

> First you'd have to go back into my mind, and the only way I can, I go back into trash, what I particularly think is trash. *I have college professors write and call me and absolutely are furious because I cut off some titles;* but in my mind, is all I can explain, and I think I said, what trash is. It is bothering my business, it is bothering my dealers, and I feel, and it is of no basic value in the city. I feel that I distribute, of the over-all trash, 10 per cent.

Surges in an earlier meeting had been asked if he couldn't get permission from the distributors to give out lists which "they" compiled of books not to be distributed. Surges replied to the committee "that the books they were talking about *are such that they cannot get any convictions against them.*"

Assemblyman Manders wants even more accomplished. Some drug stores in his eighth district in Milwaukee have "bad magazines." He is particularly concerned with five or six magazines in Mattioli's drug store, on 35th and National streets. Aschmann replied to Manders, "If Mr. Mattioli said to me tomorrow, 'You cut those off,' I would do it; and if I had enough complaints of that nature, I would cut it off in the city." By this time Manders has found the magic word to erase his troubles and he now uses it: "I think if you are going to *cooperate* with the committee at all that you should lead the way in cutting them off yourself." And with this question, the illegality of the program is broached. Surges takes over the questioning:

> Q. If you did cut these magazines off voluntarily, what would occur to you from the standpoint of what the Federal Communications Commission would do? [Surges probably means the Federal Trade Commission.]
> A. You mean if I started to control the distribution of certain publishers illegally?

Q. Yes, sir.

A. They would bring—

CHAIRMAN POTTER: (interrupting) Well, what makes it illegal?

A. Well, let me answer this with a further question: If I cut them off—and it is confusing in my mind—when I'm talking about a small amount of titles remaining, the distribution of these, there is no doubt in my mind that, let's say, Ben-Mor would pick up a lot of these titles because we are talking about *Playboy*. There is no doubt in my mind that the postman would deliver it to Mr. Ben-Mor. Now, I wonder if we are solving the problem. I would be—

CHAIRMAN POTTER: (interrupting) That is not my question.

Q. In answer to Mr. Surges' leading question, you stated if you did it illegally, and I was wondering what would be more illegal about that than what you have already done?

A. Well, I have contracts with my publishers, and it explicitly says that I will distribute legal merchandise.

Q. I see. It is a matter of contract?

A. Not only is it a matter of contract—yes, it is a matter of contract—not only is it a matter of contract, but I think if I—well, I think what he's talking about is I don't think I want to get into the problem of being—getting too big and the Government stepping in and busting me up. And I think it's pretty close to that. It's a simple thing for the publishers to run over small distributors, but *it's another thing when they have to fool with a distribution company of our size.*

And if the FTC thinks that we are of that stature and getting bigger, there is no doubt in my mind that they would not let us consolidate further area.

Potter asked for further clarification, and the enormity of the censorship operation that Aschmann and Surges are conducting grows. Aschmann replies:

A. To illustrate: I have letters in my files that I have taken on Racine and Kenosha and that because I have taken them on I have—talking about my non-franchise public—that I have eliminated distributions in these areas previously enjoyed and never complained about, and they wanted an explanation.

Q. Who wanted an explanation?

A. The publisher. *There has been no complaints, there has been no action, and they wanted an explanation.* Now, I don't know about the legal aspect, I'm not a lawyer, but I think this puts me on quite a touchy ground.

Potter, however, could still think of nothing in the way of laws that would be further violated. Aschmann, though, *is* on shaky ground, as he reveals here:

Q. Yes, I can understand on contract, but I can't understand a violation of any other law, to be very frank, and—
A. (interrupting) *Well, I have been investigated by the FTC people.*
Q. For what?
A. Well, increasing of size.
Q. Yes.
A. And *I* THINK *the subject was brought up.*

Which means, of course, cutting through Aschmann's understandably reluctant and euphemistic approach to the whole distasteful FTC investigation, that the subject was, indeed, brought up. Assemblyman Alexander R. Grant then brings the whole thing into the open with:

Let me ask this: Would it be possible for a publisher to commence action against him [Aschmann] on the basis that he was imposing upon a community—or for any private individual, for that matter—to commence an action that he was imposing upon the community his own set standard of morals and so forth in violation of the First Amendment to the Constitution? I think that the problem—
CHAIRMAN POTTER: (interrupting) *He has done this already, though, Al.*
ASSEMBLYMAN GRANT: Yes, he has, *but it has been done quietly,* it has been done for the general benefit of the public. It would seem to me, under the circumstances throughout his testimony, over the course of the last three or four years, that there has been a gradual decrease in this type of thing and you just don't pick up all this type of magazines and pitch them in the river all at once. I think that I agree with this gentleman very much as far as that it's a self-censorship thing. You can censor John Potter, you can censor myself, but if I was to impose my definition, for example, my definition of what is good

and what is bad and so forth undoubtedly differs from Adrian's [Assemblyman Manders].

CHAIRMAN POTTER: The point I'm trying to make is—and I think Mr. Aschmann's attitude is excellent, I think what he has done has been excellent; what Mr. Surges has done has been excellent in this regard—but *these two gentlemen have proposed now to this committee that the most probable solution to the problem is this matter of cooperation and self-censorship.* And then when Mr. Aschmann throws in that elimination of titles puts him in an unlawful category, then *I start to wonder whether or not their proposed solution is the right one if it's illegal.*

At this Surges asks, "May I throw some light on that again through the form of questioning, Senator?" Surges elicits from Aschmann answers disclosing how titles can be eliminated. Actions are brought against certain magazines, and declaratory judgments given, which relieve Aschmann from having to fulfill his contractual obligations. These magazines then serve as an obscenity gauge for other magazines in the same category which are eliminated *without* legal actions. But if the publisher threatens legal actions, as in the case of *Playboy,* then the magazine is left alone. At least that is the implication. However, there are still other ways of getting rid of girlie magazines and books "below the standards" besides subverting the declaratory judgment act. If a request comes *from the dealer,* then Aschmann can legitimately not distribute the title. Aschmann tells, under Surges' questioning, how these "requests" can be arranged.

A. If I say there are 12 titles in your area [Assemblyman Manders' district], I know in your area I have worked very strongly with, let's say, the Knights of Columbus out at Cudahy and that area, and they have asked me off the side, "Don't ship to this store and that store," and it has cooperated; and I have even talked to dealers. I think one of the—most progressive things that ever happened in this city was the efforts of Mr. Surges on the downtown corner stands, and this was in view of the fact of the strong stand set up by the *Milwaukee Journal. But the minute we said that this was a list of titles that the newsstand operators themselves came up with, then I don't think there*

was any room for criticism. Am I correct on that, Mr. Surges?
Q. *That is correct. We went down to all the newsstands, as a matter of fact, and they agreed not to sell any type of girlie-girlie magazine from any source whatsoever.* Is that correct Mr. Aschmann?

Unbelievably, Surges incriminates himself, despite Aschmann's effort to avoid it.

A. That is right.
Q. That is what occurred. And *this was in an effort to save those newsstands* and the operation of those newsstands because it was considered that through those newsstands is disseminated a great deal of good literature and especially good newspapers that have no other distribution point in this city except on the newsstands, and we didn't want to lose for the benefit of the city those distribution points for the newspapers and other good magazines.

Concern for newsstands so they can deliver newspapers, however, does not extend to sensational tabloids. Those would not be sold after June 18, 1964, Surges told Chairman Potter.

This whole program of distributor cooperation, though, Surges cautioned the committee, might be "considered despotic."

To aid his dealers who keep magazines under the counter, Aschmann provides signs, as well as instructions. Manders is asking the questions:

Q. Now, do you inform these distributors to keep them under the—
A. (interrupting) I have tried to use reasonable judgment. [Aschmann is extremely alert to coming "awkward" questions about his operations.]
Q. (continuing)—keep them under the counter?
A. Yes, I have. The drug people in particular. They are not in business to sell magazines. The only reason they keep *Playboy* is because people want them. Now, *Playboy* sells 2,600,000 copies a month, and I know I had an occasion to talk to some druggists, and they asked me to help them so I prepared a— *which I think is illegal,* TOO—"We have the current issue of

Playboy. Please ask your druggist for it." Their general purpose is to keep it away from the juveniles. I think they are trying hard to *cooperate*. I think *with some pulls that you are going to get the answers you want,* and I know the south side really in the last three or four years, has cleaned up far and superior to the whole city and *it's because of, I think, of the system. I know we have talked down there.* We told them the system in that area of yours.

Manders wished to continue the conversation, but Potter at this point said, "Let's have a recess. I think our reporter needs a break."

Aschmann is caught between Surges and the publishers, and when Surges asks him about pressures, Aschmann reveals that there are some which might affect his monopoly:

Q. Now, as a result of your taking—rather, suggesting that these titles are beneath the standards of this community, have you had any repercussions?
A. Well, I certainly have. I feel that the pressure is extreme. I basically feel that I don't want to handle them, but I do feel that because of the laws—and the laws of Wisconsin are probably stronger than many, many states in the Union—that they feel basically, these publishers feel, they have a chance to win it in Court. So eventually if we break the string I think you are going to definitely have a second distributor in the City of Milwaukee.
Q. Has that threat been made to you?
A. Well, I can't specifically, and I don't think it will be fair to me to make a statement in this. But through innuendoes it definitely has.

Surges points out that there are monetary compensations also in his "program" for the distributor:

Q. I think this will be of interest to the entire panel here, *and for the record:* Since you have engaged in this policy of *assisting the District Attorney's Office* and the community of Milwaukee in removing obscene literature or the girlie-girlie type magazine, *whether it could be judicially declared to be obscene or not,* what effect has that had on your business, in a monetary manner now? [Still, Surges continues self-incrimination!]

A. Well . . . we have been able to crack through the barrier of the supermarkets, and . . . our business has doubled or almost tripled.

And if someone fails to comply with what Surges and Asch-mann want done, and distributes "trash," as they suggest is the case with bookseller Joseph Chobot, Aschmann declares, "I don't give him service. I require that he comes into my place of business and pick up the merchandise."

Other booksellers in Milwaukee are not so belligerent as Chobot. Sheldon Bordow, a bookseller who appears to be in be-tween Chobot and the "respectable" Milwaukee booksellers, was subpoenaed for the hearings at the last moment. (Chobot, too, was summoned at the last moment, and one wonders if this was an intentional harassment of them on the part of Surges.) Bordow operates a liquor and paperback book store at 506 West Wisconsin Avenue in Milwaukee. Surges reveals his bookstore technique in this exchange:

Q. Mr. Bordow, *on several occasions,* myself, in the presence of officers of the vice squad, have come into your establishment; is that correct?

A. Yes, sir, *periodically.*

Q. *Yes.* And on those occasions, we have asked you to take certain books off the stand; is that correct?

A. Yes, sir.

Q. As a matter of fact, on some of those occasions, your brother, who is an *attorney at law,* was also present; is that right?

A. Yes, sir; right.

Q. And at the time any of those requests were made, you com-plied with them; is that correct?

A. Yes, sir.

All these books are not just the "trash" books either. Listen to Chairman Potter question Bordow:

Q. Now, has the District Attorney's office asked you to take any books off your shelves that you have not taken off?

A. I have never taken—I have always taken off any one that he's ever told me. In fact, it just happened recently where the issue *Candy*, I had received some copies from Milwaukee News . . . which was probably a mistake, but he told me to take them off, and that I did. In fact, I only had them for two hours then.

Senator Holger B. Rasmusen surmised that most dealers would be fearful of the adverse publicity if they didn't comply with Surges' requests. Surges implies that this is his source of power over Bordow:

> SURGES: Some dealers are and some dealers aren't. Mr. Bordow would be, as he has expressed in the past himself, and through his brother who is secretary of the company, and an attorney at law, they would be concerned about adverse publicity. Some dealers, one dealer particularly in this community, enjoys the infamy of an action or criticism of any kind. He wants it. He desires it, as a matter of fact, because it brings more people to his place. It's a sad commentary on civilization, but it is a fact, regardless.

Surges is sorrowfully complaining about Chobot.

While questioning the Madison newsstand operator Elery Johnson, the Committee ran into difficulty on the *scienter* question—if a bookseller does not know about the content of a book or magazine, he cannot be held responsible for selling it. Chairman Potter called upon help from Surges. Johnson quickly heeled and in the following exchange we can see how Surges' program can be extended in Wisconsin:

> CHAIRMAN POTTER: Mr. Surges, in Milwaukee there was suggesting, well, at any rate, that perhaps the control of a lot of this literature could be best achieved through cooperation with the distributor and the retailer and the local law enforcement agencies, and I know that you have worked that end in Milwaukee. Perhaps some questions of Mr. Johnson as to, and he already has expressed his intent to cooperate, perhaps we might get his views as to whether or not this would be an effective way to handle this type of situation.
>
> MR. SURGES: I understand your statement, Senator.
>
> Q. You stated, Mr. Johnson, that you don't feel qualified to

make determinations as to whether books are or are not obscene.
A. That's correct.
Q. And you also said that you do not want to be in the business of selling obscene material, is that correct?
A. That's right.
Q. Do you think that through the cooperation of the several dealers in Madison, including yourself, and the distributing company in Madison, that a program of policing which may be incorporated, some expert advice on the subject of what is not obscene would be of help to you in this department?
A. Well, anything would be of help to me if they'd just draw the line so that I know where I'm at.
Q. Would you participate in such a program, Mr. Johnson?
A. I will cooperate 100%.
Q. You would like to have some help in that direction?
A. That's right. The way it is I have no borderlines to draw anything.
Q. I see, and you would participate in a program which is sort of a *policing*—

Aschmann and Surges indicate that all other booksellers in the *Milwaukee* area "have been highly cooperative" (except for Chobot). And such proved to be the case in the personal interviews I had with the booksellers in Milwaukee. Most did not want any trouble. Others reported "no trouble." Still others were hostile to my inquiries.[26] Lawyer Leonard Zubrensky speaks with some bitterness about one bookseller who refused to be a witness or to be publicly involved in any way in the Supreme Court case[27] involving his fellow bookseller Joseph Chobot, who served several years after being convicted of selling pornography. In the downtown area, the booksellers will say, "I don't want *anything* to do with controversy. I run a clean store, not like those across the river."

"Across the river," in Bordow's liquor and paperback store, which also deals in "girlie" magazines, and has a close watch kept on it by police as well as citizens, the manager said, "Sure, the police look at my books and say, 'This one looks pretty bad.' And then I take it off the shelves. But they're just doing their job. Just like I am, selling books." He pointed proudly to a sign which he says keeps a large percentage of trouble from his door. The sign reads: "No Minors Allowed." His biggest readers, he said, were "priests and do-gooders." [28]

What could happen to a bookseller who refuses to abide by the rules of the "program" is illustrated by Joseph Chobot. Zubrensky, his legal counsel, has stated that Chobot started out with the "worst kind" of pornography and so got a "poor reputation," and now has lessened such activities. But Chobot is a harassed man. He will speak freely to anyone about his bouts with the District Attorney and the Milwaukee police (as he did in a letter to me January 27, 1962). He speaks of illegal raids and petty harassing arrests—some of which his counsel advises me to take with a grain of salt. But when I asked Zubrensky if perhaps Surges were not overzealous, he replied:

> Sure. The best example is that he has persecuted Joseph Chobot, a client who was found guilty of selling obscene literature. He has been arrested several times. Most recently a couple of months ago, for possessing girlie magazines, the kind sold around the state.
>
> It's pure harassment to try to continue to arrest this man. I'm not certain why they select him and nobody else. *I think that this is at the least overzealousness,* at the most it is worse than that—persecution. For what reason, I don't know.
>
> I think that Chobot has been persecuted by the police and by the District Attorney's Office.

Another bookseller with troubles is Fred Blair, manager of Mary's Bookshop. In other years, he said, the citizen groups were more concerned with getting such magazines as the *Progressive,* the *Nation,* and the *New Republic* off newsstands and out of neighborhood drug stores. He adds:

> Our store has a different problem, though we are affected by the censorship nuts. We do not handle sensational periodicals, nudist magazines, the controversial sex books, etc. Our interests lie primarily in scholastic material, classics, history, etc., with our specialty being Marxist literature. We therefore are under attack continually as a "Communist bookshop." There is pressure, which we naturally ignore. *Our business is damaged by*

local police and the FBI contacting our customers and throw-
ing a scare into them by asking all sorts of questions about us.
Then there are clumsy attempts once in a while to entrap us by
asking us to order books that were or are under attack. *The*
word is generally spread around that any person entering our
store is photographed and may suffer reprisals.

The first line of defense against censorship is the bookseller.
In Milwaukee, it appears, there is no "first line." The days
when most booksellers would risk "not only their livelihoods,
but their lives, in the age-old contest against the suppression of
ideas," [29] appears to be past, except for a few hold-outs. They
will sacrifice the relatively small profit from the sale of books
blacklisted by law enforcement officials, or NODL, or the CDL,
or the Wisconsin Pharmaceutical Association, or the super-
market list, for the sake of the larger profit derived from the
general trade with contented customers. The gross profit on
the sale of paperbound books in 1953 was 5½ cents on a 25-
cent book. With rising costs and prices, the gross per copy is
not much more today.

Surges takes advantage of the booksellers' ignorance of their
legal rights. He ignored the *scienter* ruling in the *Smith v. Cali-*
fornia case of 1959, for example, in trying to get David
Wolkenstein, proprietor of the Mid-Towne Pharmacy, to admit
to some responsibility for publications in his store in the smut
committee hearings.

The declaratory judgment act does not benefit the booksellers in Milwaukee. Zubrensky wrote to Rice before the
passage of the act:

> The reasoning behind 231S [the declaratory judgment act]
> was that if the book or movie were made the defendant, the
> exhibitor or distributor *would not fold up the way they do now*
> *and that freedom of expression would gain as a result.*[30]

When booksellers were queried about the declaratory judgment
act, when *Cancer* was being tried under it, and the newspapers
had publicized it, bookseller after bookseller was ignorant of its
purpose. Even Chobot knew nothing of it. Surges, of course, did

not inform them. But then, none expressed any interest in it to me.

Back in 1960 a legal observer commented:

> One probable effect of the Wisconsin statute is that some obstreperous district attorneys will merely add it to their arsenal of coercive weapons. Undoubtedly this cannot, of itself, create constitutional objections to the statute. But argument can be made that a further probable effect of the statute is its imposition of a previous restraint on distributors of literature.[31]

How Surges uses the declaratory judgment act in his "program of guardianship" to break contracts was related earlier. It is also illustrated in the following exchange with Senator Rasmusen.

SENATOR RASMUSEN: [Speaking to Bordow.] Referring to the magazines that the District Attorney's Office requested you to take out of circulation, suppose you had not removed them, could legal action have been taken against him?

SURGES: You are asking me that question, then, sir?

RASMUSEN: Yes.

SURGES: Well, there has been quite a few of them and in every instance, I cannot honestly say that we could bring a legal action against the magazines that this man took off his racks.

RASMUSEN: I mean against the man that had them.

SURGES: I would never attempt to bring an action against the man that had them on the basis of these magazines, sir. We attempt, first of all, to bring declaratory judgment against this particular type of magazine because it's so close to the line that to sustain our position under a criminal case wherein we must prove *beyond a reasonable doubt* that the person is guilty, we do not take that chance unless it is of a very, what is sometimes referred to as a hard-core type of pornography, we don't. We bring first an action under the declaratory judgment statute. But I can say that several of the books that Mr. Bordow did take off the stand, I don't think that at that particular time we could have sustained a criminal action against him; and in some instances we would have had difficulty sustaining a position, a judgment, against the book itself under the declaratory judgment statute.

And this, no doubt, was the reason the Milwaukee Junior Bar Association president, William Randall, in 1961, regretted the deletion of the phrase "beyond a reasonable doubt" in the final version of the declaratory judgment act. Originally that phrase was in the proposed law. "The Milwaukee Junior Bar Association," Randall added, "is not satisfied with the law." [32]

In surveying the Milwaukee censorship scene, little needs to be said of the drug stores and supermarkets in Milwaukee. (There are some three hundred of each.) Knowing what we do of their self-censorship practices, and having Surges' assurance that "pharmacists in Milwaukee are doing a fantastic job of policing this literature in their stores," we have a fairly good idea of what is happening here.

What about the libraries in Milwaukee? The Milwaukee Public Library was one of the 113 answering the 151 questionnaires sent out in that survey by the *Library Journal*. The library appeared to have many of the twenty controversial books on the questionnaire, but under City Librarian Richard E. Krug the library has its own little guardianship program. The library has

> grades of restriction. Restricted . . . means "for adult circulation only"; "reference" means for adults only and restricted to use in the library. Eight of the listed titles [of the survey] were in the first category, and three were *confined to quarters*.[33]

The three? Erskine Caldwell's *Jenny by Nature,* Irving Wallace's *The Chapman Report,* and, of course, Henry Miller's *Tropic of Cancer*. Some books can't be taken out of the library, said Krug, because some "misguided adults would pass them along to children." He cheerfully admitted to being a censor: "That's what we're here for, to make a selection. We're professionals." [34] Krug, however, might heed the advice of Alec Craig, who observes, "The practice of withdrawing books from the open shelves is objectionable because it distorts the view of the literary situation which the library's selection gives to the visitor." The librarian should resort to this only "where political pressure makes it the only alternative to not acquiring a book at all." [35]

The study of the Milwaukee newspapers' performance before and during Surges' implementation of his "program of guardianship" is of central importance in determining the censorship setting of that city. An assault of censorship upon book publishing and circulation, of course, should be of serious concern to any newspaperman. How, then, have the *Milwaukee Sentinel* and the *Milwaukee Journal* reacted to what has taken place in Milwaukee? They performed more in the manner of "guardians" than watchdogs.

The *Milwaukee Sentinel,* until 1962 one of Hearst's many sensational newspapers, was not concerned with the extralegal and illegal practices going on in that city. Several times it was the instigator of "pornography probes" by citizen groups, and it may have helped form the proper public opinion climate for Surges to bring action against *Cancer.*

The *Milwaukee Journal* presents a picture of vacillation and lethargy in this fight against censorship of freedom of expression strangely out of keeping with its reputation (renewed from year to year by various newspaper ratings) as one of the great newspapers in this country. Everything, and more, that has been related in this chapter was known to some newspapermen of the *Journal* staff. Was there ever a concerted campaign against such censorship practices carried on by the *Journal*? A reading of the editorials on the subject from the files of the *Journal* office itself from the year 1949 up to the present shows that there was not. Among the factors possibly keeping the *Milwaukee Journal* from fighting this "obscenity" censorship were these: First of all, the opposition newspaper, the *Sentinel,* actively campaigned and supported citizen groups engaged in censorship early in Milwaukee's censorship history. For the *Journal* to launch such a campaign against these groups while a sister newspaper supported them would have been unpopular. After the *Journal* had acquired the *Sentinel* in 1962 and had obtained a monopoly in Milwaukee, for one reason or another the *Journal* had lost its crusading zeal. Perhaps, having made its reputation, it was now content to rest upon it. Perhaps some of its executives are Catholics and hence more vulnerable to the pressures of Catholic censorship groups. Perhaps it was a combination of all these things, meshed with the don't-make-ripples feeling that comes with being a contented "fat cat." Through it all was the belief that "dirty books" were not necessarily under the protection of that constantly invoked journalistic phrase—freedom of the press. "Obscenity" was not worth defending—or not worth defending at the price the *Journal* would have had to pay.

The Milwaukee Literary Commission was founded in 1949, with the *Journal*'s blessing. The Movie Commission was operating from 1949 on, too, having been authorized by an ordinance of 1917. What editorials were written from 1950 to 1963, on the subject of questionable literature and censorship in Milwaukee? From 1950 through 1953, there were six. Three were written in 1952 and a similar number in 1953. From 1954 through 1956 there were four. Two came in each of the years 1955 and 1956. There were four editorials on the subject in 1957. But from 1958 to 1964, there is the incredibly low number of two. And this at a time when citizen groups across the nation were organizing and, when strong, forcing their designs upon booksellers, distributors and district attorneys throughout the country—and especially in Milwaukee.

Apparently, the stronger the censorship forces grew in Milwaukee, the fewer the editorials against censorship. And of the editorials just cited two were of a questionable nature so far as being a statement *against* censorship. For example, in 1952, an editorial concluded that self-censorship was needed to clean up the filth on the newsstands.[36] And in 1955 the editorial writer (a Mr. John Baker) while decrying censorship also railed against the type of violence and "distortion" portrayed in the film *The Blackboard Jungle*.[37] (Since that editorial, of course, Milwaukee has had its share of blackboard jungle incidents.) Of the editorials studied in these thirteen years, from 1950 through 1963, only four were direct and forceful statements against what was taking place in Milwaukee.

Other editorials on obscene literature, and censorship related to it, *were* published in the *Journal,* true. But they were statements on things happening in *other* parts of the country. In the years just cited (from 1950–1963) there were seven such editorials. Editorials on happenings in other parts of Wisconsin in this area numbered four from 1959 through 1964.

To bring the editorial study of the *Journal* in this subject matter more up to date, an editorial on January 28, 1964, noted that the Milwaukee District Attorney's Office was about to form a panel of ten persons to help determine whether certain books or magazines were obscene. They were to be selected by McCauley and one assistant (Surges, no doubt), and a person to be named. Now, did the *Journal,* recalling its past experiences with such literary committees, blast the announcement of such a proposal? No. Meekly, it cautioned the District Attorney to the effect that book burners, zealots, and civic meddlers might be appointed to such a committee.

Two strong *Journal* editorials were written about a Surges survey ("Why the Dragnet"),[38] and about the city common council's street-zoning committee's threat to take away newsstand licenses because of girlie magazine displays.[39]

Finally, on February 4, 1965, the *Journal* took the CDL to task for its "requests" tactics; but all these editorial efforts were nullified by a favorable story on the current CDL campaign, featuring the CDL president and Richard Surges.[40]

Still unwilling to accept the evidence of the *Journal*'s own editorial files and seeking an explanation to what had occurred in these editorial offices, I arranged to interview two editorial writers of the *Journal,* Perry Hill and Donald Olesen.

"Are you aware of the program of 'cooperation' now in existence in Milwaukee?" I asked each separately.

"Yes." They were aware of it. No surprise registered on their faces. I tried again.

"Are you aware that policemen tell booksellers to take magazines and books off their shelves after thumbing through them a few minutes?"

"Yes." They were informed of this. Once more, I tried.

"Are you aware that Assistant District Attorney Surges, a

man Hill described as a 'zealot' in an editorial, works hand in hand with the distributor Aschmann and so controls the flow of literature into Milwaukee County?"

"Yes." *Still* no surprise on the faces.

At this moment I began to understand why, at the time of the initial action against *Cancer* when I informed Richard D. Kemplin, court reporter for the *Journal,* of the unofficial censoring going on by police and other officials, he refused to believe it. And then commented that he had to get away for a *Journal* picnic being held that afternoon.[41]

Perry Hill said that the *Journal* didn't *like* the idea of what the police and Surges were doing, and that maybe "we haven't said enough." We have always complained, he said, about the booksellers and theater managers "cooperating." Olesen said that there is a "traditional feeling of unease at this censorship, on the *Journal,* but no unanimity of opinion on what to do." McCauley, it seems, would come to the *Journal* office and complain about any editorial written on the subject. "The movie situation," Olesen said, *"is* disgraceful."

"What would happen to the *Journal,"* I asked Olesen, "if it were to launch a full-scale sustained editorial attack against the guardianship program existing in Milwaukee?"

"Such a campaign," Olesen replied, "requires complete cooperation of the newspaper from the top on down." There was some feeling, he said, that a "little censorship" was needed. "There is a need for some kind of censorship control of hardcore pornography. That is the consensus of editorial writers here."

But what is "hard-core pornography" to the *Journal* editorial writers undoubtedly falls into the less objectionable "girlie magazine" category of the Supreme Court.

As I got ready to leave his office and the impressive *Journal* building, Olesen remarked to me: "If you come across anything that I can work on, let me know." I looked at him. "I mean it," he added.

It is fitting to recall here the concluding cheerful and chilling remarks of Chairman Potter, of the "smut" committee:

Well, it has become obvious to me, anyway, that since this Committee was formed and the legislation implementing the Committee was passed there have been decisions which make this matter of *policing* obscene literature most difficult, and I think that *one of the recommendations* will no doubt come out of this Committee, and *it will be that local law enforcement agencies attempt to cooperate with people like Mr. Boyd and Mr. Johnson, distributors and retailers,* and so far we have received only enthusiastic support from retailers and distributors and I think that much can be achieved in the State of Wisconsin without resorting to any censorship, and without causing a hardship on men like Mr. Boyd, Mr. Wilson, and Mr. Johnson for making a sincere effort to only have material on their stands which complied and conformed to the standards of our society and of law and one of the reasons we have you here is to get your attitude and your thoughts on that, and your expression corroborates the expressions of the dealers in the Milwaukee area.

A close scrutiny of Milwaukee reveals that city as being overrun by censorship groups, and its newsstands and bookstores emasculated of any serious literature smacking of "obscenity" by those groups and the law enforcement officers of the city. On the part of the latter, this is outright illegal censorship. Through it all, the *Milwaukee Journal,* one of the perennially ranked top-ten newspapers of the country, has discreetly kept a hands-off attitude, except when the most flagrant violations of freedom of the press were exposed. And those exposés were not made by staff members of that newspaper. Theirs was a failure to realize that freedom of the press is indivisible, a lesson which was to be brought home to them in the State Supreme Court political campaign that followed the Milwaukee trial of *Cancer.*

12
CANCER IN MILWAUKEE

As was the case in so many other places in the country, nothing happened to the hardcover edition of *Cancer* in Milwaukee. Leonard Zubrensky remarked on this, "I have a vague recollection that as long as the book sold in hardcover there was an understanding that the District Attorney would not prosecute. But if it was sold in softcover, they would, and did."

The paperback edition of *Tropic of Cancer,* published October 10, 1961, was distributed in Milwaukee the same day. On October 14, the *Milwaukee Sentinel* printed a story under the headline, "Mothers Still Fight Pornography," in which Mrs. Merten told how fifty parishes had formed committees to fight the problem. They used NODL methods and lists. *Cancer* was placed on the NODL list, John S. Brennan, assistant executive secretary of NODL, wrote me, for "portrayal of sex facts offensively." [1] On October 15, the *Sentinel* reported that a probe of smut had revealed an increase in bad literature. The paper ran the results of the probe on Sunday. As a result of the story, the *Sentinel* reported, "Public opinion began to rally around the drive against salacious picture magazines." (Hearst newspapers, no matter how many sensational stories they run, are against books like *Cancer.*)

For the three days it was allowed to sell in Milwaukee, the

paperback *Cancer* had excellent sales. Aschmann reported at the trial of the book that 3000 copies were put into his three bookmobiles on October 9 or 10. When the rest of the copies were returned on October 13, some 2460 copies had been sold. Milwaukeeans evidently thought they *really* "ought to know" about the Miller novel. Aschmann said, however, that there were about ten calls from dealers who did not want to sell the book. *Cancer* was not distributed to any supermarkets, and only some 300 copies were sold in drug stores.[2]

Surges told the *Sentinel* that he was tipped off about the book by William Aschmann. A United Press International news story reported the same thing.[3] Surges must have thought it better for his "program" presentation to the smut-investigating committee to have a *bookseller* notify him of the novel instead of the distributor, because he testified to this at the committee hearings. Bookseller Bordow, under questioning, said that it was *he* who first approached Surges about the book.[4] And in the trial of *Cancer* an unnamed citizen was supposed to have complained![5] Once having been tipped (by Aschmann, Bordow, or "a citizen"), Surges said that he "only read parts of it." Then he read "parts of it" to District Attorney McCauley. (Surely a strange way to go about the whole business of banning, because by now every intelligent person knew that the book had to be judged *as a whole* before any determination could be made. Stranger still is Surges' confession of his actions to the newspapers.)

After hearing these parts of *Cancer,* McCauley agreed to be the plaintiff, acting as an individual, in the civil court action. Meanwhile, parts of the book were also read by Captain Harry Kuszewski of the Milwaukee Police Department. "I think it's obscene," he said to the newspapers. "Absolutely rotten." If McCauley hadn't brought the action against the book, Captain Kuszewski declared, "I would have." [6] (Less than two years later, the *Milwaukee Sentinel* reported that the same Captain Kuszewski had been suspended after being accused by a madam of a house of prostitution in Milwaukee of accepting pay-offs for protection. The madam was a convicted prostitute.[7] He was brought to trial in 1964 for misconduct in office and for filing a false income tax return. He was convicted on six tax counts of the indictment. The misconduct in office counts were dismissed. He was fined a total of $3000.

After being briefed on the book, the two vice squad detectives, James Donnelley and Robert Gaurke, nosed around Milwaukee bookstores for a copy and couldn't find one, according to newspaper accounts. (But trial testimony has one of the men buying the book from a bookstore and showing it to Surges.) Bookseller Schwartz told the *Sentinel,* "No, it wasn't the police that called. Some people called and warned us." [8] But Schwartz, on October 13, had sent this telegram to Grove Press: "POLICE BANNED TROPIC OF CANCER CANCEL ORDER FOR 100 PAPER."

If Donnelley and Gaurke *couldn't* find a copy of *Cancer* in a Milwaukee bookstore, and if they didn't "nudge" any off the cooperating dealers' shelves, then *Cancer* disappeared because the bookstores had already been notified by District Attorney McCauley to take the book off the shelves. A Marquette University student clerk working at Schwartz's bookstore said that McCauley had indeed called up Schwartz and told him to take the book off.[9] Bookseller Erwin Belau told me that he had read *enough* of *Tropic of Cancer* to "throw it off the shelves. Perhaps I'm old-fashioned," he concluded. Zubrensky, asked if he knew anything about McCauley ordering *Cancer* off the shelves, said that McCauley "suggested" that they take it off. McCauley, Zubrensky said, "doesn't want to have trouble with outraged citizens." Aschmann agreed that McCauley "took a personal interest in *Cancer.*"

What happened to *Cancer* in the first few days in Milwaukee illustrates the blatant illegal suppression that goes unnoticed and unchecked in many American cities. The declaratory judgment act, under which the novel was being prosecuted, provided for a thirty-day period in which a trial was to take place. During this period, under that act, and until a judgment is rendered, the bookseller and distributor were supposedly free to sell and distribute the book. Zubrensky said, "The declaratory judgment law hasn't worked. It has had an opposite effect as far as *Cancer* is concerned. There is no legal threat—but booksellers stopped —they want to stay out of trouble. They are eager to have the D.A. advise them. Very." [10]

The protests that occurred when the distributor "mandatorily removed" *Cancer* from distribution have been mentioned earlier. In an interview, Aschmann told me that there was a "tremendous upheaval," that he "lost prestige." "What value does *Cancer* have on the newsstand?" he ruefully asked. "Only the style of writing. Publicity sold it." As it had sold *Lady Chatterley's Lover* five years before, he added, 60,000 copies of it. But another Milwaukeean, a lawyer, did not think citizens as a whole were "particularly perturbed save as there was the usual division of opinion; and I think a good deal depended on whether a man was a Catholic or greatly concerned to have the city as lily white as possible." [11]

Aschmann told me in an interview in January 1962 that the Literary Commission had read *Cancer* and recommended that it be removed from the stands. Surges, in an interview the day before, had told me the same thing. However, when I called up Professor of Journalism David R. Host of Marquette University, chairman of the Literary Commission, and asked him if this were true, he denied it vehemently. "Literary Commission? I don't know whether there is one or not. It never met." Surges, he said, had determined that *Cancer* was obscene.[12]

What did Surges think of Miller's novel? In our January interview, four months before the trial, he said that *Tropic of Cancer* and similar works were "advanced techniques" of obscenity which could destroy confidence in the written word. "The great defender of freedom of the press," he said, "is the First Amendment. It should not be pandered away." Had he read *Pornography and the Law*? (The Kronhausens' book, besides calling *Cancer* an example of "erotic realism," says that Henry Miller is "certainly not 'obscene.'")[13] "Yes," Surges said, but "they don't deal with the people we run into." What did he, Surges, think Miller was trying to do in *Cancer*? Surges replied, "I think he was dabbling." Henry Miller was "capable of stream of consciousness." Miller was "trying to show that there was a lot of rot in the world," and he "shows nothing of the good things in Paris." The purpose of Miller's book, Surges said, was to say, "Get healthy with sex." Turning his head away, Surges said that Miller, when he wrote the book, had just been married and that his inhibitions were released. Miller thought that if he talked about sex he'd release his inhibitions.

What did Circuit Judge Ronold A. Drechsler, who was to preside at the trial, think of the book? According to Surges, Drechsler had said it was a "terrible book, terrible."

"How far will this case go?" I asked Surges.

"I am reasonably certain," he replied, "that this case will be carried to the U.S. Supreme Court."

Surges stated that he was going to prosecute the book on the basis that the community standards of Milwaukee were such that the book was not up to them.

"What *are* the community standards of Milwaukee?" I asked.

"I can't answer that," Surges, very indignant, replied. "I can't write a book. It would take a book." He said later, after cooling down, that you would have to extend yourself, the same as a judge or a reasonable man would have to, to come up with an answer.

McCauley, acting through Surges, filed a complaint against *Cancer* in the Circuit Court of Milwaukee County. It was one of many such *in rem* proceedings sparked by *Cancer* (in which the book itself is tried instead of the bookseller—something which the ACLU calls a "new approach to obscenity prosecutions"). Judge Drechsler, after examining the book and agreeing that McCauley had reasonable cause for complaint, on October 18, 1961, issued an order to show cause why the book should not be banned. The defendants were Henry Miller, Grove Press, and Macfadden Publications, Inc. (the distributors).

In their answer, filed by Milwaukee attorneys David B. Bartell and William J. Panagis, the book's defenders said that a finding of obscenity would violate a provision of article I, section 3, of the state constitution, which says: "Every person may freely speak, write and publish his sentiments on all subjects, being responsible for the abuse of that right, and no law shall be passed to restrain or abridge liberty of speech or of the press."

The defense said a ban would violate that part of the first amendment to the federal Constitution which says: "Congress shall make no law . . . abridging the freedom of speech, or of the press."

The defense asserted that an obscenity finding also would deprive the author and publishers of property without due process of law, in violation of article 14, section 1, of the federal Constitution.[14]

They too were ready to go to the highest court in the land.[15]

January 9, 1962, was set as the start of a jury trial by Judge Drechsler, with December 26, 1962, set for hearing motions before the trial. Through mutual agreement at this hearing the trial, without jury, was set for May 15, 1962. But from October 15, 1961, until the trial next year on May 15 (a critical period for sales), *Cancer* could *not* be purchased in Milwaukee. At first it was suppressed illegally, then, through Surges' recommendations, an amendment to the declaratory judgment act made the ban legal.

That amendment should be briefly discussed here because of its importance to the declaratory judgment act, and because it is also very important to Surges' designs on questionable literature. It eventually passed through the Wisconsin legislature and was signed into law without the notice of, or any show of concern by, Wisconsin's press and its libertarians.

While this first real test of Wisconsin's new declaratory judgment act was in the legal mills, Surges was no doubt aware that curtailing *Cancer* sales was illegal while litigation under the civil act was in progress. And so he must have been anxiously watching the legislative efforts of Senator Allen Busby of Milwaukee.

Busby had introduced a substitute amendment to a bill proposing to amend the act on July 28, 1961, and he was shepherding it through the legislature. Newspapers ran a story in November to the effect that the amendment would give "authorities a freer hand in stopping the flow of obscene literature." The bill, the journalists pointed out to their readers, "would permit a district attorney to get an injunction to halt distribution of allegedly obscene material *as soon as the case was before the courts*." [16]

The original act provided for sales to *continue* while the litigation was in progress, so recognizing the economics of bookselling and the bookseller. The Busby amendment did away with such safeguards. The Madison CLU head, in the state capital, was unaware of the amendment until I notified him.

"Newspapers and magazines," he then said, "would be hit hard." He decided to try to get the Governor to veto the bill, but by then, December 9, 1961, it was too late. Zubrensky and the Milwaukee Junior Bar Association, originators of the original bill, were also unaware of the amendment. When I told Assistant District Attorney Nager of Madison about the amendment and that no citizen groups or newspapers seemed to be aroused by it he was incredulous:

"Are they willing to give seventy-two district attorneys in Wisconsin censorship powers?" he asked.

Apparently they were. The amendment was passed by the Assembly unanimously, 89 to 0, on November 8, 1961. Governor Gaylord Nelson signed it into law on December 10.

What this new law also did was to allow the actions brought against publications to be brought in the name of the state instead of the district attorney concerned. Why this is of some importance to Surges is explained in the next paragraphs of the news story:

> In case the State loses, the county treasury would pay the cost and *not the district attorney personally*.
>
> The law also makes it easier to remove *subsequent issues* of weekly or biweekly publications from sale pending a case involving an earlier issue.[17]

There is also a psychological advantage for the prosecutor. Instead of his name as a complainant in a legal action, it is the state of Wisconsin *versus* whoever is the defendant, with all the power and grandeur a state's name can engender backing up the action. The "subsequent issues" comment of the amendment reeks of prior restraint—precensorship.

13

THE MILWAUKEE CANCER TRIAL

"An important new (1957) Wisconsin law will be put to first use, in Milwaukee county at least, by . . . McCauley's civil complaint against . . . *Cancer,* as being obscene." So editorialized the *Milwaukee Journal* on October 19, 1961. After stressing that the law prevents economic loss to sellers and telling how "it gives anybody involved in creating, producing, distributing, selling or exhibiting the material 30 days to step up and defend it," the *Journal* concludes:

> Most importantly, it seems to accommodate both those who are more concerned with fighting obscenity and those more worried about the dangers of censorship. It eliminates the unwholesome pressure of "requests for cooperation" in suppressing material on the advice of a "literary commission," such as Milwaukee county *used* to have. [Italics added.]

The usual pattern for the defense in the many *Cancer* cases followed the general brief written by Grove attorney Charles Rembar and included in the Grove legal packet. The defense presented the statements by critics and reviewers on the merits of *Cancer*, then critics and other expert witnesses were called to testify or to submit sworn affidavits in support of the novel. The expert would identify himself, declare his familiarity with the book and Miller's writings. He would state his position in the case, list his qualifications and then proceed to defend the book, beginning usually with some comments on the nature of artistic merit.

The prosecution, meanwhile, would assemble a "plain-as-mud" jury with whom the prosecuting attorney tried to ally himself and would dismiss "all such learned experts as strange eggheads who in no sense understand the 'average man' whose sensibilities are supposed to have been assaulted by the book." [1]

To counter the usual anti-intellectual pattern of the prosecution, *Cancer* was defended on the ground that it is a work of art[2] and as such protected by the First Amendment.

Across America this was the general pattern of *Cancer* litigation. But in the Milwaukee trial, which ran from May 15 to 18, 1962, there were some important variations. First of all both parties waived a jury. The novel's fate would be decided by Circuit Judge Ronold A. Drechsler, a man described as "a very strict Lutheran" by one of his contemporaries.[3] The judge had already remarked to Surges, as we know, that *Cancer* was a "terrible book, terrible." As a member of the judiciary Judge Drechsler would reserve final judgment until all the evidence was in, but under the circumstances we can understand why Surges was more sympathetic than most *Cancer* prosecutors to the defense lawyers' request to waive a jury trial. Bartell and Panagis did not, of course, know about the comment Drechsler had made to Surges. Even if they had, according to Panagis, that would not have deterred them because of the faith they had in the judge.

"We knew he was quite strict in his religion," Panagis said. "But we knew the case was going up on appeal, regardless of Drechsler's decision, all the way to the U.S. Supreme Court if necessary. We waived a jury trial because it would create difficulty as far as a practical matter was concerned." The practical matter, Panagis said, was the question of how the book would be presented to the jury. "Reading the book aloud might be shocking to the jury," he explained. "You might get someone to read it, but this is time-consuming and then that person would have to read in a monotone without inflection—or else the tone of the voice could be contested or at least questioned privately by the jury." In these cases, Panagis said, usually it's better to try the book before the judge. "We could've given the jury twelve books to read, but then you would've wondered if they had read the book. We *knew* the Supreme Court would read the book." Bartell and he had the utmost faith, Panagis said, in the book's being under the protection of the First Amendment.[4]

But there are arguments for a jury trial in obscenity cases over that of a court trial with only a judge presiding. A jury, drawn indiscriminately from all classes, is, in theory, representative of a community's standards. (And Surges would base his all on "community standards.") U.S. Supreme Court Justice Brennan, in recommending a jury trial in obscenity cases, once wrote that it "has a special aptitude for reflecting the view of the average person."[5] "A valuable principle for obscenity cases," Zechariah Chafee declares, is "that *a single person should not in fact be able to suppress any book or periodical or work of art.*"[6] Professor L. M. Alpert considers it "beyond the capacity of an average judge to apply the 'absurd' laws of obscenity to works of literature."[7] Most judges, too, according to Alec Craig, "are apt to represent the less defensible aspect of yesterday's morals and fashions."[8] Lockhart and McClure noted:

> Judges . . . are seldom equipped by training or experience to evaluate the literary, educational, and scientific values of a book. Some of them of course don't recognize their limitations; to them, the obscene is self-evident, and they neither need nor want the help of evidence concerning a book's values in these respects. Fortunately, few judges are afflicted with this form of bigotry and obtuseness. Today, most courts readily consider some form of evidence of the literary, educational, or scientific values of the book under attack. But they do not always agree on what kinds of evidence it is proper to consider. Some of them consider the published book reviews and appraisals of competent critics. Others admit the testimony of expert witnesses.

And one court has even gone so far as to receive and consider the solicited letters of persons qualified to appraise the book.[9]

There is a central dilemma in obscenity cases. On the one hand, the judgment is a sensitive constitutional one and cannot be locked in by a jury verdict. On the other hand, the defendant is entitled to a trial by jury. The dilemma is sometimes resolved by saying that if a jury does not exonerate him, then the defendant may ask the court for a constitutional judgment in his favor. Until recent decisions, many judges were unsure of what to do in this situation, but civil liberties advocates feel that the basic principle should be, when reasonable men differ, the issue should be resolved against censorship.

The second variation from the national pattern of *Cancer* cases in the Milwaukee trial came when defense attorney Bartell sought to prove that the novel had literary, cultural, and educational as well as social values, and hence was not obscene. To this purpose he attempted to introduce as evidence quotations provided by the Grove Press legal packet from T. S. Eliot, Aldous Huxley, George Orwell, Lawrence Durrell, John Ciardi and Norman Cousins. These statements in praise of the book by these respected men of letters had been introduced in countless other *Cancer* trials. But they were not allowed to be entered by Judge Drechsler. Unless these men could appear in the court and be cross-examined, their statements would be "hearsay," he ruled. (Such limitations were not imposed by Wisconsin's declaratory act.) Judge Drechsler doubted, too, if those experts knew the standards prevailing in Milwaukee.

> Surges, who had said before the trial that he was not interested in what "eggheads from all over the country" thought about the book, had won an important point. Every witness had to prove that he knew the "average Milwaukeean" in order to testify.[10]

Robert W. Wells of the *Milwaukee Journal* gives a rich description of the courtroom personalities:

> The characters in the courtroom drama fit their roles. On the one hand was . . . Surges, a tall, lean, intense man. Grouped

with him were representatives of the clergy—a minister, a priest and a rabbi, forming a classic tableau of moral authority closing ranks against the sins of the flesh.

On the other side was the chief spokesman for the defense, Bartell, a short, mild seeming man, who seldom raised his voice or missed an opening. His principal support came from educators, men to whom books have a special meaning and who feel that writers—serious writers, at least—are artists and must be free to follow the artistic gleam into unlikely byways.[11]

Surges' witnesses were distributor Aschmann; Louis J. Swichkow, a rabbi; William B. Furie, a Jewish director of education; Father John Michael Murphy, a priest who taught literature at a Catholic seminary; George W. Mueller, a deputy chief probation officer for Milwaukee County; and the Lutheran pastor who was a member of the CDL, Hoover T. Grimsby. Surges considered his witnesses those who were in the best position to evaluate the standards of the Milwaukee community and "what would appeal to the prurient interest of the average person within that community." [12] All his witnesses agreed that the book would have a deleterious effect upon the average Milwaukeean—i.e., would appeal to his prurient interests.[13]

"*Cancer*," said Rabbi Swichkow, "is nauseating as a whole because of its morbid description of sex relations and sexual acts . . . sex is perverted by an author and capitalized on." Education director Furie said that "*Cancer* when viewed as a whole has no cultural value except for negative manifestations." Under cross-examination he said:

> When I finished reading the book . . . I felt revulsion.
>
> Certain parts of the book left me with an itching feeling. As a result of my experience, my background and status, and so forth, reading the book didn't have a permanent deleterious effect . . . I think that the multiplicity of all these books (including . . . *Cancer* and *Lady Chatterley's Lover*) reflects the abysmal moral bankruptcy of our time.

(Furie, with the foregoing statements, labels himself as at least a sensitive reader. Miller would have approved of the effects of the reading.)

The most literate witness of the group on this matter was Father Murphy. His thoughts on prurient interest were:

> Prurient interest is that interest which is concerned with the sexual function of a man. If a person is normal he has a prurient interest. The effect of prurient interest is to set in motion within us those powers which are meant to terminate in intercourse. Pruriency can also cause a person to terminate this urge in morbid thoughts, or a number of what psychologists call perversions. The morbid thought mentioned would be what I as a priest would call sin, that is, an offense against the law of God as shown by Scriptures.

Although *Cancer,* for Father Murphy, had "moments of brilliance, and the comic element was the best part," there was too much "unrelieved emphasis on vulgarity," and references to sex were in "bad taste." Miller's effect has been "to in a sense dehumanize man, as he draws it. That is to make man less noble, less spiritual, less charitable, thoughtful of others." To someone who had not known corruption previously, the book could be "very corrupting." Some sophisticated persons could read it but not the average Milwaukeean.[14] *"Cancer,"* Father Murphy insisted, "does not have educational value."

Under cross-examination, Father Murphy revealed, "I had a feeling of disgust and revulsion when I finished the book."

Probation Officer Mueller felt that parts of the book "aroused lustful desires." The only social values in the book were negative ones. The Reverend Mr. Grimsby admitted that the novel presented a reasonable description of a "pocket of society" in Paris in the thirties, but believed that the book would have a "deteriorating effect on the moral structure of society in Milwaukee" because *Cancer* represented a "lower standard of morality than we have, generally speaking, in . . . Milwaukee."

Witnesses called for the defense were Professor Paul L. Wiley, of the University of Wisconsin English Department; Professor Norman Solkoff, of the University of Wisconsin-Milwaukee Psychology Department; John Dulka, University of Wisconsin-Milwaukee reference librarian; and Morgan Gibson, poet and faculty member of UW-M. All agreed that *Cancer* did not appeal to the prurient interests of the average Milwaukeean. Gibson thought the book would *purge* the reader of prurient interests.[15]

Professor Wiley testified:

> In assessing the literary value of a book as an English Literature professor I take into account the literary intention of the book, that is, the overall intention, the form of the book, the quality of the language, the adequacy generally of the writing to the probable intention of the author.[16]

Cancer had literary merit, Professor Wiley said; how great, he was not prepared to estimate.

> The form—autobiographical fiction—was adequate to the author's aim, which was to portray "a group of people who were unhappy, sometimes ill, living in a metropolitan world," a "sick society," during the Depression; and the language, though perhaps crude, was honest, the "purple passages" being necessary for the effect, which was not to appeal to the prurient interest.[17]

Psychologist Solkoff said that he knew of "no experimental evidence that erotic reading causes erotic behavior." The book had social importance for these reasons:

> It depicts an individual who has many so-called friends in society; many people feel like this man felt in *Tropic of Cancer,* and it depicts this in a most realistic fashion, allowing many individuals, who feel as frustrated, as confused, as miserable, to identify themselves with this man and perhaps in this way be able to take some kind of an appropriate action concerning his own life. The central theme is a man fighting against very intolerable odds. Against these odds, he becomes exceedingly frustrated—helpless—quite depressed. The depressive aspect was very, very intense to me.[18]

Librarian Dulka said that he believed Miller held a good place in American literature and that *Cancer* was a well-written book whose dominant theme was affirmation of life.[19] Under Surges' cross-examination he admitted that he did not know what the moral standards in Milwaukee were, but said he had heard *Cancer*'s four-letter words (some of them) used in Milwaukee County. He added in reply to harsh cross-examination:

> I use these four-letter words in my home in the course of my conversation. I have used the four-letter word beginning with an "f" in my family circle. I don't have any children. . . . When I attend church functions I do not use these four-letter words. I don't use these four-letter words at meetings either. I try not to use the four-letter words at mixed meetings. The people that I generally communicate with do not use the four-letter words. The people that I talk to generally in the course of my day's activities, do not use the four-letter words nor do they go into detail about their sexual enterprises.[20]

Morgan Gibson testified that it was extraordinarily difficult to assess Miller's place in literature because some of his major books have been "unavailable as a result of misguided attempts to suppress his work." Surges objected to the answer and he was promptly sustained by Judge Drechsler. Gibson offered this interpretation of the book:

> In a cancerous civilization, among warped and desperate people, Henry Miller . . . struggles for personal salvation from sexual and social compulsions. He liberates himself by writing about "that which is omitted in books." The book that we have, then, is about a man writing the book that we have. The character moves from the cancerous chaos of life into the imaginative release of art, back and forth, nourishing his vitality to the point where it explodes into a vision of a new life which is ecstatic, delirious, Dionysian, in which body and spirit are one, and man is natural and free. Since this apocalyptic vision springs out of a sense of death, the book is often disturbing, paradoxical, and revolting. The experiences which he presents do not appeal to the prurient interest because of the suffering, frustration, and failure associated with sex, and because of Miller's efforts to transcend sexual compulsion. The tone, moreover, varies from horror to wild satire to visionary ecstasy, leaving the reader anything but aroused sexually. . . . The form of the book would lead a reader from unfreedom through sympathetic suffering to the kind of imaginative release that Miller achieves

by the end of the book, a feeling that he has found his creative self.[21]

Cancer, said Gibson, could "raise the cultural standards of any community, including Milwaukee."

Milwaukeeans who see an Ingmar Bergman movie which is now playing in this city about an incestuous relationship between brother and sister, are probably capable of reading a serious work of literature, such as *Tropic of Cancer,* and understanding its full significance.[22]

Gibson was the last witness.

If this case were going to be decided on the basis of how the novel would affect the average Milwaukee reader, Surges clearly held the advantage so far. His witnesses were in a variety of occupations which brought them close to the people, and all were of the opinion that the book appealed to prurient interest. The defense witnesses, on the other hand, were all on the staff of the University of Wisconsin. One lived in Madison, while one of the UW-M faculty members, Gibson, had lived in Milwaukee only eight months.

Through it all Judge Drechsler, according to Gibson,

was good-humored, polite to everyone, and—mysterious. It was impossible to know what was going on behind his wrinkled face. Everyone spoke volumes, but he. And yet he alone would decide . . . Would he, like Judge Epstein of Chicago, hand down an eloquent defense of the right to read? [23]

As it turned out, Judge Drechsler was no Epstein.

In his decision Judge Drechsler reviewed the testimony, faithfully recording the number of years each witness had lived in Milwaukee. He cited the reviews and newspaper articles which had been received in evidence and quoted from three passages which declared the book to be obscene in one way or another. He faithfully noted that Aschmann had said that in his opinion "supermarkets would not permit the display of the book on their racks, if there were no litigation, nor would 98 per cent of the drug stores." [24] And so Surges' private guardianship program is taken at face value for something entirely different.

Directing his attention to the novel itself, Judge Drechsler, following the lead of the Massachusetts Supreme Court, turned "counter": "vulgar, vile, profane, and indecent words or language was found upon 112 pages," he said. And although he was loath to do so, Judge Drechsler listed the four- and five-letter words. There were twenty, at a conservative count, in the four-letter category:

> Namely, the one most frequently used beginning with "f" and ending with "k"; cunt, next most used, designating women or a portion of their anatomy; slut, bone, cock, hole, putz, twat, sexy, laid, make, heat, suck, come, clap, dose, fart, shit, piss, leak. Ten 5-letter words, frequently used, are: prick, bitch, whore, semen, turds, shits, balls, juice, crack and fairy. While the use of those words alone do [*sic*] not make the book obscene, they do tend to establish, the court believes, that the book as a whole has no significant literary, cultural or educational character. Together, those words make the 4-letter words of "dirt" and "smut."
>
> That conclusion is further supported by the statements such as on page 199, "if only once she had slipped me a piece of a— once in a while"; and on page 214, a character let a Lesbian suck her off for 200 francs. The word above as "a—" is spelled out on the reference page.[25]

What quirk led Judge Drechsler to spell out the words that he did and leave "a—" as it is here? The picture of that strict Lutheran patiently tabulating the results of his reading of *Cancer* is a painful one. Furthermore, in his tabulation, he was not accurate! He counted only thirty-five "descriptions or portrayals of sexual acts, bouts, or episodes" appearing on some "75 pages, beginning with page 16 and ending with page 263." The Massachusetts Supreme Court was far superior in its methods. That august body counted eighty-five sex episodes. But then, that is a higher court.

Because of these things, although there were some passages of merit, Judge Drechsler found the dominant effect of the whole book to be obscene. "It would have no appeal nor attraction to book buyers and readers." (One wonders who bought those 2459 copies of *Cancer* in the first three days of sale in Milwaukee.) Furthermore, said the judge, Miller admits that he is *for* obscenity and that there is obscenity in the book, on page 225. Judge Drechsler wrote:

> On that page, there are four sentences which include the word "obscene." The two mildest ones, which sufficiently show his attitude, are these:
>> "If anyone knew what it meant to read the riddle of that thing which today is called a 'crack' or a 'hole,' if anyone had the least feeling of mystery about the phenomena which are labeled 'obscene,' this world would crack asunder."

and

> "More obscene than anything is inertia."

One begins to question Judge Drechsler's ability to interpret a serious literary work about the time he begins to comment on the number of particular words on a page. One becomes more dubious of his literary qualifications with the first *Cancer* quotation he cites above. One is convinced that he is an unqualified critic when, attempting to show that Miller is *for* obscenity, he quotes the second passage: "More obscene than anything is inertia." Judge Drechsler, by the way, stated that he had read the book carefully three times.

The declaratory judgment act, according to Judge Drechsler,

> is a valid exercise of the police power of Wisconsin, in the interest of promoting public welfare and morals, *for the suppression of obscene literature*. It was enacted for the protection of its citizens.[26]

Citing *State of Wisconsin v. Chobot,*[27] Drechsler wrote:

> If the dominant theme of material taken as a whole, considered by contemporary community standards, appeals to prurient interest, it is "obscene" within the statute, sec. 944.21 (1), proscribing the sale or possession for sale of such matter. . . . The witnesses of the plaintiff, in the instant case, were of the opinion, under such test, included in the language of the questions to them, that the book under such standards appeals

to the prurient interest of the average person in the community of Milwaukee.

He added:

The dominant theme of *Tropic of Cancer* taken as a whole, to the average person in the community, applying the contemporary standards of the community, appeals to the prurient interest within the rule of the *Chobot* and *Roth* cases, and it is obscene within that section of the statutes.

The Wisconsin legislature enacted the declaratory judgment act, according to Judge Drechsler, because it recognized that society could become decadent when exposed to such material as *Cancer*. (Later, a dissenting State Supreme Court justice reviewing Drechsler's decision was also to misconstrue the reason for the passage of Wisconsin's declaratory judgment act —as espoused by the Milwaukee Junior Bar Association.)

Judge Drechsler then paid Milwaukee this supreme compliment:

One of the foundations upon which this nation rests is its morality. The level of morality in this area is at a higher plane than that in others of similar or larger population. Books such as *Tropic of Cancer* both corrode and erode that foundation; and would lower the plane of morality towards that of other places. May it never be lowered to that of the scene of the theme of the book.

"Let the judgment be entered," he wrote finally, "that the book *Tropic of Cancer* is obscene." The date of the decision was June 22, 1962. Judgment was entered June 27, 1962.

14

THE WISCONSIN APPEAL

In their appeal to the Wisconsin Supreme Court the following year (May 1963), Bartell and Panagis reviewed the evidence, and then, citing the Butler, Schenck and Roth cases, said that *Cancer* was protected by the First Amendment because it is not obscene.

Wisconsin legal counsel seem drawn to the state of Massachusetts in matters of obscenity, and the attorneys for the appellants were no exception. (The Massachusetts opinion was at that time, however, the only recent reviewing-court opinion on *Cancer*.) The Massachusetts Supreme Court had held *Cancer* not obscene, they argued, and:

> The record in the case at bar is substantially the same as that which was before the Massachusetts court and that the decision of the Massachusetts court is authority for the proposition that the book is not "obscene" and is therefore entitled to the protection of the First Amendment of the United States Constitution.[1]

That court, they declared, had rejected the test of obscenity in *Regina v. Hicklin,* and had recognized that the Roth case had given constitutional protection to ideas with even the "slightest redeeming social importance."

The Massachusetts Supreme Court had also held that according to some principles established in the Roth case, only hard-core pornography was "utterly without redeeming social importance" and so not within the protection of the First Amendment. "The portrayal of sex, e.g., in art, literature and scientific works," they added, "is not itself sufficient reason to deny material the constitutional protection of freedom of speech and press." Aside from these and other principles, the Massachusetts Court had also ruled that what the U.S. Supreme Court had meant by "obscenity" must be determined by what it had done in other cases. Analyzing the other cases, including the Kingsley Books, Inc., and the four *per curiam* decisions (October term, 1957), along with *Kingsley Intl. Pictures Corp., Manual Enterprises, Grove Press, Inc. v. Christenberry, Eastman Kodak Co. v. Hendricks* (262 F. 2d 392) and *People v. Richmond County News, Inc.,* the Massachusetts Court concluded, "with respect to material designed for general circulation, only predominantly 'hard-core' pornography, without redeeming social significance, is obscene in the constitutional sense."

Citing still further the Massachusetts decision, Bartell and Panagis wrote:

> whether *Tropic* is "obscene" . . . depends upon whether the appeal . . . to the normal adult is predominantly prurient. It is not relevant that we think that the book at many places is repulsive, vulgar, and grossly offensive in the use of four-letter words, and in the detailed and coarse statements of sexual episodes. That a serious work uses four-letter words and has a grossly offensive tone does not mean that the work is not entitled to constitutional protection.

And so, resting much of the weight of their argument on the Massachusetts high court's action, the attorneys for the appellants asked that the judgment be reversed and the complaint against *Cancer* dismissed.

A more effective brief for the appellants was filed by the Wisconsin chapter of the American Civil Liberties Union as a friend of the court. Attorneys for the WCLU were Walstead, Anderson, Bylsma and Eisenberg, a Madison law firm. Professor Emeritus William Rice of the University of Wisconsin, president of the Wisconsin CLU, instigated the brief. The Milwaukee chapter of the CLU, oddly enough, did not participate, in any way, in the *Cancer* campaign.

The WCLU brief emphasized the fact that there was a disparity of opinion concerning the literary, cultural, and educational character of the novel in the record and that this meant, as a matter of law, that *Cancer* was not "without the slightest redeeming social importance." The brief continued:

> It is quite another thing to say, as the trial court said in its opinion: "Whether or not the book has even the slightest redeeming social importance does not place it within the protection of the First Amendment if it is obscene." *The trial court completely misinterprets* the . . . opinion in *Roth* . . . The trial court's opinion rather clearly turns the language of the *Roth* case right around and uses it to prove contrary to the language of *Roth* that something which has even the "slightest redeeming social importance" may nevertheless be obscene. This is an interpretation of the *Roth* case, which neither that case, nor subsequent cases, permit.

The point of protection of books with social importance was stressed with an extensive citation from Judge Epstein's decision, including a brief analysis of three U.S. Supreme Court *per curiam* opinions that followed the Roth case: *One, Inc. v. Olesen, Sunshine Book Co.,* and *Times Film Corp.* "These three decisions," Judge Epstein had said in his Chicago decision, "point unmistakably to the determination of the court to restrict obscenity to hard-core pornography."

The statements about *Cancer* from eminent men of letters which were not received by Judge Drechsler were included in the WCLU brief.

The Manual Enterprises decision was then discussed, and the WCLU brief added: "*Manual* makes clear that the legal test of obscenity is not only whether to the average person, the dominant theme of the material, taken as a whole, appeals to prurient interest, but also, the material must be patently offensive." Certainly, the WCLU brief continued, after *Manual,* it cannot be said that while homosexual magazines, to quote Justice Harlan, "cannot, under any permissible constitutional standard, be deemed to be beyond the pale of contemporary notions of rudimentary decency" and it might be added, *while these homosexual magazines are freely to be purchased in Milwaukee,* a literary work by a well known American writer, whom many consider one of the literary giants of this century, is to be banned. How could Milwaukee be a better, indeed, intellectually freer city, when it bans a literary work that many feel has great artistic value while at the same time the normal and the abnormal have the opportunity to read magazines obviously without such value? [2]

The WCLU attorneys, being from Madison, apparently did not know that those homosexual magazines, especially *Manual,* were *not* freely purchased in Milwaukee because of Surges' "program of guardianship."

Pointing out that there was no evidence of anyone's being corrupted by reading, the WCLU brief then argued that "the community in terms of whose standards of decency the issue of obscenity must be decided is not any local community but the national community as a whole." And this struck at the heart of Surges' argument. U.S. Supreme Court Justice Harlan's decision on *Manual* was cited: "We think that the proper test under this federal statute, reaching as it does all parts of the United States whose population reflects many different ethnic and cultural backgrounds, is a national standard of decency." What would such a thing mean to Wisconsin, the WCLU brief asked, if the situation were otherwise?

Persons of greater intellectual perspicacity feeling that they did not have the same opportunities of choice available to the citizens of the so-called more "sophisticated" states would tend to move to those states in order to have the greater freedom of choice. . . . Can anyone doubt that such a situation would tend to create a more divisive nation?

In the concluding argument the brief states:

A logical extension of modern notions of the democratic ideal requires that there be a national conscience with reference to freedom to choose books, magazines and all forms of written material. A nation which prides itself on the freedom of individual choice can ill afford to permit artificial boundaries such as state lines to be the determining factor in whether its citizens shall be able to make the free choice it broadcasts to the world that its citizens enjoy. We live in a nation in which the interstate concept of equal freedom and opportunity of all our citizens constantly takes on more realistic proportions. We started in this imperfect world with an ideal which we have ever striven to reduce to reality. Notions of equality of opportunity exist the world over. America, more than any other nation in the world, has achieved realization of this ideal. We have enabled more people to own their own homes, to determine at what jobs or professions they shall work, to pick their own spouses, to mention just a few of the choices, than any other nation in the world. To move in the direction of restricting their choice of reading material based on artificial boundaries would be a step backward, which in all good conscience, men who are so free cannot lightly take.

Surges' brief countered the Massachusetts Supreme Court decision citations with the *State v. Chobot* decision. The Wisconsin Supreme Court was not bound by a sister state's decision, Surges wrote, especially since in *Chobot* the Wisconsin Court had reached different conclusions on the *per curiam* decisions of 1957 than had the Massachusetts Court. In *Chobot,* Surges argued:

> Analysis of the cases discloses that the tests of obscenity there applied were not the tests set forth and approved in the *Roth Case*. It is apparent that the United States Supreme Court, in citing the *Roth Case* in each such reversal, has insisted that the test to be applied is that approved in the *Roth Case*.

Furthermore, no witnesses testified in Massachusetts on community standards, only evidence was considered, whereas "many reputable, qualified, long-time residents of Milwaukee County" testified that the book appealed to the prurient interest of the average Milwaukeean. Librarian John Dulka "made" Surges' brief here for using "the four-letter word beginning with F in his home and family circle."

The "term community in the definition or test of obscenity," Surges argued, "refers to an indistinct geographic area part of and attached to a metropolitan center. The city of Madison constitutes the center of a community as does the city and county of Milwaukee. . . .

"The difference between pornography and hard-core pornography," Surges continued, "is an extralegal mythical distinction being hyperbolized by disseminators of obscene literature to undermine the clear effect of the definition in the *Roth Case*." He added:

> It is difficult to understand how men vitally interested in literature, and therefore concerned with written expression, can justify varying or changing the meaning of words, the tools of their trade and of thought, in an attempt to vary or change the thought which these words had when written. It is an absolute prostitution of truth, which is the avowed product of protected free speech.

The contention that any book with redeeming social importance cannot be obscene, Surges held, was without merit. Surges cited Aschmann's testimony on the reluctance of supermarkets and drug stores to carry *Cancer* and audaciously added, "We submit that the testimony of Mr. Aschmann provides a veritable mathematical conclusion reflecting the standards of the community of Milwaukee."

Surges summarized the testimony of those witnesses he deemed in the best positions to judge the standards of Milwaukee, and asked that the lower court judgment be affirmed.

The Supreme Court of Wisconsin reversed and remanded the lower court judgment with directions to dismiss the complaint.[3] The vote was four to three, with Justice Thomas Fairchild writing the majority opinion.

The definition of "obscene" in the Roth case, Justice Fairchild wrote, is the same as that previously determined by the state court in *Chobot*. Quoting freely from the 1960 article by Lockhart and McClure,[4] Justice Fairchild pointed out that the Roth case had laid down only two constitutional requirements for determining what is obscene: that the material be judged as a whole, and that it be judged by its impact upon the average person. The four *per curiam* decisions, Lockhart and McClure wrote, had made it "clear that the court was applying the constitutional guaranties of freedom of expression to confine obscenity censorship within very narrow limits indeed." Ideas with even the slightest redeeming importance must have constitutional protection. Justice Fairchild ruled:

> Under the capsule statement of the Roth test, the question of whether the work is obscene is to be answered in the process of identifying the dominant theme and the degree of its appeal to the prurient interest. A balancing of factors is undoubtedly necessary in the application of the test, and we are of the opinion that where a work of apparent serious purpose is involved, the scales will not readily be tipped toward the determination of obscenity.

To be weighed in reaching any determination of obscenity were the "seriousness of the author's purpose, the social importance of the idea expressed, or the artistic quality of expression." The Massachusetts decision was cited in support of the Wisconsin Supreme Court's expression of the balancing concept:

> We think, in the light of the decisions reviewed . . . that the First Amendment protects material which has value because of ideas, news, or artistic, literary, or scientific attributes. If the appeal of material (taken as a whole) to adults is not predominantly prurient, adults cannot be denied the material. When the public risks of suppressing ideas are weighed against the risks of permitting their circulation, the guaranties of the First Amendment must be given controlling effect. The dangers of subjective judgments in the matter of censorship lead to a strong presupposition against suppression.

Although much of the language in *Cancer* would be offensive to many,

> It seems a reasonable conclusion that the use of crude language contributed to the force with which the author expressed his ideas. Although some of these words would not be tolerated in

our society if inflicted on unwilling listeners, an offended reader need only close the book in order to escape.

Also considered in this opinion was the role of the appellate court in obscenity cases. Calling upon Lockhart and McClure again, Justice Fairchild cited this passage:

> There is a view that when the constitutional protection is claimed, the judge or appellate court must make an independent review of the material to determine whether it is obscene, and the concept that obscenity is a fact issue has been criticized.
>
> That a judgment of obscenity is not a fact issue of the ordinary type is obvious.[5]

Just as the Massachusetts Supreme Court resolved the dilemma by relying upon the rule that where the evidence is documentary the appellate court is not bound by trial court inferences, so, too, wrote Justice Fairchild, does the Wisconsin Court recognize a similar rule.

> Although there was more conflict in the expert testimony in this case than there appears to have been in the Massachusetts case, we deem the reading of the book to constitute the most weighty factor in the determination, and do not consider ourselves bound by the decision of the trial court, based on his reading of it.

Too much weight, he continued, was given to vulgar language by the lower court and to

> the fact that the incidents related violate our standards of acceptable conduct, and insufficient consideration to the fact that the book has commanded serious attention as a literary work of some importance.

As for community standards, once again Justice Fairchild cited Lockhart and McClure to the effect that the term has reference to the standards of society as a whole, and not reference to any locality. Justice Fairchild added this telling observation:

> We conclude that for the purposes of our statute, no distinction ought to be made between the standards of different com-

munities within the state. We doubt whether standards which are relevant to the question of obscenity differ significantly from one locality to another in Wisconsin. Furthermore, our statute, sec. 269.565 (6), Stats., permits a judgment of obscenity to be used in a criminal trial of any person who was served with notice of it before the alleged violation. Under it a judgment obtained in Milwaukee County could be so used anywhere in the state. Clearly this should not be so if the particular matter could be obscene in one area and not in another.

In his summary, Justice Fairchild noted that *Cancer* had received serious attention from the critics as an important book, and that it appeared to be a truthful portrayal of an unsavory segment of life.

Some of the episodes, taken alone, appeal to prurient interests, but, in our opinion, the dominant theme of the book, taken as a whole, does not.

Our reading of the book has engendered no enthusiasm. We do not endorse it. Our judgment will preserve its access to the market place where Wisconsin readers may buy it if they choose. In terms of the good that this particular book is likely to accomplish, we probably do no great thing in preserving it. Our function, however, is not to determine the quality of a book. Our duty is to respect and enforce in full measure the freedom of expression guaranteed by state and federal constitutions.

Judgment reversed, cause remanded with directions to dismiss the complaint.

Concurring with Justice Fairchild in this May 20, 1963, decision were Justices Horace Wilkie, Myron Gordon, and William Dieterich. Chief Justice Timothy Brown wrote a dissenting opinion supported by Justices George Currie and J. Harold Hallows. Hallows also wrote a separate dissent.

In his dissent, Chief Justice Brown said that the lower court finding was not against the "great weight and clear preponderance of the evidence."

Whatever we may think, individually, of the public policy of suppressing any writing, as a court we may not declare our personal opposing preferences to be the law and thus subvert the public policy determined by legislature. . . . The judgment of the trial court must be affirmed unless . . . we can find that upon perusal of the book itself we find as a matter of law that *Tropic of Cancer* is not constitutionally obscene.

By the Roth test alone, the Chief Justice argued, *Cancer* is obscene. But if the book must also be shown to be "patently offensive," then there is no difficulty in finding this element too in the novel.

The book is a collection of anecdotes which, with few exceptions, describe in detail the sexual proclivities of a number of depraved men whose central character appears to be the author. His account of their practices and perversions in the erotica arena are described in the vilest terms known to the English language.

"I agree emphatically with the Massachusetts dissenters," Chief Justice Brown concluded. "*Tropic of Cancer* is saturated with filth in its substance and in its expression. The judgment should be affirmed."

Justice Hallows, in what has been termed "an exceedingly colorful dissent," [6] rejected the idea that *Roth* and the *per curiam* decisions limited the definition of obscenity to "hardcore" pornography. Nor could he see that any "balancing" was included in the state statute. (The reader will recall that this is the Justice Hallows whose wife in 1953, as head of the Decent Literature Committee of the Milwaukee Archdiocesan Confraternity of Christian Mothers, used NODL lists in her program.) If a writer's dominant theme appeals to the prurient interest of the average man, continued Justice Hallows:

Applying contemporary community standards, it [the book] is not saved by its literary style. Obscenity is only increased and heightened by being couched in literary artistry. Neither can obscenity have redeeming social importance. It is fallacious to argue what would be otherwise obscene is not obscene because it has social significance or some literary merit. The end (social significance or literary merit) does not justify the means (appeal to the prurient interest).

And as for the differences between obscenity, pornography, and hard-core pornography, Justice Hallows argued, "All pornography is obscene. 'Hard-core' can only mean a greater degree of obscenity, but can it be said that any pornography or obscenity is good?" And the "less patent obscenity becomes, the more insidious the appeal to prurient interests."

Justice Hallows then called the court's attention to what distributor Aschmann had testified:

> He testified supermarkets and drug stores were selective in what they displayed because they did not want books on their racks which would embarrass them in the eyes of their customers and none of the 170 super markets would accept *Tropic of Cancer* on their racks and 98 per cent of the drug stores refused it. *This certainly is of some importance and indication of what the contemporary community standard is.*[7]

And so, in good faith, does a Justice of the Supreme Court of Wisconsin take what Surges' "program of guardianship" has wrought and accept it as evidence of Milwaukee's contemporary standards.

With the Wisconsin Supreme Court decision *Tropic of Cancer* was allowed to circulate in Milwaukee County. But this decision did not mark the end of Surges' efforts to ban the novel. In Surges' brief in support of a motion for a rehearing of the *Cancer* case, he again raised the specter of reading and antisocial conduct,[8] and argued that a determination of obscenity must be made "without considering the existence of social redeeming value in the book." Free expression, he said, is a facet of liberty in whose name "many sins are committed." A cordon of reviewers, Surges said,

> not present in court to have their opinions subjected to cross-examination caused the testimony of several students of human nature, literature, education and civic benefit, proffered by state to be cast aside, a classic determination of a trial judge, who followed the dictate of precedent in arriving at his carefully prepared, pensive, studied opinion is disregarded and upset, the legislative effort is thwarted, and *the public is rendered defenseless before the spew of a semen and feces saturated book.*[9]

Were these critics and reviewers writing honestly of books such as *Cancer?* No, said Surges:

> It is natural, in our estimation, that these writers, turned critics, are impelled to formulate favorable reviews out of a desire to create a cushion of latitude for themselves. It does not seem correct that their *self-serving opinions* should be accorded more legal weight than judicial opinions and the objective opinions of persons whose only interest is to serve and benefit society.[10]

Surges also chided the court for citing so freely, and evidently following, the advice proffered by Lockhart and McClure in the matter of contemporary community standards and the *per curiam* decisions of 1957.

And in the following paragraph Surges casts aspersions on the four defense witnesses' testimony, while holding up the prosecution's witnesses' mannerisms as evidence, in effect, of high character:

> The appellate court in reading a transcript is incapable of hearing the voices and tones of voices of the witnesses, or of recognizing the spontaneity of answers, the depth in the manner of presentation, the *time lapses showing evasiveness, the physical attributes and mannerisms.* Our respect for the appellate court is far too deep to conceive that it conjectures that courts must rise above these mundane considerations. We daresay even appellate justices evaluate their friends and associates by these standards for many, and delicate reasons, amongst them the fact that by such many signs the thoughts, dispositions, habits and characteristics of a person are made known.[11]

Surges concluded with a statement to the effect that he (along with McCauley) hoped "that the spirit of controversy has not carried us beyond the place accorded an advocate in this, the highest, most dignified forum in the State of Wisconsin."

The Supreme Court rejected the petition for rehearing on its ruling.[12]

15

THE WISCONSIN PRESS AND CANCER

How did the Wisconsin press react to the *Cancer* trials? To such an attack on freedom of the press involving a sister mass communication medium? Most of the press remained mute except for superficial news stories. No one, it seemed, wanted to be caught defending a "dirty book." Almost no one editorialized against *Cancer,* either—for obvious reasons—but there were a few instances of this.

The Milwaukee trial attracted surprisingly little interest throughout the state. In October of 1961 most of the newspapers ran the announcement that *Cancer* would be tried, but the trial itself, in May 1962, was reported in few Wisconsin papers outside of Madison and Milwaukee. It was covered dutifully each day by the *Milwaukee Sentinel* and the *Milwaukee Journal,* however, and at the end of the four and a half days of testimony, Robert W. Wells of the *Journal* wrote an excellent summary which was carried on page one.[1]

After the trial was over, and before Judge Drechsler delivered his decision, two Wisconsin dailies under the same ownership editorialized against *Cancer.* The editorial appeared on the same day, May 19, 1962, in both the *Green Bay Press-Gazette* and the *Appleton Post-Crescent. Tropic of Cancer* was a "disgusting book," but the "question of prohibiting any book to adults is a difficult one and the matter of how to do it is perplexing." Sales soared, with obscenity charges, and paperbacks made the book handy for everyone. This criticism was relatively mild, but the *Press-Gazette* made up for it later, in commenting on the Wisconsin Supreme Court decision.

Titling that editorial "A Controversial Book," the *Press-Gazette* reviewed the decision and remarked: "The court appeared to be unanimous on one thing. That is, that this book is a pretty dirty article." The newspaper editorial decried the fact that local community standards had been cast aside. It concluded:

> Where a matter of doubt exists, it is probably better for the courts to err on the side of permitting the circulation of the book. But in a case such as this one where apparently all concerned are in substantial agreement that the book is obscene, it is very doubtful if the case of freedom is helped by ruling in the book's favor. As Justice Hallows said, it is not a right to be obscene. And when the court tolerates the sprinkling of obscenities and vulgarities through a book merely to promote its sales it is merely inviting other obscenities.[2]

In Racine, Wisconsin, the District Attorney expressed surprise at the Supreme Court ruling, but said that he would abide by it.[3] However, that front-page columnist of the *Racine Journal-Times,* Tex Reynolds, held firm: "I hesitate to argue with the august justices. But speaking personally, if that book isn't obscene, I've never read one that is."[4] The *Appleton Post-Crescent,* meanwhile, took the easy way out and on July 23, 1963, under the headline, "What Others Are Saying in Wisconsin, High Court Wrong in Defending *Tropic of Cancer,*" reprinted an editorial from the Catholic *Green Bay Register* criticizing the decision.

But these papers are the exceptions. Most of the state's daily newspapers simply carried the Associated Press or United Press International stories on the State Supreme Court decision, or else ignored it completely. The 258 Wisconsin weeklies did not report it at all, so far as I can determine.[5]

After the *Wausau Daily Record-Herald* carried the Associated Press story of the decision on May 20 (three paragraphs out of the eight that were dispatched), on May 23 it ran an editorial entitled "Is Smut Increasing in Mails?" "Stamp it out," it advocated. The *Marinette Eagle Star,* which ran the same Associated Press story on May 20, wrote an editorial May 25 on a bookseller in Poughkeepsie, New York, who in that month was evicted because of highway building. In protest he allowed his 200,000 volumes, which were moved to the sidewalks, to be ruined by the elements. The *Star* lamented this waste, and sagely observed that the wisdom stored in books can never be replaced. The *Daily Citizen* of Beaver Dam, attorney Howard Boyle's home town, ran the United Press International story on the Supreme Court decision on May 20, devoting two paragraphs to it. In the same issue it ran a five-paragraph story on Radcliffe girls staging a Harvard panty raid.

Editorially and otherwise there were lapses in the Milwaukee papers' coverage. On the eve of requesting the Supreme Court for a rehearing, Surges spoke at a Milwaukee Public Affairs Forum. The *Journal* reported what he had to say under the headline " 'TROPIC' BAN STILL SOUGHT HERE." After reporting that the D.A.'s Office would ask the Wisconsin Supreme Court to reconsider its decision, the paper quoted Surges as saying that the Supreme Court "did not adequately consider either the average man or community standards." From a legal point of view, Surges said, if a book appealed to "prurient (lustful) interests of the average man, it was obscene." Speaking in opposition, Attorney David L. Walther, perhaps looking into the future, or else in answer to something Surges said *which wasn't reported,* said:

> The supreme court is not necessarily in favor of dirty books because it rules that it is unconstitutional not to allow publication of the book . . .
> This represents the minimum safeguard we can give to literature.[6]

Why the *Milwaukee Journal,* that newspaper with a national reputation, did not print what Surges actually did say I do not know. The *Milwaukee Sentinel* did not have such reservations. On the same day the *Journal* story appeared, under the headline "COURT'S 'TROPIC' RULING BLASTED" the *Sentinel* reported that Surges charged the court with:

> Completely ignoring law and judicial precedent and "foisting on a defenseless public" a "patently obscene" book . . .
>
> Surges . . . said that the court ignored legislative intent and its own previous decisions and substituted its own concept of obscenity for that of the "average man."
>
> "The judges . . . from their ivory domed towers, placed themselves on a podium and decided for themselves what is obscene." The law requires that the judges apply community standards and not their own . . .
>
> The judges are "so out of touch with the day to day human conflict" that they cannot render a proper decision in an obscenity case . . .
>
> Surges . . . charged that the court threw "all the rules out the window" merely because Miller was considered a "great author" and his book had been praised by critics.
>
> The court placed Miller above the rules of society, Surges insisted.[7]

Five days later, possibly to atone for its reporting omission, the *Journal* editorially censured Surges for his outburst:

> A lawyer who told a court to its face what . . . Surges said about the Wisconsin supreme court on a public platform last week could be found in contempt.
>
> A zealot against what he himself regards as obscenity, Surges let the sting of defeat go to his tongue. . . . He covered the court with abuse and ridicule.[8]

The *Sentinel* did not comment editorially on the Supreme Court decision. By then it was no longer a Hearst paper, having been bought by the *Journal* in 1962.

The *Journal,* aroused (temporarily), said that the court had "taken the logical path out of an absurd and confusing quagmire" in its ruling. The "community standards" formula, the *Journal* said, was "vague, unworkable and close to ridiculous. How do you locate the 'average person' in a community, and how do you determine what arouses his 'prurient interest'?" The court majority took no stand on the literary merits of *Cancer,* said the editorial. Neither did the *Journal.*[9] Two months later, the *Journal* wrote an editorial entitled "On Censorship of Books," in response to the New York Supreme Court decision on *Cancer*:

> During the trial of . . . *Cancer* for obscenity in Milwaukee, it was argued that Milwaukeeans are so much less sophisticated than the residents of New York that a different moral yardstick applies.
>
> Ironically, Miller's book is now judged permissible for us unsophisticates, while the New York court of appeals has ruled that the book is too obscene for the cultured Manhattanites.[10]

Cancer would not have had its sales had it not been for bans, the *Journal* said:

> The censors and would-be censors, sincere though they may be, have been responsible for the sale of the books they deplore more than anyone else. Despite them, the literary pendulum has swung toward a point where almost every novelist now feels he must include some Anglo-Saxon terms and a few bedroom scenes to show he's up to date.
>
> One of these days, the serious writers will realize that the fight for freedom to write as frankly as they please has been won, except for occasional rear guard actions. Perhaps then some of them will no longer feel required to prove an already proven point and will permit their characters to use longer words and to deal with less Freudian problems.[11]

The reason for the *Journal*'s refusal to defend the literary merits of *Cancer* now becomes apparent. The "serious writers" of today (and no doubt yesterday, e.g., Miller and D. H. Lawrence) and their subject matter are evidently unpalatable to the editorial chiefs of the *Milwaukee Journal.* But then, in that curiously vacillating way most newspapers have in such matters, the *Journal* one month later quoted a *Christian Century* article on the New York decision under the title: "To Prurient, Even Bible Is 'Dirty,' Editorial Says." The *Century* editorial said that the New York decision jeopardizes rather than protects the health of our free society.

To say this is not to defend . . . *Cancer,* but to champion something much more important: The right of the people to a free press . . .

[*Cancer*] is a book which the healthy can take in stride—and the sick mind is apt to find as much appeal to prurient interest in the Bible as in Miller's sordid descriptions.[12]

What can result from such vacillation and apathy in the face of such censorship forces as those in Milwaukee was strikingly illustrated for the *Journal,* and Wisconsin, in just a few months. For among those four justices who voted that *Cancer* was not obscene was one who would shortly be running for re-election to the Supreme Court of Wisconsin.

16
THE CANCER ELECTION

One wonders whether, as Justice Horace W. Wilkie sat at the Wisconsin Supreme Court table and cast his vote to free *Tropic of Cancer* for sale in his state, he paused momentarily and thought about the Supreme Court race for re-election that he would be in the following year. Perhaps he thought briefly that some unpleasant comments might be made, to the effect that his vote had tipped the decision in favor of Miller's controversial novel, since he was the only one of the four anticensorship justices up for re-election in 1964. Perhaps. But neither Wilkie nor his bitterest foe could have dreamed of the judicial Pandora's box his ballot opened. Chances are that Wisconsin lawyers and judges will never forget the unprecedented judicial campaign that raged around one vote and one book.

One of the "bitterest, most controversial high court campaigns on record in the state" [1] began with Howard H. Boyle, Jr., of Beaver Dam, entering the March 10 primary for the Supreme Court and attacking Wilkie for siding with the majority of the Supreme Court in the *Cancer* case. Before all was over on April 7, the independence of the elective state judiciary was endangered, the Wisconsin Supreme Court bench itself felt threatened, and freedom of the press became the issue. [2] "Decent literature" groups backed Boyle, while other groups, calling for freedom of expression, formed to back Wilkie.

"It was that book," one newspaperman remarked, "which caused the controversy and catapulted Boyle from relative political obscurity to a prominence as a public figure which he had never known before. At the same time an unprecedented number of endorsements to Wilkie changed the entire tone from previous judicial contests." [3]

In 1964, Wisconsin was one of fifteen states that chose its justices in nonpartisan elections. The term of office was ten years. With no party campaigns involved, the judiciary elections are placid affairs normally, but in 1964 the Boyle-Wilkie contest became only slightly less important than the Democratic presidential preferential primary contest between Alabama Governor George Wallace and Wisconsin Governor John Reynolds.

Horace W. Wilkie, forty-seven, of Madison, had received the LL.B. degree from George Washington University in 1944. As a Democratic candidate for Congress from the 2nd District, he was defeated in 1948, 1950, and 1952. From January 1957 to June 1962, Wilkie served as a Democratic State Senator from the City of Madison. Appointed to the Supreme Court on June 5, 1962, by Governor Gaylord Nelson—to fill out a term that had two years to run—he had been practicing law in Madison for seventeen years when the honor was bestowed. He had been associated first with the law firm of Wilkie, Toebaas, Hart, Kraege and Jackman, then with Wilkie, Anderson, Bylsma and Eisenberg. His specialization was general trial work and appeals in all fields. Wilkie was married and had five daughters.

Howard H. Boyle, Jr., forty-two, of Beaver Dam, had received his B.S. degree from Holy Cross College. From 1942 to 1946 he had served with the U.S. Navy. He earned a law degree from Marquette University Law School in 1950, and was editor-in-chief of the *Marquette Law Review* during his final three semesters in school. Boyle held no public office; from 1950 onward he was a practicing attorney, and from 1946 to 1963 he was on the faculty of the University of Minnesota, where he taught principles of economics and business law. From 1961 to 1963 Boyle served as chairman of the Milwaukee Bar Association Committee on Judicial Qualifications. He received from the MBA in 1962 an award "in recognition of special efforts on behalf of MBA and the lawyers of Wisconsin in furtherance of the high standards and ideals of the legal profession during the past year." In 1963 he spoke at the Wisconsin State Bar Association convention for the fourth consecutive year. At the time of the election he was the father of nine children.

Boyle, like Wilkie, was a "visible" candidate. He had become known to Wisconsin voters by earlier running as an independent against Senator Wiley in a Republican primary for the U.S. Senate. He polled less than 20,000 votes. The next year he again ran as an independent in a special primary to select candidates for the seat of the late Senator Joseph McCarthy. In this election he received a little more than 20,000 votes.

Boyle was publicly tagged as a right-wing Republican. Jack Ladinsky found him to be "a sincere and dedicated man, strongly committed to the conservative philosophy, but not particularly politically sophisticated." On the eve of the election Boyle told the newspapers, "For many years I have been active combatting the evils of obscenity." [4]

Wilkie announced his candidacy for the ten-year, $24,000-a-year term on the Supreme Court bench on July 1, 1963, and began what appeared to be an uneventful campaign. Attorney Harry E. Larsen, fifty-three, entered the race too but created little political stir. A University of Wisconsin graduate, Larsen had opened a law office in Superior, Wisconsin, in 1936.

When Boyle announced his determination to run, he immediately attacked Wilkie for his part in the Supreme Court decision on *Cancer*. Pornography, said Boyle, would be his main issue. In his campaign he made it appear that he was against the sale of pornography and that Wilkie was not. Boyle received "considerable support from Roman Catholic sources, and he ran exceptionally well in Catholic areas." [5]

Wilkie initially centered his campaign on continued implementation of the court reorganization program of 1962, which was an attempt to step up the time element in cases before all Wisconsin courts and eliminate backlogs of cases. He also favored retention of the system of electing Wisconsin's judges.

Larsen did not feel, he said, that judges were "sacred cows" —above reproach. He criticized Wilkie's six-point program to improve judicial administration, calling them the "six platitudes of Wilkie." Larsen became especially critical of Wilkie when he learned that Wilkie had in effect endorsed a former legislative colleague, State Senator Lynn Stalbaum of Racine, a Democratic candidate for Congress, although Wisconsin Supreme Court elections are supposed to be nonpartisan. At a dinner for Stalbaum Wilkie was quoted as saying that although he couldn't endorse his colleague, he hadn't driven 150 miles just for the dinner. Most of the newspapers that caught this incident criticized Wilkie for it, and Wilkie himself considered it a serious campaign error which probably cost him endorsements and votes.

In the primary Boyle did not do much direct campaigning but his attacks on Wilkie received wide publicity. The primary results disclosed that Boyle was an "iceberg candidate," with most of his support invisible before the primary. Although he spent little money on his campaign, Boyle's attack on the "liberal" judicial philosophy of the court, as exemplified by the *Cancer* decision, won him a surprise nomination.

The final tally of the primary on March 10 showed Wilkie with 141,041, Boyle with 127,020, and Larsen, who was eliminated, with 108,187. In Milwaukee County, significantly enough, Boyle was only 36 votes behind Wilkie. He received 61,930 votes while Wilkie got 61,966. Larsen pulled 54,384 votes there.

Wilkie's primary edge over Boyle, about 14,000 votes, came mainly from his home county, Dane—which includes Madison —where he had 15,849 to Boyle's 3,727. Most of Wilkie's strength came from the south central area of the state, where he carried, by comfortable margins, most of the counties. Boyle made his best showing in the Fox River Valley area, "reflecting strong conservative sentiment there." Larsen, meanwhile, ran well ahead up in his home area and also "made good showings in Kenosha, Racine, Waukesha and Milwaukee counties." [6]

And so the two main characters were cast for the April 7 election stage. Ordinarily Wisconsin judicial elections are distinguished by voter apathy. One explanation is that voters just can't get excited about electing judges on a nonparty, nonpartisan ticket. Another possible reason is that the issues which arouse voters are often lacking in judicial elections. The turbulence of the primary campaign, however, indicated that the 1964 Wisconsin judicial election would be something more than "a placid affair."

The primary election set off an "alarm chorus among lawyers, judges, newspaper editorial writers, and others." [7] The liberal Madison paper, the *Capital Times,* blared a call to arms to the state's newspapers the day after the primary. Never known for euphemisms, the *Times* called Boyle a "right-wing extremist of the Birch type, a flaming follower of the late Senator Joe McCarthy." The editorial, headed "Boyle Presents a Frightening Prospect in Court Race," continued:

> His campaign issue for the Supreme Court race is pornography—one of the issues which Birchites have been using to butt in on what people can read and what can be taught in schools.
>
> We had an example of this kind of meddling in Eagle River last year when Birchites on the school board sought to bar the *New York Times* magazine and the *Saturday Review* because they were obscene. . . .
>
> In Wisconsin we are threatened with this type of thinking on our Supreme Court as a result of Tuesday's primary.
>
> *The newspapers in this state, which have most to lose from the censorship type of mind on our courts, have a job to do between now and April 7.* [8]

The *Racine Journal-Times* two days later ran an editorial entitled "Boyle Plainly Violates Ethics." Boyle's attack was "vicious and indefensible . . . with the broad implication that

Justice Wilkie favors pornographic literature." [9] Columnist Tex
Reynolds ("If that book isn't obscene . . .") had nothing to
say in this newspaper at this time.

The *Stevens Point Journal* gently scored Boyle for his pornography techniques of campaigning and ended with: "One
thing now seems certain. The campaigning in the next three
weeks will be quite different from the usual run of academic
discussions of judicial administration." [10]

Among other things, money talked in the judicial election.
In the primary campaign Boyle had spent, personally, only
$545.72. Seven clubs contributed $1,344.12. Larsen spent
$1,080. Wilkie personally reported spending $4,749.83. Three
Wilkie clubs added $18,685 to his campaign coffers. Boyle's
campaign costs, then, totaled $1,889.84, while Wilkie's came
to almost his new annual salary—$23,434.83.

The ratio of expenditures between the two would be cut in
the election campaign, yet Wilkie spent nearly four times more
than Boyle. Boyle reported $13,211, and Wilkie reported
$55,954 to the secretary of the state of Wisconsin at the end
of that election.[11]

The main issue in the judicial election had been set by Boyle
in the primary. Given the choice, Wilkie would have liked to
run in the incumbent's traditional manner—and to have been
elected in the traditional manner: without much of a struggle.
But Boyle dictated what the main issue was to be, and Wilkie,
powerless to do anything about it, had to fight for his judicial
life.

"A vote for Boyle is a vote against obscenity." This is what
Boyle said, this is what Boyle believed.[12] The issue drew strong
Catholic support.

Other issues, hidden issues, drew Catholic votes that Boyle
had no control over, and made no pronouncements about. But
they were there, and Boyle's supporters made the most of them.
One was the school bus issue. As a state senator, Wilkie had
voted three times against the Manders School Bus Law which
would have provided transportation for parochial school children at the expense of the state. Wilkie's previous legislative

stand on the parochial school bus law was used by Boyle supporters to draw votes.[13]

In a statement to the press, Justice Wilkie spoke of his
campaign in this way:

> The only proper issue now, as when I began this campaign nine
> months ago, is which candidate is best qualified in terms of legal
> ability and experience, integrity, and judicial temperament to
> be justice . . . My credentials have been presented to the
> voters: 1—Service on the Supreme Court for two years [56
> opinions and 300 decisions]; 2—Support by all three ex-chief
> justices of Wisconsin; 3—Endorsement by every one of the 19
> daily newspapers that have taken a position in the contest; 4—
> Support by lawyers and other interested groups from every
> corner of the state.
>
> There is a fundamental difference in legal philosophy between
> myself as the incumbent justice on the Supreme Court and my
> challenger. I am irrevocably committed to an independent ju-
> diciary in which a judge rules on the facts and law in the case
> at hand, without seeking to impose on others his own self-de-
> termined moral code or his own preconceived view of what is
> popular or what he would wish the law to be (not what it
> actually is). My opponent does not agree with the fundamental
> concept of the role of a judge. Above all, an appellate judge
> must be impartial.

Boyle summed up his campaign beliefs to the press in these
strong and revealing terms. (Curiously, he refers to himself,
here and in other communications, in the third person.)

> No matter how violent be the attack on Boyle, or how vicious
> be the attempt to smear his reputation, one fact in this Supreme
> Court campaign stands out clearly. Horace Wilkie is one of
> four judges who made it possible for pornography of the most
> insidious kind to be available to our children. In the *Tropic of
> Cancer* decision, these four judges took it upon themselves, to
> extend the constitutional protection of free speech to one of
> the filthiest books ever published—a book which the court's
> chief justice described as being "saturated with filth in its
> substance and in its expression." This means that as long as
> these four men continue to sit in combination on the Wisconsin

Supreme Court, the circulation among our youth of obscene writings of the *Tropic of Cancer* type will be protected by law. Thus Justice Wilkie and the other three judges have effectively nullified laws which the people have enacted to protect against lewd, obscene and indecent written matter in their communities.

Protection of Constitutional guaranties did not require these four judges to do this. The Guaranty of Free Speech suffered no restriction whatsoever over the many years when legal favor was withheld from morally depraved writings like those in question. The only thing which Justice Wilkie and the other three have done here is to extend the constitutional guaranty of free speech to cover acknowledged obscenity. By so doing, teenage abortion, venereal disease, unwed motherhood and other transgressions of youth which are encouraged by obscene written matter have been promoted by merely four men who hold a powerful position.

The problem of obscenity is deadly serious from yet another view. Today our sacred national principles are facing challenge from an alien, Godless ideology. Resisting the onslaught of this enemy force will require the strongest moral fiber in our youth, on whom will fall the onus of battle.

The legalization of the type of pornography in question is a clear indication of Justice Wilkie's legal philosophy. And such a way of thinking promises greater damage to our law than has already been worked. Do the people of Wisconsin want a man with such a way of thinking to represent them on their Supreme Court?

The diabolic cunning of the adversary is shown by the nature of the counter-attack. The real issue is ignored because Boyle's stand is right. Instead the opposition attempts to smear Boyle by falsehoods and unreasonable accusations. Boyle is charged with violating ethics, extremism and censorship, all of which charges are false. It is said that the issue is a "Catholic" one, which is an insult to the decent-minded persons of every other faith. No amount of foul innuendo is being spared, and the cause of decency ignored.

I am trying to keep our children clean. I will fight to the end for this purpose.[14]

How did Boyle campaign for the Wisconsin Supreme Court, a campaign he considered a "moral crusade"? The public furor that he raised when he used the *Cancer* decision as a focal point for his attack had been in effect most of Boyle's campaign up to within ten days of the election. But the amount of news time and space devoted to the campaign itself were, in the words of one newspaperman, "phenomenal": up to March 29 Boyle had made only six formal appearances, yet he remained in the "public eye and attracted a respectable amount of support." [15]

Boyle ran what is called a "loose" campaign. Too loose, according to one student of the campaign, Jack Ladinsky. "Boyle failed to do many of the things a good campaigner would do," Ladinsky said.

"Many people have contacted me indicating their concern over this obscenity problem," Boyle told one newsman. "Much of my time has been spent in attempting to help them get organized." [16]

Boyle had no campaign staff. He depended on volunteers, and what organizations they could develop and influence, to do the bulk of his campaigning. Still, he put in a full day almost every day of the week:

> "I usually get started early, about 6 in the morning. There is travel to some part of the state for speeches and organizing work until I get back home some time after dinner, maybe about 10 p.m. Then I usually spend several hours answering letters that call for an immediate reply and preparing statements deemed necessary because of developments in the campaign."

The far north and western parts of Wisconsin he ignored because of practical limitations of time and money. He realized the need for support in the south-central part of Wisconsin and especially in Dane County. "Except for Dane County, I would have received the most votes in the primary," he said. "I'm trying to do more campaigning in the area, but I'm just not well acquainted there, and that is a hardship." The campaign cost Boyle more than he could afford, he admitted. "My law practice has definitely suffered."

And so for the first time in recent Wisconsin history, a judge was challenged by his opponent on the basis of his vote. And not only was the judge challenged, but also the bench. Boyle charged at Appleton:

> The obscenity issue which I raise in the campaign is not a matter of censorship or bookburning. The point is that a Supreme Court justice does not have the power to impose his own personal morality on the people.
> The nature of obscenity . . . must be dealt with by the people through their Legislature, not by a small group of judges like Mr. Wilkie and company.[17]

Calling an *Appleton Post-Crescent* editorial "false and malicious," Boyle denied that he had violated ethics in criticizing Wilkie's decision:

> If the day ever comes when a judge is thus not answerable to the people, the lamp of our liberty will have been extinguished. . . . [Wilkie opened the door to pornography. Wilkie made] a vicious and personal attack on Howard H. Boyle, Jr. . . . Is this how you serve your community in all weighty matters? Why have you done this? Is it because you want the law to protect the purveyors of obscenity rather than the morals of our youth? [18]

The *Post-Crescent* had opposed the *Cancer* decision. Nevertheless, it editorialized against Boyle.

"Everyone *had* to come out for Wilkie," Leonard Zubrensky remarked:

> The campaign was so patently unfair and so outrageous that I suppose when you see an outrage being perpetrated in front of your eyes *you don't mind engaging in something which might be a little bit critically improper,* when you see . . . a terrible thing.[19]

Boyle's attack had a great chance of succeeding because, in judicial elections and out, obscenity in the courts and law ethics are not familiar to the voter. In his campaign, Boyle wanted to reach the man in the street.[20] With his down-to-earth tactics, he did just that.

In the end, Wilkie, because of the public response to Boyle's tactics, was dramatically forced to explain his own *Cancer* vote to the public. This was *what he had said in the beginning he could not and would not do.*

Boyle's supporters included many Catholic voters because of the reasons presented earlier, and because of the obscenity issue. But always Boyle insisted that in this campaign obscene literature was a religious issue but not a denominational one. Hundreds of priests and nuns came out for Boyle, with the largest single gathering from Marquette University High School in Milwaukee.[21] Other church and civic groups were also attracted to Boyle by his stand on obscenity.[22] And, wrote John Wyngaard, "Boyle's previous appeals have been to the hardcore conservatives—the radicals of the Right—and it may be presumed that some of that association remains to bring him some votes."[23] That association had indeed remained.

On Wisconsin Conservative Party stationery, Chairman W. B. Olson wrote a letter to the *Burlington Standard* espousing the same line against Wilkie that Boyle was using.[24] (On the whole conservative lawyers, however, according to Ladinsky, did not support Boyle.) Another letter writer to the same paper was Merrill Stalbaum, GOP assemblyman from Racine County.[25] This man, brother of the Lynn Stalbaum who was "semi-endorsed" by Wilkie at the testimonial dinner, seconded Olson's remarks in his letter to the editor. The Young Republicans of Milwaukee County affirmed their belief, publicly, that a judicial election candidate *could* be criticized.[26] The Non Partisan League for an Informed Electorate came out for Boyle. The secretary of that organization, Ralph D. Pennings, was also listed on the Seventh Congressional District ballot as a presidential convention delegate for Governor George Wallace. The John Birch Society was linked to the campaign tenuously through a campaign contribution, and probably even more so in other ways—under Catholic front groups and so-called nonpartisan groups such as the Citizens for Educational Freedom.[27] Many prominent Kohler officials backed Boyle's campaign financially, as did other companies with known extreme right persuasion.[28] (Ex-governor Walter J. Kohler, Jr., a prominent Republican, however, publicly endorsed Wilkie.)

The *Milwaukee Journal* remarked, right after the primary, "Boyle . . . apparently won strong support from citizens and religious groups combating pornographic literature on the basis of his attack on the . . . *Cancer* decision." [29] The churches and the Citizens for Decent Literature were very much in the campaign, especially the churches in Milwaukee and Green Bay. *Journal* reporter Edward S. Kerstein on April 12, 1964, reported that at least one church society passed out leaflets urging parishioners to vote against Wilkie:

> At SS. Cyril and Methodius church [in Milwaukee] parishioners were advised that the *Tropic of Cancer* was obscene and that reading such a book was sinful.
>
> At Sacred Heart parish, 3640 S. Kinnickinnic Ave., St. Francis, the printed church bulletin stated: "Be sure to vote for the judge who is opposed to obscenity, Howard Boyle."
>
> Other church bulletins maintained that "a moral issue" was involved in the Wilkie-Boyle contest.
>
> Some parochial school children were advised by their Catholic nun teachers to tell their parents to cast their ballots for Boyle.[30]

The Reverend Ralph E. Brushaber, pastor of the Warner Memorial Chapel in Milwaukee (a Church of God congregation), said in a church bulletin that members now

> have an opportunity to voice your belief that the majority of the court were in error in the recent ruling reversing the lower court's ruling against dirty literature.
>
> Justice Wilkie voted that certain pornographic books were not illegally being sold. . . . We believe in freedom of speech, but that doesn't mean freedom to be filthy.[31]

From the pulpit there were other exhortations to vote for Boyle. By and large, Catholic priests were very careful not to mention the school bus issue from the pulpit, but it was omnipresent. "Vote for the man against obscenity," was the public word.[32]

Another "decency" literature sheet, called "What the Experts Say!" listed what Drechsler, Chief Justice Brown, the prosecution witnesses, New York and Massachusetts high court officials, and (of course) J. Edgar Hoover, had to say about *Cancer* and obscenity and juvenile delinquency and then asked at the bottom of the page: "What's Your Decision?" Flyers proclaimed that if you wanted to protect your child from pornography, the man to vote for was Boyle. "A Vote for Boyle Is a Vote *Against* Smut—A Vote *for* Decency!"

As early as February the CDL of Greater Milwaukee had mobilized for action by endorsing Boyle.

The Non Partisan League for an Informed Electorate, with Chairman Robert J. Perz in control—Perz is the mayor of Antigo, Wisconsin—engaged in one of the oddest actions of the campaign. The Non Partisan League came to the notice of Grove Press through a telegram from a Stevens Point Methodist minister, Lee A. Burress, Jr., the same Burress who had surveyed censorship in Wisconsin public schools. This was his telegram of March 27, 1964:

SIR THE MARCH 26 STEVENS POINT WIS JOURNAL ALLEGES THAT R DAVID PENNINGS OF MOSINEE WIS IS SPOKESMAN FOR THE NON PARTISAN LEAGUE . . . WHICH IS CIRCULATING A LETTER CONTAINING 19 PASSAGES FROM TROPIC OF CANCER   THE LETTER IS ALLEGEDLY SIGNED BY ROBERT J PERZ. . . . IT IS A WAY OF ATTACKING JUSTICE . . . WILKIE WHO VOTED THAT THE BOOK IS NOT OBSCENE   HE IS RUNNING FOR RE ELECTION   HIS OPPONENT HOWARD BOYLE HAS ATTACKED HIM AS FAVORING DISTRIBUTION OF OBSCENITY IN THE STATE   BOYLE IS ALLEGED TO FAVOR THE RESTRICTED DISTRIBUTION OF THE LETTER   I URGE YOU TO CONSIDER AN INJUNCTION OR OTHER LEGAL MEANS OF PREVENTING WHAT APPEARS TO BE PLAGIARISM DESIGNED TO HARASS JUDGES WHO FAVOR FREE DISTRIBUTION OF LITERATURE

Milton Perlman of Grove Press answered Burress:

CONDEMN UNDISCIPLINED . . . ACTION NON PARTISAN LEAGUE REGRET OUR INABILITY TO PURSUE LEGAL TACTIC [33]

Perz *had* engaged in this "undisciplined" action, as his name at the bottom of the letter attached to the material testified. The Non Partisan League had taken a page from the Chicago CDL's obscenity book. When Judge Epstein had ruled *Cancer* not obscene in Chicago, the CDL immediately printed a pamphlet entitled "Citizen Protest over legal opinion concerning 'Tropic of Cancer.' " Running selections from *Cancer* on one page, at the top of another page of text attempting to refute Judge Epstein's arguments was this question: "Judge Epstein considers the book NOT LEGALLY OBSCENE. What do you think?" A careful comparison of the typography of the excerpts from the Chicago printing and the Wisconsin printing (two full 8½ x 11 pages) reveals that the two come from the same "make-up" of type. Excerpts from pages 6, 16, 41, 53, 80, 93, 115, 5, 126, 131, 140, 155, 187, 209, 214, 223, 232 and 262 were the same, and in this order. (The page 5 excerpt falls out of its natural numerical order in both printings.)

The excerpts, along with a letter signed by Perz and the sheet called "What the Experts Say!" were sent to an "exclusive list" of community leaders throughout the state. The letter pointed out that as a responsible leader the recipient was no doubt aware of the *Cancer* decision, but it outlined what had happened anyway, naming the judges who had voted against the book, and singling out Justice Wilkie as coming up for election.

Boyle said that he had not seen the NPL material before it was sent out but that he supported "restricted distribution" of it.[34] Had he had control of the situation, he added later, he wouldn't have used it; but the use of the letter "was not a serious error."

An even more unpleasant aspect of the race for Justice of the Supreme Court of Wisconsin was the telephone calls and letters received by Justice Wilkie and his family. Although Justice Wilkie denied receiving *many* messages, in a telephone interview with me, others connected with the race insist that this was not so.

"Before the campaign was through," Zubrensky declared, "Wilkie and his wife went through a fantastic ordeal. Friends began looking at Mrs. Wilkie as though she were running a smut trade in Madison. The Wilkies were actually stunned by this campaign to make *Cancer* the only issue in that race." Mrs.

Lisa Tarkow, a prominent Madison Democrat, said that the Wilkies "received thousands of messages that were not very friendly. By mail and telephone." Mrs. Tarkow said, "I even got a call, and I wasn't even listed as being on his committee." One or two other friends of the family have indicated that the campaign was carried to the Wilkies in this way. As active as the CDL of Greater Milwaukee was, Justice Wilkie, no doubt for reasons of his own, is abstaining from comment on what must have been a painful episode. A board of directors member of the Milwaukee CDL branch wrote me:

> Our function in educating the public explains what steps they can take to encourage more enforcement of existing laws, *more letter-writing to* Mayors, public officials and *supreme court justices,* to show the Community standards.[35]

And one Milwaukee woman, who merely confronted Boyle with the freedom of expression issue during one of his talks, received abusive letters and telephone calls from throughout the state.[36]

Against all this, what were Wilkie's tactics? He traveled. More than 25,000 miles. He made more than 250 speeches, and most of those were before civic clubs.[37]

"In a judicial race, you can't put too much vinegar in a speech," he said, early in the race. "I can't expect to switch many votes, but I hope to activate my supporters." Wilkie spoke mostly on the issues given earlier in his campaign summary.[38]

Who were Wilkie's supporters? "One of the most noteworthy features of the campaign," Ladinsky remarked, "was the strong bipartisan support for Wilkie, particularly of lawyers. For example, Carroll P. Callahan, past president of the Wisconsin State Bar Association, was President of the Wisconsin Lawyers for Justice Wilkie." (Callahan had been campaign manager for Wilbur Renk when this Republican ran for governor.) Wilkie's supporters included persons from both major political parties.

For several months Wilkie spent only two or three days a

week on the road, campaigning quietly while keeping up his Supreme Court work. After the primary, he increased his campaigning to four or five days a week.

In one typical day he spent eleven hours in Dodge and Jefferson counties. He had an 8:30 A.M. equal-time interview on radio station WBEV, Beaver Dam (the third time he had been in Boyle's home town). According to one newspaperman, Wilkie was held to his Dodge County schedule with tight comfortableness by County Judge Joseph Schultz, who had also been an active Democrat before rising to the bench. During this day Wilkie visited with lawyers in Beaver Dam, Waupun, Mayville, Juneau, Watertown and Ft. Atkinson. He had from 90 to 100 per cent turnout. His picture was taken with attorneys and judges, and most of these pictures appeared in the daily or weekly newspapers. At the pleasure of his hosts he spoke about the Beatles, juvenile delinquency, and—his candidacy.[39]

At Mayville, every lawyer in town turned out to greet him in the office of Attorney Lloyd Allen. Wilkie stopped briefly to visit with Ed Marolla, Horicon weekly newspaper publisher, en route to Juneau. He had a ten-minute visit with Robert Hemmy, secretary of Midland Mutual in Horicon, a long-time friend. Hemmy offered to mail 25,000 post cards backing Wilkie's candidacy at his own expense, as the result of a casual remark of Wilkie's that he often left fifteen or twenty such cards with friends to use on his behalf. At the Juneau county courthouse he spoke to nonpartisan and bipartisan lawyers and judges. He was interviewed on radio stations in Watertown and Ft. Atkinson. "A judicial candidate can't actually offer a platform, as a candidate for partisan office can," he repeatedly said. "He can only offer his qualifications and pledge his independence to make his decision on the law and the fact."

Wilkie skirted the "cloaked issue" of the school bus law in his campaign. But in Ladinsky's words, he knew that it "was damned important." Ladinsky feels that Boyle didn't realize its importance, although in the weekend before the elections handouts on the issue were passed out in front of Catholic churches in Milwaukee, Madison and Fond du Lac.[40]

In the closing week of his very strategic and well-organized campaign, Wilkie made his strongest speeches. The first, on April 2, defended the *Cancer* decision as correct under the law.

"Of course, I myself and the whole court are against obscenity," Wilkie said. "Any charge that this decision opens the door to pornography in this state is completely ridiculous." What was really involved in the campaign, Wilkie charged, "is the most serious attack on the judiciary" ever made in a Supreme Court election.

"If my opponent's ideas prevail," Wilkie said, "a judge will no longer rule on the facts and the law in the case at hand. Instead, after looking out the window to take a Gallup poll of views of the populace, he will decide the case accordingly, without any concern for the facts or applicable law." The court had ruled on *Tropic of Cancer,* Wilkie asserted, on the basis of the Constitution, the facts of the case, *and the need to preserve freedom of the press.*[41]

By April 15, "one of the most powerful coalitions of influence and opinion-making" ever observed in a Wisconsin judicial election had been formed behind Wilkie.[42] He received strong support from organized Democrats. The AFL-CIO council backed him. Three former governors of Wisconsin threw their support in his favor (Walter J. Kohler, Jr., Republican governor 1951–57; Gaylord A. Nelson, Democratic governor 1959–63; and Philip F. La Follette, Progressive governor 1931–33 and 1935–39). And Governor Reynolds, in an unprecedented extension of the executive branch of government into the judicial branch, gave Wilkie a public endorsement. Nine state senators declared their support of Wilkie in a public statement. (Among the signers, Senator Allen J. Busby of Milwaukee.)

Virtually all of the University of Wisconsin Law School faculty backed Wilkie in a semiofficial public statement, prompted to do so by Boyle's campaign. Shortly thereafter seventy-five UW law students also signed a statement criticizing Boyle's tactics. The majority of the faculty of the Marquette University Law School (Boyle's alma mater) endorsed Wilkie individually.

Shaken by the vicious attack on a member of their court and upon the Supreme Court itself, six of the seven justices, through Judge Myron L. Gordon (who had voted with the *Cancer* majority), made a formal statement at a meeting of the Milwaukee Junior Bar Association. Gordon denied that the *Cancer* decision had opened the doors to pornography. Judges, Gordon observed, are often aware of the popular opinion which must be disregarded in reaching Supreme Court decisions.

Justice Hallows, the "colorful dissenter" in the *Cancer* case, stated explicitly that he wanted to identify himself as the one justice who did not support Justice Gordon's statement. Hallows thought it improper "to resort to a public forum to defend a decision of the supreme court."

As a result of their actions, the justices were praised editorially by the *Milwaukee Journal* and criticized severely by the *Milwaukee Sentinel*. For the first time in Wisconsin judicial history the Supreme Court had defended a decision in such a manner.

The American Bar Association adopted in 1953 a "Statement on the Freedom to Read." Part of it says simply: "Resolved that the freedom to read is a corollary of the constitutional guarantee of freedom of the press and American lawyers should oppose efforts to restrict it." But none of the Wisconsin lawyers spoke in terms of freedom to read *Cancer*. Instead, they addressed themselves to Boyle's campaign tactics. However, no newspapers had defended *Cancer* in terms of its literary merits, either.

The most celebrated censure of Boyle took place in the Milwaukee Junior Bar Association. Although there was no consensus among the members as to the appropriate way to campaign, the executive board of the MJBA censured Boyle for criticizing Wilkie's *Cancer* vote. The censure caused fourteen MJBA members to form a Lawyers Non Partisan Committee. "The executive board's censure," it reported after its investigation, was "based on a misunderstanding of the law, showed poor judgment and violated the intent and spirit of the association's constitution and by-laws." [43] According to Ladinsky, it is indeed possible to say that the MJBA was in error. There is no specific rule against challenging a judge on the basis of his vote in the Wisconsin state canons. Although there is an American Bar canon against a judicial candidate's stating how he would vote on a particular issue, this canon was not adopted by Wisconsin lawyers. Adding to the MJBA embarrassment, a Racine lawyer asked the MJBA to censure Wilkie for appearing at that testimonial dinner for the candidate for Congress.

But it is time to turn to the now *alerted* Wisconsin press and examine the lifesaving role it played in this critical judicial campaign.

17

THE PRESS TO THE RESCUE

Although the Wisconsin lawyers' support for Justice Wilkie was indispensable for his campaign, without almost overwhelming press support it is doubtful that he could have won.

Boyle accused Wilkie of opening the Wisconsin doors to pornography. One of the most effective and striking answers to this campaign charge was to saturate the newspapers with an advertisement showing Justice Wilkie seated at his dining room table surrounded by a happy wife and five attractive smiling daughters from early teens to the twenties. Wilkie for pornography? With such an All-American family of young women?

The power of the press was worked into the Wilkie advertising campaign, also. Under headlines ENDORSED! ACCLAIMED! appeared the mastheads of many of Wisconsin's leading dailies, including, ironically, the *Green Bay Press-Gazette, The Racine Journal Times,* the *Appleton Post-Crescent* and the *Milwaukee Sentinel.* And this, of course, was not false advertising. All of the daily Wisconsin press that expressed itself editorially had indeed come out for Wilkie—that same Wilkie who had voted for the "dirty" book that few newspapers in Wisconsin, if any, defended on literary grounds. Some of these supporting papers had even scored the decision clearing Miller's novel.

In addition to Wilkie's daily-press support, when the weeklies took any stance it was usually for him. So thorough was the newspaper alignment that the *Green Bay Register,* a diocesan paper, bitterly editorialized:

> We cannot recall an election that has been preceded with as much unity on the part of the daily newspapers of the state as in the currently impending election of a new Supreme Court Justice.
>
> We have neither heard nor seen a paper that has given any support to the candidate who has announced himself in favor of printed decency in this state. On the other hand every paper has lined up robot-like fashion behind the liberal views of the candidate who concurred in a court decision May 20, 1963, to permit the dissemination of a pornographic book in our state.
>
> What is singular in the unanimity of the State's papers is not so much their total support of one candidate as is the vehemence of their concerted attack upon the other.
>
> A sort of howl has gone up from daily and Sunday editorial pages charging that freedom of speech will be seriously impaired in Wisconsin if the pro-decency man is elected.[1]

Realizing rather belatedly that freedom of the press was in jeopardy, the state press *had* lined up in something like robot fashion—although a kinder observer might have commented that "the press had closed ranks against a common foe." All scored Boyle's tactics as sensational and dishonest. Freedom of expression and of the press was mentioned repeatedly. Presaged by its editorial against Boyle the day after the primary, the *Capital Times* did the most thorough job on Boyle—a job which Boyle later said cost him the election.[2]

Miles McMillan wrote in its "Hello Wisconsin" front-page column two days after the primary:

> The issue in the Supreme Court race is not pornography, no matter what Howard Boyle says. The issue is censorship. I don't want Howard Boyle or anyone else telling me what books I can read in this state. That's what he wants to do as Supreme Court Justice. He wants to substitute his judgment for mine about what I can read and what my children can read. This is what

is at stake in the Supreme Court race. Boyle admits it. He says it's *the* issue.

Boyle, a Birch-type thinker and one of those flaming true-believers in the revelations of the late Joe McCarthy, does not think I should have the right to read *Tropic of Cancer*.[3]

When Allen Schraufnagel, superintendent of schools at Elroy, Wisconsin, wrote in attacking the *Times* for rejecting the ideas of censorship Boyle was campaigning on, the *Times* answered editorially. There was disagreement throughout the country on *Cancer* and *Fanny Hill,* the *Times* pointed out:

> Our position is that we do not want right-wingers of the Howard Boyle and Allen Schraufnagel stripe setting themselves up as the arbiters of what we and the rest of the people of Wisconsin can read.
>
> No one knows where their censoring would stop.
>
> In Eagle River last year some like-minded censors started to clean up the high school library. Before long they were denouncing the *New York Times Magazine,* the *Saturday Review,* the *Christian Science Monitor* and the *Capital Times*.[4]

The editorial then tells how McCarthy censored *these* periodicals for Communist taints: the *Capital Times,* the *New York Times,* the *Washington Post,* the *St. Louis Post-Dispatch,* and the *Saturday Evening Post.*

When Boyle protested being called a "right-wing extremist of the Birch type," the *Capital Times* replied by quoting a letter Boyle had sent to the *Milwaukee Journal* September 10, 1955:

> Because I believe that your paper in its editorial policy and in its manner of portraying news stories advocates the liberal-istic cause of godless disregard of the principles of our founding fathers, thereby undermining ideals of freedom and equality, I do not want your support in the question of my possible candidacy for the United States Senate.[5]

Slightly less impressive, and playing a huge role in Wilkie's narrow victory in Milwaukee County, was the *Milwaukee Journal.* Temporarily aroused to the dangers of censorship embodied in such persons as Boyle, it too kept up a steady anti-Boyle drumbeat, from late March up to election day.

Only the *Burlington Standard-Press,* a weekly, strongly supported Boyle editorially for the race. Why? The people didn't like the unfair way Wilkie's backers treated Boyle!

Few television stations in Wisconsin have specific editorial programs. One that does is WMTV in Madison. In the midst of the Wilkie campaign, WMTV ran an editorial supporting the crusade against *Cancer.* The editorial resulted from a Middleton, Wisconsin, incident involving the removal of magazines from a hotel newsstand there, which the Madison CLU had protested vigorously. In contrast, WMTV telecast this to its viewers:

Because the State Supreme Court did not find the controversial novel *Tropic of Cancer* obscene, does not necessarily mean it should be accepted as desirable or recommended reading.

Furthermore, the Supreme Court's ruling should not be construed as meaning our magazine and book counters are free of reading material ranging from generally undesirable to downright filthy. And, because the Supreme Court failed to label the particular *Tropic of Cancer* novel as obscene, doesn't mean that steps cannot be taken to curb the availability, especially to youths, of undesirable books and magazines.

An example still in the making, we've noted with interest, is the concern expressed by County Board member EDWIN HICKMAN of Middleton. We applaud his action and determination in working with city of Middleton officials in a move to discourage the sale of obscene, or near-obscene, books and magazines in his city . . . the kind that so often wind up in the hands of youngsters, including pre-teens.

We can't help but feel Hickman will be successful in his campaign.

Similar action should be encouraged in all communities, with PTA groups and service clubs leading the way toward developing community pressure that could bring about the end of trashy movie magazines, filthy novels, and suggestive stories aimed at reaching the teenager.

Such a goal should be of genuine concern to every community and neighborhood.[6]

Someone *always* fails to get the word. Now either WMTV was not notified by the National Association of Broadcasters three years before, or its staff does not read the *New York Times*. The motion picture, television, radio, and book industries agreed on February 20, 1961, to join forces in fighting censorship. The *Times* news story by Murray Schumach on February 21 reads in part: "When book publishers are confronted with a censorship dispute they will count on support from the movie, television and radio industries." The NAB had represented the television industry in the pact. WMTV should have been defending, not attacking, *Cancer*.

An ironic incident also took place in Milwaukee. Certainly the Milwaukee papers had earned the right to display some support for the principle of freedom of expression anyway (having ignored the practice for so long), without incurring the displeasure of the censors. But the ungrateful citizens' censorship groups did not grant the newspapers even this small luxury. Both papers were attacked by word of mouth and in print.

A printed attack came on April 6, 1964, in the form of a paid advertisement in the *Journal*. Under a two-column headline there appeared this "letter to the editors" from L. B. Leith Hartman, M.D., 2821 E. Belleview Place, Milwaukee:

WANTED: A NEWSPAPER FOR
THE CITY OF MILWAUKEE

To the Editors of the Journal and Sentinel:
Dear Sirs: I am writing this because, in my opinion (based on personal observation of your "news" coverage), there is no longer, in the true sense of the word, a free press in this city.

In the interest of fair play and common decency I feel compelled to use this limited forum to speak out concerning what I consider a vitally important issue: The candidacy of Mr. Boyle for Judge in the State Supreme Court (a candidacy which has been vigorously opposed by both *The Milwaukee Journal* and *The Milwaukee Sentinel*).

How a person votes in an election is nobody else's business, but the vote of a Supreme Court justice on an issue that affects everybody in the state is very properly a matter of public record.

Personally, I can think of no better issue on which to determine the basic moral values of a candidate than the one involved in the current election, i.e., whether or not the sale of the book *Tropic of Cancer* should be made legal in this state.

New York is not known as being unkind to the arts, but *Tropic of Cancer* is considered too filthy to be sold there.

It has been stated that Mr. Boyle has been unethical in criticizing Judge Wilkie's decision. If this were true (which, of course, it is not) then every judicial decision that has ever been handed down would be immune to criticism.

Great harm can be done by making a book such as *Tropic of Cancer* available to the young at drug stores, newsstands, etc., and we are fortunate to have a man of Mr. Boyle's courage running for office.

I am not a Catholic and do not know Mr. Boyle, but believe very strongly that a vote for him would be a vote for common decency.

In my opinion the opposition of the *Journal* and *Sentinel* to Mr. Boyle's candidacy is the best moral indorsement he could get.

Two months after the election Hartman inserted a similar advertisement on June 27, 1964, under these headlines:

STILL WANTED FOR THE CITY OF MILWAUKEE: A NEWSPAPER THAT WILL FAIRLY AND OBJECTIVELY REPORT THE NEWS AND KEEP THE PUBLIC INFORMED ON BOTH SIDES OF ALL IMPORTANT CONTROVERSIAL ISSUES

Wilkie won the April election, with 556,639 votes to Boyle's 489,703. Boyle was about 70,000 votes short of polling as many votes as Wallace and Republican John Byrnes did together in the presidential preferential primary race. Twenty-two of the state's seventy-two counties cast a majority for Boyle. As expected, the most substantial contribution to Wilkie's margin came from Dane County, where he polled 46,056 votes to Boyle's 16,385. In Milwaukee County, Wilkie eked out a 6000-vote margin over Boyle—152,831 to 146,580.

And so the campaign ended, but not the comments made about it. An executive director of the American Judicature Society, Glenn R. Winters, said that not much was done right by anybody throughout the campaign; that the State Bar and the Milwaukee Bar Association should have followed the Milwaukee Junior Bar Association's lead and given guidance to the voters, and that the Supreme Court justices acted improperly in defending Wilkie. (Ladinsky's impression from interview material is that the large majority of Wisconsin lawyers agree.) Wilkie was subject to criticism for defending himself against Boyle's charges. Boyle was wrong in criticizing the *Cancer* decision. As reported in the press, in fact, Winters was opposed to the whole campaign:

> The narrow squeak by which Justice Wilkie won is scant comfort to the next judge who will face the voters; and the fact that other judges swallowed their inhibitions and joined in the public statement is "eloquent proof that they are not insensitive to what such pressures may mean."
>   . . . it is difficult enough at best to reconcile the judicial office with any kind of an election campaign. "Surely, the most a judge can say is that if he is elected he will continue to do his best to do justice to all who come before him. To use his campaign as a forum in which to reinact the controversial issues in which he has participated is simply unthinkable." [7]

"Almost surely," commented one newsman, "the story as a whole will figure in a revived argument about reorganizing the judicial selection process." [8]

Winters found:

> That the newspapers of the state carried their responsibilities in a most commendable manner and "in my opinion, their *close coverage* of the campaign and their editorial comment probably was sufficient to account for the narrow margin by which Justice Wilkie won." [9]

Leonard Zubrensky had some reservations about the press's performance during the campaign. "In playing up Boyle's sensational attacks on Wilkie, the newspapers served Boyle in much the same manner newspapers served McCarthy," he said. "Against front-page denunciation of Wilkie, they matched some editorial comment on the editorial page. Many persons read the front page," he pointed out. "Very few read the editorial page. The way McCarthy was ultimately fought in Wisconsin was to 'shut him out,' " Zubrensky added. "This was what should have been done with Boyle. The battle was won," he said, "but the war was lost. Since the judicial campaign, politicians have been frightened by the obscenity issue." Lockhart agreed: "There is no doubt this race will influence judges. There is no question about it." [10]

The *Stevens Point Journal,* evidently having learned little from the whole *Cancer* banning, editorialized:

> [The vote may be interpreted to show] that there is a substantial group of people who desire improvement in this matter of grave public concern. . . .
>
> The need is for laws that will make it clear that books like *Tropic of Cancer* and some of the foul magazines and pictures that pass today for literature and art can be labeled as "abuse of that right." [11]

After the fright that Boyle threw into the Wisconsin judiciary, the vindication of the Wisconsin Supreme Court *Cancer* decision by the United States Supreme Court came as small solace. Because by that time the judiciary all knew that another Supreme Court race was coming up in 1965, and that Boyle in all probability would enter it. He did. And he once again brought *Cancer* in as an issue.

In this race against Justice Nathan Heffernan, Boyle said that the *Cancer* decision was "symptomatic of the liberal philosophy of the Supreme Court." Heffernan, the incumbent, had not even participated in the *Cancer* decision, having been appointed to a vacancy in the Court after the decision. Although Boyle lost this race too—in April 1965—he had developed a little more political acumen, and he took fifty-three of the seventy-two Wisconsin counties. Heffernan gathered more than a third of his votes in Dane, Milwaukee and Sheboygan counties (he is from Sheboygan). In this race, Boyle, a candidate representing forces and attitudes dangerous to freedom of the press, was endorsed by two dailies (Ft. Atkinson and Beaver Dam) and eighteen weeklies.

18

CANCER BEFORE THE U.S. SUPREME COURT—THE JACOBELLIS DECISION

The obscenity taint that had badly foxed *Tropic of Cancer*'s pages for thirty years was partially eradicated by the Jacobellis decision in 1964. How *Cancer* finally landed on the desks of the Supreme Court justices for a stamp of approval made American legal history.

The U.S. Supreme Court can consider a case coming from a state court if it is appealed on the ground that the state statute is unconstitutional or that in some other way the party has been deprived of a federal constitutional right. Although the lawyers handling the *Cancer* case in Florida had waived all constitutional issues, Grove Press nevertheless attempted to get the Florida case into the Supreme Court by petition for certiorari.[1]

To the surprise of many of those concerned, the Supreme Court took the case—and handled it in an extraordinary way. (At the moment the Supreme Court handed down the Jacobellis decision, Rembar and Gertz were also working out the details of the Illinois certiorari petition.)

To some without special legal background, to anyone who had followed the trail of *Tropic of Cancer* across the nation for the three years previous to the U.S. Supreme Court's decision on *Cancer,* it would have been suprising if the petition for certiorari had been turned down by that learned tribunal, regardless of the niceties of law involved. Possibly the Supreme Court simply decided that *Cancer* had undergone enough trial by brushfire censorship. With five state supreme courts dividing three to two on whether the novel was obscene, with the lower courts across the country equally divisive in their verdicts, with the confusion which would have reigned had the Jacobellis decision (*Jacobellis v. State of Ohio*) been rendered without including another decision on the most censored book in modern times, it was only natural that at this propitious moment the U.S. Supreme Court would have sought a way to give direction and guidance to the lower courts. That way was through Grove Press's petition for certiorari.

The Jacobellis decision suggests strongly that it was written by the Supreme Court to apply not only to movies but also to books and other materials. *Cancer* itself represents a kind of extreme in realistic writing that corresponds neatly to the explicit delineations of sexual love shown in *The Lovers,* the film which the Jacobellis decision declared was not obscene. *Cancer,* cleared of obscenity charges, would serve nicely as an illustration of just how far the Supreme Court was willing to go in allowing "questionable books" to circulate. *The Lovers* would serve the same purpose in the area of film.

To the censor, to the prude, *Cancer* was going very far indeed. As Los Angeles lawyer Stanley Fleishman said to *Time,* "To be obscene, . . . a book has to go significantly beyond what has already been declared not obscene, and that is impossible. You can't talk about sex any more frankly than is being done now" in books such as *Cancer.*[2]

In Florida, in an injunctive proceeding under a Florida obscenity statute, a circuit court found *Cancer* obscene and the injunction was granted. The novel, according to the court, narrated a succession of sexual episodes replete with filth. The District Court of Appeal in 1963 affirmed the finding (*Grove Press v. Florida*).[3]

Since there were no briefs on the merits in the case that the Supreme Court decided, the reader may recall at this time the Grove Press general brief described earlier. (Perhaps the Supreme Court had followed the state supreme court cases involving *Cancer* and felt sufficiently acquainted with the issues involved.) Here is the decision of the Supreme Court:

> 718—Grove Press, Inc., v. Gerstein et al. on petition for writ of certiorari to the District Court of Appeal of Florida. Per curiam. Petition for a writ of certiorari granted, and judgment reversed. Justices Black and Douglas would reverse for the reasons stated in the opinion of Justice Black in Jacobellis v. Ohio, no. 11, ante p. Justices Brennan and Goldberg would reverse for the reasons stated in the opinion of Justice Brennan in Jacobellis, ante p. Justice Stewart would reverse for the reasons stated in his opinion in Jacobellis, ante p. The Chief Justice, and Justices Clark, Harlan, and White of opinion certiorari should be denied.

And so we must check the Jacobellis decision for the various justices' reasons for reversing the Florida *Cancer* decision.

The Ohio Jacobellis case was argued before the U.S. Supreme Court on March 26, 1963, and was restored to calendar for reargument for April 1, 1964. The case was decided June 22, 1964. Nico Jacobellis, manager of the Heights Art Theatre in Cleveland Heights, Ohio, exhibited the film *Les Amants* (*The Lovers*) and was convicted on two counts for *possessing* and *exhibiting* an obscene film in violation of an Ohio obscenity statute. Waiving trial by jury, Jacobellis was fined $500 on the first count and $2,000 on the second by a court of three judges. If the fines were not paid, Jacobellis was to be imprisoned in the workhouse. His conviction was affirmed by an intermediate appellate court and by the Supreme Court of Ohio.[4]

Former Grove Press counsel Ephraim London, as it happened, argued the case before the U.S. Supreme Court for Jacobellis and won. He argued that *The Lovers* was not obscene by any standard—but that a nationwide standard must be applied. If the First Amendment guaranteed free speech to all states, he held, then free speech must be uniformly protected everywhere. The prosecuting attorney of Cuyahoga County in Ohio, John T. Corrigan, defended Jacobellis' conviction.

"Why, pray tell," Corrigan asked, "should Ohio be governed by standards outside Ohio?"

When Justice Potter Stewart wanted to know how one could find a national standard—"Is it the lowest common denominator?"—London agreed that the problem was a difficult one. What people are reading, looking at and tolerating throughout the nation should be considered, he said. *The Lovers* was a classic example of how a national standard might be applied. Shown in forty-four states, it won two prizes and was nominated for a "ten best films" award by the *New York Times* and others.[5]

The Jacobellis judgment was announced by Justice Brennan, joined by Justice Goldberg. Brennan clarified statements made in the Roth decision, and reaffirmed the principle that:

> In "obscenity" cases as in all others involving rights derived from the First Amendment guarantees of free expression, this court cannot avoid making an independent constitutional judgment on the facts of the case as to whether the material involved is constitutionally protected.

He allowed that the proper standard for making the determination—"whether to the average person, applying contemporary community standards, the dominant theme of the material taken as a whole appeals to prurient interest"—had been the subject of much discussion and controversy since the Roth decision. This test for obscenity, he admitted, making perhaps the most magnificent understatement of any Supreme Court decision, "is not perfect." Any substitute, however, "would raise equally difficult problems, and we therefore adhere to that standard."

Justice Brennan re-emphasized the "social importance" concept and rejected any "weighing" of a work's social importance against its prurient appeal, as was done in the Milwaukee decision and the Wisconsin Supreme Court decision. And literary merit, among other values, constitutes social importance:

We would reiterate, however, our recognition in Roth that obscenity is excluded from the constitutional protection only because it is "utterly without redeeming social importance," and that "the portrayal of sex, e.g., in art, literature and scientific works, is not itself sufficient reason to deny material the constitutional protection of freedom of speech and press." . . . It follows that material dealing with sex in a manner that advocates ideas, *Kingsley Int'l Pictures Corp. v. Regents* . . . or that has literary or scientific or artistic value or any other form of social importance, may not be branded as obscenity and denied the constitutional protection. Nor may the constitutional status of the material be made to turn on a "weighing" of its social importance against its prurient appeal, for a work cannot be proscribed unless it is "utterly" without social importance.

"It should also be recognized," Justice Brennan continued, "that the Roth standard requires in the first instance a finding that the material 'goes substantially beyond customary limits of candor in description or representation of such matters.' " Furthermore, "contemporary community standards"—as the Wisconsin Supreme Court decided—should not be interpreted to mean "standards of the particular local community from which the case arises. *This is an incorrect reading of Roth*." [6] (Demolishing Surges' arguments, of course.)

"It is after all," Justice Brennan said, "a national Constitution we are expounding."

Recognizing that there was a legitimate interest in preventing dissemination of material deemed harmful to children, Justice Brennan suggested:

State and local authorities might well consider whether their objectives in this area would be better served by laws aimed specifically at preventing distribution of objectionable material to children, rather than at totally prohibiting its dissemination. Since the present conviction is based upon exhibition of the film to the public at large and not upon its exhibition to children, the judgment must be reviewed under the strict standard applicable in determining the scope of the expression that is protected by the Constitution.

Reviewing *The Lovers,* Justice Brennan said that it dealt with a woman who abandons her husband and family for a young archeologist with whom she has fallen in love. The state's objections were based almost entirely on an explicit love scene late in the film. Having "viewed the film, in the light of the record made in the trial court, . . . we conclude that it is not obscene within the standards enunciated" in the Roth decision.

Certainly considering Justice Brennan's remarks, the censors received a setback. However, Brennan leaves other devastating possibilities open by suggesting that state and local authorities enact laws aimed at preventing dissemination of objectionable material to children. This would seem to be material not obscene under a national standard, yet still forbidden for children. The obvious arguments against such legislation and the dangers have been succinctly stated by Lockhart and McClure:

> To insist that dealers in books and magazines determine at their peril which ones must not be sold to adolescents would be asking the impossible of them and therefore would probably violate the constitutional requirement of *scienter.* To prohibit dealers from exhibiting within the view of adolescents books and magazines that can be sold only to adults would raise the additional problem of undue interference with the material's primary audience. Beyond these obstacles is the disrupting effect of "adult only" counters or shelves in book stores and at newsstands, for the "adult only" label would serve only to attract adolescents eager for a look at the forbidden fruit and would make it difficult for the dealer to prevent adolescent shoplifting of the books and magazines. To avoid these difficulties cautious dealers might well decide to abandon all books and magazines claimed by anyone to be unsuitable for adolescents. For these reasons, we suspect that the Supreme Court might well invalidate statutes designed to deny a peripheral adolescent audience access to books and magazines aimed at a primary audience of sexually mature adults, because of the tendency to reduce adult reading material to a level suitable for adolescents.[7]

The Wisconsin legislature immediately seized upon this censorship outlet and attempted to enact legislation against selling obscenity to children.[8]

Regardless of this factor, however, as a result of this U.S. Supreme Court decision, all unfavorable state supreme court decisions and similar lower court decisions on *Cancer* should have been regarded as overruled.

But just as the 1959 U.S. Supreme Court decision on school integration did not bring about compliance in the South, the *Cancer* decision did not produce full compliance in the rest of the United States. Rosset wrote to me in January 1965, six months after the decision:

> As of now, we still do not have permission to sell *Tropic of Cancer* in the very area of Florida from whence the final case came. The judge there still stubbornly holds to the view that the book is obscene and will continue to be so until the Florida courts specifically say that it is not. There, with the help of the Civil Liberties Union, we are still pursuing the matter and must get a final clearance.
>
> In Philadelphia we have a more serious matter. A judge quite a while ago placed an injunction against the sale of the book in Philadelphia. After the Supreme Court decision, it was erroneously assumed by our order department that it was safe to fill orders in the Philadelphia area. As a result, a few weeks ago, two booksellers were arrested in the middle of the night and taken in handcuffs to police stations and booked for selling obscene books.
>
> Later, Grove Press was cited for contempt of court. Since then we've been trying to clear ourselves of contempt. The judge holds that despite the Supreme Court decision he had not lifted the injunction and therefore our action was in contempt. We have agreed not to sell further copies of the book until the judge lifts the injunction. In order to lift the injunction we have had to file yet another separate action in that state.
>
> Approximately two weeks ago in Los Angeles County a bookseller was arrested for selling *Tropic of Cancer* to a minor. This is remarkable. The California Supreme Court had given perhaps the best decision rendered on the book: that the book was a work of art and should not be subjected to legal suppression.

The Philadelphia and Florida cases were finally settled the summer of 1966.

A few comments about the Supreme Court dissents in the Jacobellis case should be made before concluding this chapter, even though the dissenters did not participate in the Florida *Cancer* case.

Chief Justice Warren, with whom Justice Clark joined in dissenting, rejected the national-standard interpretation of the Roth case in favor of community standards. He decried the possibility of defining "hard-core pornography" with any more clarity than "obscenity," and said if we retreated to the position that only hard-core pornography is denied First Amendment protection, "we would soon be faced with the need to define that term."

"The more I see of these obscenity cases," Justice Harlan said in his dissent,

> the more convinced I become that in permitting the States wide, but not federally unrestricted, scope in this field, while holding the Federal Government with a tight rein, lies the best promise for achieving a sensible accommodation between the public interest sought to be served by obscenity laws . . . and protection of genuine rights of free expression.

The Jacobellis and *Cancer* opinions were delivered June 22, 1964. In September, while presidential candidate Barry Goldwater talked about the decay in the nation's morality, nine highly respected clergymen "exploded in furious criticism" of the Supreme Court over the two decisions. They were Presiding Bishop Lloyd C. Wicke of the Methodist Church New York Conference; the Rev. Wilburn C. West, Eastern States Mission President of the Church of Jesus Christ of Latter-Day Saints; the Rev. W. Scott Morton, director of New York's Presbyterian University Christian Foundation; Catholic Bishops Leo A. Pursley of Fort Wayne, Aloysius J. Willinger of Monterey-Fresno, California, and John King Mussio of Steubenville, Ohio; and New York Rabbis Chaim Lipschitz, Julius G. Neumann and Jehuda Melber.

The clergymen's document charged that in its decisions the Supreme Court had "virtually promulgated degeneracy as the standard way of American life":

> In finding that the Constitution was intended as a guarantee for the dissemination of filth, and a device to deprive the public of the right to protect itself against vile and corrupt publications, the "under God" foundations of the United States were implied to be irrelevant.
>
> These decisions cannot be accepted quietly by the American people if this nation is to survive. Giving free rein to the vile depiction of violence, perversion, illicit sex and, in consequence, to their performance, is an unerring sign of progressive decay and decline. Further, it gives prophetic meaning to the Soviet intent to "bury" America.
>
> We urge that religious leaders of all faiths in all communities stand together in vociferously decrying the fact that the court has presumed to recast the moral law.[9]

Those clergymen need not have worried about rousing their religious leaders nor their congregations, nor their communities. Had they but looked about before setting off for their New York conference they could have discovered brooding censors in their communities tilling with renewed fury their own little guardianship programs.

These forces were not deterred by the U.S. Supreme Court *Cancer* decision. The *Cancer* campaign itself appeared to have served as a testing ground for their tactics. Rather than emerge from the campaign disheartened and defeated, they closed ranks and marched off as battle-hardened veterans searching for new, and old, foes. By the mid-sixties some ten thousand groups scattered about the countryside—Catholic and non-Catholic—referred to NODL lists which included two hundred magazines and three hundred and fifty books. *Cancer,* of course, is on this list because it is not recommended for children. The CDL passed the three-hundred-fifty mark in the number of chapters formed across the nation. The Birch Society and other extremist groups were joining these ranks. And the U.S. Supreme Court with the Ginzburg decision in 1965 not only gave these forces aid and comfort, but presented them with a formidable censorship weapon. That decision was the first backward step taken by the Court since the *Times* Film Corp. case in 1961.

Now the publisher and seller must be concerned with the "setting" in which the publication is presented. This involves advertising and promotion of the material. If the description is such that it stimulates the reader to accept the material as prurient and indicates that the claim to "social importance" is pretense, then this may be used as evidence that the material is obscene, even though that same material described in different ways, perhaps by a different ad agency, would *not* be considered obscene.

According to the Civil Liberties Union the post-Ginzburg period is marked by increased censorship, official and unofficial, at every level of government.[10] Obviously the same is true of private groups, which have been given a new lease on life.

In Minneapolis, for example, the Metropolitan Airports Commission banned some books from airport newsstands because they offended the tastes of the commission members. Whose books were among those banned? Henry Miller's.

19

IN THE WAKE OF THE BATTLE

as good almost kill a Man as kill a good Book: who kills a Man kills a reasonable creature, Gods Image; but hee who destroyes a good Booke, kills reason it selfe, kills the Image of God.
—John Milton

Would it have mattered after all, if *Tropic of Cancer,* instead of surviving, had been destroyed? If Henry Miller, instead of swimming through the Sargasso Sea of censorship, had drowned? Would it have mattered to have given the censors their way with just this one book and one man?

Suppression of one book or one man's ideas in the past has invariably led to other suppressions, suppressions of still other ideas and freedoms. To place these ideas and freedoms under anyone's control would be catastrophic.

In America the primary device for learning, for transmitting our heritage, is the printed word. The foundation of the communications industry, truly, is the book. It offers Americans the wide variety of views so important to a society during an increasingly monolithic trend. And the right to read is so ingrained in American life that to encroach upon it ever so slightly would be to shake the pillars of this democracy.

But this is an *obscene* book. Does it matter if one of *those* is suppressed? And after reiterating the arguments from the preceding paragraphs, one should add in answering that precisely because *Cancer is* an *obscene* book it should be defended. Henry Steele Commager has said that every generation has to win anew its right to freedom of expression. In our time this freedom of inquiry, criticism, and dissent is embodied in the battle against censorship of literature.

As our mirror on the *Cancer* trail has reflected, censorship of literature is directly related to freedom of the press. Obscenity is such a vague term that it lends itself readily to censors' designs to suppress books and magazines questioning contemporary social, political, and religious beliefs. Censors, as we have seen, are all too ready to circumvent the law by whatever means are available.

Literature is life—part of learning. And life is something that cannot be censored. To experience and learn through books is more efficient, less costly, and less heartbreaking than to learn through empirical experience. Through literature important social problems are aired and discussed and solutions offered. Had it not been for such books as *Cancer,* newspapers and television today would not be able to discuss so openly problems of birth control, venereal disease, and sex. "Under our system of government," as Justice Douglas observed, "there is an accommodation for the widest varieties of tastes and ideas . . . [A] requirement that literature or art conform to some norm prescribed by an official smacks of an ideology foreign to our system." Had the freedom to explore in literature been effectively curtailed by censors in the early years, socially and politically we would still be in the Middle Ages.

On the whole the American press, the guardian of our freedoms, is not fully aware of the bonds between the journalist and the artist. Whether he wants to or not, the journalist with his stories of life acquaints child and adult with the social, political, and economic maelstroms of this world, and the frustrations, hostilities, and crimes accompanying them. The artist does the same thing. In so doing, both journalist and artist favor a realistic education for life. Once again, it is better that this education come primarily through the press and literature.

Certainly both journalist and artist seek the truth, and in seeking they are both observer and participant. Both have had to fight for the freedom to express this truth in plain prose. Both have groped in forbidden places, uncovering horrors conveniently forgotten by an all-too-forgetful public. Both have had to face the wrath of the public when it was confronted with the unpleasantness it has bred. Both function under unwritten laws requiring them to report life scrupulously—and when they do otherwise, both are guilty of romanticizing and falsifying that life. Both, in reporting life truthfully, in a society as conventional as America's, are committing antisocial acts.

A true journalist can no more falsify the facts and distort the story he has been assigned to write than an artist can paint an untrue picture of the life he sees. For the journalist it is fatal if someone places restrictions upon, say, the material he is to use in preparing a series of articles exposing graft in government. Many are the journalists who have had just such restrictions placed upon them and have found them intolerable. Freedom to say what we know to be true, and believe to be true, in the way we want to say it, has always been one of the true artist's tenets.

Had a journalist been assigned to do a documentary on the bohemian low road of Paris in the thirties he would have described just what Henry Miller described. To report what he saw and heard honestly, that journalist would have had to use the words Henry Miller used. He would have had to describe the sex episodes Miller described. Unfortunately, no journalist was ever assigned to this task. And for just that reason all journalists should rejoice that a fellow writer *did* assign *himself* that chore and scrupulously report what he saw to the world.

Journalists should openly welcome the artist into this battle to tell the truth. Many times the journalist, like the historian, is bound by the facts, and so prevented from telling the whole truth. The artist has no such restrictions placed upon his creative faculties. Because of this he makes a valuable comrade-in-arms.

Both journalist and artist, through their interpretations, seek to bring about a better society. Embattled Henry Miller gave Americans an interpretation of their society at variance with the often romanticized interpretations found in the mass media. Using sexuality and four-letter words to jolt the complacent, he spoke of a shallow, mechanistic society—criticisms that applied equally well to the world. After living through mass murders and war miseries and problems brought about by technology and urbanization to a point where, in America, there are almost as many jails and insane asylums as there are high schools and colleges, we can see that Miller's social and political maledictions have been more than the maundering flights of a butterfly artist. And as artists frequently do after exploring a problem, Miller has offered a solution to this problematical society—self-realization and affirmation. The average journalist, not having access to editorial columns but having that same desire to bring about a better life, should applaud Miller's efforts.

The American press, always so conscious of most censorship (especially when it comes from government officials), so conscious of its "watchdog" functions, curiously has ambiguous feelings when confronted with obscenity censorship: *Newsweek* and *Reader's Digest* have contributed money to CDL. *Time* wanted to do a cover story about Miller recently, but he refused because of the unfair treatment *Time* has always accorded him. And a literary editor of *Newsweek* has called Miller the funniest American writer since Mark Twain. On the one hand the press is able to realize the cancerous spread of censorship (and that this is just one strain), but on the other hand, reflecting public opinion as it does, the press is painfully aware that defending "dirty books" is extremely unpopular. And so it conveniently forgets that it also has a duty to *lead* public opinion, to pave the climatic way for an understanding of the arts. It conveniently forgets, too, that within its own columns and channels there is enough sexual stimulation to wreak as much harm as the sexiest of novels—if only because of wider distribution and readership. This is sometimes forgotten when the moment arrives to comment about and defend a "dirty book." Constantly the press has to be reminded of the persistent encroachment of irrational influences upon freedom of expression. Constantly it has to be reminded that *all* books are entitled to protection as a part of the "press." Constantly it has to be reminded that the rights of the minority must be protected against the majority. Constantly it has to be reminded that it has a responsibility to do all these things because of the position of responsibility it occupies with the decreasing number of mass media voices in America. Constantly it has to be reminded that good books and bad books, like good newspapers and bad newspapers, have a right to exist.

What can happen in a community when censorship forces with their haptic visions start operating on obscenity charges and the press looks the other way was illustrated in Milwaukee and throughout Wisconsin during the campaign to ban *Cancer*.

What can happen to a country immersed in such conflict remains to be seen. The harm that has been done and is being done in America may never be known. But we do know that this conspiracy of silence has delayed until now free and open discussion of birth control, one of the most pressing problems of the world today; that decency taboos have wrought untold social damage and misery by delaying scientific inquiry into venereal disease; that imposed secrecy in the area of sex has resulted in untold marital difficulties and divorces. No one knows just how many human souls have been damaged by these taboos.

To argue that censorship does not attain its ends is to ignore yesteryear's ignorance on such subjects. Or, indeed, to ignore such ignorance in present-day life. Such "decency" control, legal or extralegal, is truly a deterrent to intelligent knowledge of life and life forces.

Because each is a fresh interpretation of life, every work of art is bound to rouse conflict. If what the artist renders is not fresh, then it is not art, but a repetition of what has gone before. A country needs artists and publishers like Henry Miller and Barney Rosset to prick its conscience, to awaken it to internal and external dangers. Whether the fires they set should be smothered by censors or allowed to blaze freely until they die of their own accord—or become larger conflagrations—is the choice that should be left to American citizens. Not to censors.

Americans generally believe they live in a country that nurtures and cherishes freedom. So basic to that freedom is the freedom to read that the vast majority of them *should have* been shocked to learn in 1961 that a fellow American's work had been banned from circulation in these United States for thirty years. Had that author and his major works been universally condemned as "poor" by the literati, then the banning would have been shocking enough. But to learn that the author in question has an international reputation and influence (an influence felt even in America, despite the ban), and to learn that the banned books were actually acclaimed by responsible critics at home and abroad (and read freely by "foreigners")— all of this *should have* been a traumatic experience for freedom-loving Americans everywhere. All of this *should have* been. That it *wasn't* is an American disgrace.

Henry Miller's lament seems entirely justified. He wrote to me on October 20, 1964: "This battle with negative forces will go on perpetually. You win here and lose there. After a few years it starts up again, on some other level."

What is heartening, however, as we have seen on *Tropic of Cancer*'s journey through the looking glass, is that the level is constantly being raised—at the expense of the censors.

GROVE PRESS

is proud to announce the publication of the first
American edition of a great international classic

HENRY MILLER'S
Tropic of Cancer

INTRODUCTION BY KARL SHAPIRO; PREFACE BY ANAÏS NIN

THE LITERARY WORLD has long hailed *Tropic of Cancer* as a major masterpiece. T. S. Eliot, Ezra Pound, George Orwell, Edmund Wilson, Lawrence Durrell, Norman Cousins, Sir Herbert Read, and many other leading writers of our time have characterized *Tropic of Cancer* as a modern American classic. Yet it has taken 27 years for Henry Miller's most important and, in the opinion of many, best work to be published in his own country.

LAWRENCE DURRELL: "For me, *Tropic of Cancer* stands beside *Moby Dick*. American literature today begins and ends with the meaning of what he has done. To read *Tropic of Cancer* is to understand how shockingly romantic all European writing after Rousseau has become. In Miller's book all the passions are there, stripped of their romantic envelope; it was not a book due to puritanical shock...It was the book of someone whose fidelity to himself had conquered the narrow confines in which we normally hem the range of subjects permissible to art."

SIR HERBERT READ: "One of the most significant contributions to the literature of our time."

KARL SHAPIRO: "I call Henry Miller the greatest living author because I think he is...Miller's achievement is miraculous: he is screamingly funny without making fun of sex, the way Rabelais does...Miller is accurate and poetic in the highest degree; there is not a smirk anywhere in his writings. Miller undoubtedly profited from the mistakes of his predecessors; his aim was not to write about the erotic but to write the whole truth about the life he knew..."

JOHN CIARDI: "Certainly there can be no doubt that *Tropic of Cancer* is a substantial work of art."

NORMAN COUSINS: "My congratulations on the courage and good taste which have led you to plan an American edition of Henry Miller's *Tropic of Cancer*. Henry Miller is both condiment and nutriment. With the passing of the years his fare is much less exotically remote than it once seemed. It may be that we are growing up to him. In any case, we can celebrate our return to the feast. *Tropic of Cancer* is one of the noteworthy books of this century, as Miller is one of the adornments of modern American literature."

HORACE GREGORY: "*Tropic of Cancer* is one of the very few American novels coming out of the 1930's that is better today than when it was written and twice as much alive. As I reread the book I kept thinking of Huckleberry Finn—this book is Huck Finn in Paris, a living twentieth century Huck Finn, as unique as Huck himself."

351 pages, $7.50
Now at all bookstores.
GROVE PRESS

NOTES *

I

1. Walker Winslow in *Henry Miller and the Critics,* ed. George Wickes (Carbondale, Ill., 1963), p. 65. Hereafter, Wickes.

2. Kingsley Widmer, *Henry Miller* (New York, 1963), p. 166n.

3. Alfred Perles, *My Friend, Henry Miller* (New York, 1962), p. 46.

4. Philip Rahv, "The Artist as Desperado," *New Republic,* CIV (April 21, 1941), 559.

5. Widmer, p. 133.

6. Major sources for this biographical sketch are Bern Porter's "Chronology and Bibliography" in *The Happy Rock,* pp. 152–54; Widmer's chronology, pp. 13–15; chronology in *A Henry Miller Reader,* ed. Lawrence Durrell (New York, 1959), pp. 383–91; chronology in Sydney Omarr's *Henry Miller: His World of Urania* (London, 1960), pp. 61–64; and Miller's letters to me.

7. Perles in Wickes, p. 3.

8. See Mildred Edie Brady's "The New Cult of Sex and Anarchy," *Harper's,* CXCIV (April, 1947), 312–22, for a more or less sensational account of Miller's life at Big Sur. Miller has written a more sober account in his book *Big Sur and the Oranges of Hieronymus Bosch* (New York, 1957).

---

* Space does not permit a more thorough documentation than appears in these pages. For the scholar who desires more, some 1,700 notes appear in the dissertation from which this study was composed, now on microfilm at Ann Arbor, Michigan.

9. George Wickes, *Henry Miller,* University of Minnesota Pamphlets on American Writers No. 56, 1966, p. 7.

10. Orvis Ross, *Minneapolis Star-Tribune, circa* 1960. The clipping is in the Grove Press files now at Syracuse University. Ross is a critic, composer and musician.

11. See editor George Plimpton's *Writers at Work: The Paris Review Interviews,* Second Series (New York, 1963), for Miller's comments.

12. William Carlos Williams in *The Happy Rock: A Book About Henry Miller,* ed. Bern Porter (Berkeley, Calif., 1945), p. 97.

2

1. In Sydney Omarr's *Henry Miller: His World of Urania* (London, 1960), p. 35.

2. "Defense of the Freedom to Read," in *Versions of Censorship,* eds. John McCormick and Mairi MacInnes (Garden City, N.Y., 1962), p. 226.

3. *Black Spring* (New York, 1963), p. 21.

4. Omarr, p. 65.

5. Kingsley Widmer, *Henry Miller* (New York, 1963), p. 133.

6. Eberhard and Phyllis Kronhausen, *Pornography and the Law* (New York, 1959), pp. 26–7.

7. Edward Weeks in *The First Freedom: Liberty and Justice in the World of Books,* ed. Robert B. Downs (Chicago, 1960), p. 163. Hereafter, Downs.

8. In Irene and Allen Cleaton's *Books and Battles: American Literature 1920–1930* (Boston, 1937), p. xviii.

9. *Ibid.,* p. 252.

10. In Downs, p. 277.

11. Cleaton, pp. xiii, 199.

12. John Roeburt, *The Wicked and the Banned* (New York, 1963), p. 25.

13. Cleaton, p. 232. See, too, Frederick Lewis Allen, *Only Yesterday* (New York, 1959), p. 249.

14. Wallace Fowlie, *The Age of Surrealism* (New York, 1950), pp. 15–16.

15. *Tropic of Cancer* (New York, 1961), pp. 1–2. All citations

are from the Grove paperback edition. Page numbers are given in parentheses at the end of each excerpt.

16. Widmer, p. 39.

17. Charles I. Glicksberg, "Henry Miller: Individualist in Extremis," *The Southwest Review,* XXXIII (Summer, 1948), 291–93.

18. Karl Shapiro, *In Defense of Ignorance* (New York, 1960), p. 322.

19. Widmer, p. 66.

20. In *Henry Miller and the Critics,* ed. George Wickes (Carbondale, Ill., 1963), p. 109.

21. *Ibid.*

22. *Ibid.,* p. 151.

3

1. Kenneth Rexroth, "The Neglected Henry Miller," *Nation,* CLXXXI (Nov. 5, 1955), 385.

2. Walker Winslow in *Henry Miller and the Critics,* ed. George Wickes (Carbondale, Ill., 1963), p. 64. Hereafter, Wickes.

3. Wickes, p. xvii.

4. Cited in Stanley Kauffmann's "Old Shocker Comes Home," *New Republic,* CXLV (July 10, 1961), 18.

5. Alfred Perles, *My Friend, Henry Miller* (New York, 1962), pp. 69, 157.

6. John Haverstick, "Henry Miller: Man in Quest of Life," *Saturday Review,* XL (Aug. 3, 1957), 8.

7. Robert E. Spiller ed., *A Time of Harvest, American Literature 1910–1960* (New York, 1963), pp. 40–1. Geismar's essay: "Society and the Novel."

8. *Ibid.,* p. 41.

9. Kenneth Rexroth, "Empty Zone," *Nation,* CXCIII (July 1, 1961), 16.

10. Terry Southern, "Miller: Only the Beginning," *Nation,* CXCIII (Nov. 18, 1961), 400.

11. Karl Shapiro, *In Defense of Ignorance* (New York, 1960), p. 326.

12. Kingsley Widmer, *Henry Miller* (New York, 1963), pp. 156–57. See also for similar comment, Shapiro, pp. 320, 323, 337; Leslie Fiedler, *Waiting for the End* (New York, 1964), p. 45; and

Theodore Solotaroff, "All That Cellar-Deep Jazz," *Commentary*, XXXII (October, 1961), 317.

13. Terry Southern, *et al., Writers in Revolt* (New York, 1963), p. 129.

14. Henry Heifetz, "The Anti-Social Act of Writing," *Studies on the Left*, IV (Spring, 1964), 5.

15. Shapiro, p. 326. In an essay also used as the Introduction to *Cancer* by Grove Press.

16. John Chandos ed., *To Deprave and Corrupt* (London, 1962), p. 43.

17. The full citation to this court case and all other court cases cited in this book may be found in the Appendix.

19. However, Elmer Gertz did succeed in having this particular Chicago ordinance thrown out by the U.S. Supreme Court early in 1968.

4

1. Thomas Parkinson, "The Hilarity of Henry Miller," *The Listener*, LIX (June 19, 1958), 1021. For a partial chronology on the publication of *Cancer* around the world, see the bibliography.

2. "Censorship Issues, Legal and Otherwise," *Publishers' Weekly*, CLXXIX (Jan. 16, 1961), 83.

3. Pitirim Sorokin, *The American Sex Revolution* (Boston, 1956), p. 19; Leslie Fiedler, *Waiting for the End* (New York, 1964), p. 160; David Fellman, *The Limits of Freedom* (New Brunswick, N.J., 1959), p. 81; Eric Larrabee, "The Cultural Context of Sex Censorship," *Law and Contemporary Problems*, XX (Autumn, 1955), 684.

4. William B. Lockhart and Robert C. McClure, "Literature, The Law of Obscenity, and the Constitution," *Minnesota Law Review*, XXXVIII (March, 1954), 361.

5. Alan Reitman of the American Civil Liberties Union, in a letter to me, Oct. 9, 1964. Robert B. Downs ed., *The First Freedom: Liberty and Justice in the World of Books* (Chicago, 1960), p. xiii, speaks of these groups. As *Time* does, later: "The New Pornography," *Time*, LXXXVIII (April 16, 1965), 28–9. See also Peter Jennison, "Freedom to Read." Public Affairs Pamphlet No. 344 (New York, 1963), p. 6. See Larrabee too, p. 680.

6. "Censorship Issues, Legal and Otherwise," p. 83.

7. See Jack Nelson and Gene Roberts, Jr., *The Censors and the Schools* (Boston and Toronto, 1963), p. 20, for a fuller account. And the book itself for the role the DAR plays in this area, and America's Future, Inc.

8. William B. Lockhart and Robert C. McClure, "Censorship of Obscenity: The Developing Constitutional Standards," *Minnesota Law Review*, XLV (November, 1960), 9.

9. Emphasis added. Cited by Jennison, p. 14.

10. Terence J. Murphy, *Censorship: Government and Obscenity* (Baltimore, 1963), p. 100. Emphasis added.

11. Morris L. Ernst and Alan U. Schwartz, *Censorship: The Search for the Obscene* (New York and London, 1964), pp. 114–15. Hereafter, *Censorship*.

12. Reitman letter to me, Oct. 9, 1964.

13. *Censorship*, p. 241.

14. Jason Epstein, "A Criticism of Commercial Publishing," *Daedalus*, XCII (Winter, 1963), 66. Emphasis added.

15. *Ibid.*, p. 67.

16. For an account of an unconstitutional seizure of it, see "About Evergreen Review No. 32," *Evergreen Review*, VIII (August–September, 1964), 32.

17. Henry Heifetz, "The Anti-Social Act of Writing," *Studies on the Left*, IV (Spring, 1964), 5.

18. Elmer Gertz letter to me, Feb. 16, 1965. Agreeing is Karl Shapiro, in an interview Nov. 13, 1964, University of Wisconsin. For more praise, see Peter Revell, "Propaganda and Pornography," *Library Journal*, LXXXVIII (Oct. 1, 1963), 3562.

19. Reitman letter to me, Oct. 9, 1964.

20. See, too, *Censorship*, p. 241; *Toronto Daily Star*, Oct. 17, 1962; and Trumbull Huntington, "Censorship: A Bookseller's View," *Publishers' Weekly*, CLXXXV (March 2, 1964), 57–8, for similar praise.

21. Rosset letter to Filipacchi, Aug. 26, 1959. All letters cited here are either in the Grove Press files at Syracuse University, or, if addressed to me, in my files. Unless otherwise stated, all are unpublished.

22. Samuel S. Vaughan, "Why a Book Sells Is Not as Much a Mystery as It Seems," *New York Times Book Review*, Feb. 25, 1962, p. 4.

23. Rosset letter to Guy Schoeller. Date unknown. A carbon copy was examined.

24. April 6, 1959. Emphasis added.

25. April 9, 1959.

26. May 18, 1959.

27. July 4, 1959. Emphasis added. Later, the *Economist* reported that Miller held back for the same reasons, in "Storm Over the 'Tropics.' " *Economist,* CC (July 1, 1961), 390:

" 'I don't want to be the central figure in a great controversy about my books. I don't want to take time from my writing to be interviewed on the radio and television or for the newspapers. Besides, the people whose opinion I most care about have read the books and I am not interested in those who want to buy them just to look at what they think are dirty words. . . .'

"[Miller] is a very shy man. . . . Miller has always tried hard to maintain a certain measure of isolation from the world at large."

28. Rosset letter to Miller, July 8, 1959. Emphasis added.

29. Aug. 5, 1959.

30. Rosset letter to Miller, Aug. 11, 1959.

31. Rosset letter to Filipacchi, Aug. 26, 1959. Emphasis added.

32. Jan. 18, 1960.

33. Miller letter to Rosset, Jan. 20, 1960. The "drastic changes" probably involved divorce. One year later *Newsweek* reported that Miller's wife was divorcing him for desertion in California while he "was traipsing around Europe, vainly looking for a place to settle down." "Tropic Storm," *Newsweek,* LVII (June 19, 1961), 33.

34. Henry Miller, "Another Open Letter," *New Republic,* CIX (Dec. 6, 1943), 813.

35. Feb. 11, 1960.

36. Feb. 24, 1960.

37. Feb. 3, 1965.

38. Feb. 11, 1960.

39. Robert Muller, *Daily Mail* (London, Eng.), May 13, 1960.

5

1. Grove Press News Release, May 15, 1961.

2. *Ibid.,* May 16, 1961.

3. Karl Shapiro, in an interview Nov. 13, 1964, University of Wisconsin.

4. Stanley Kauffmann, in "Old Shocker Comes Home," *New*

Republic, CXLV (July 10, 1961), 17, had this to say about the $7.50 price tag on the 351-page book:

"The interest of the price is that here it relates to the content of the book—not, as is usual, to its length or format. The publisher knows that the public knows the book's reputation and is willing to pay much more than is currently charged for books of similar production cost. . . . Rather than call it cashing in on prurience, let us say that the publisher is asking the purchaser to make a contribution to a defense fund in case of legal prosecution, although no provision is made for refunding, say, three dollars per copy if the publisher is unmolested."

However, Rosset insists that the price is quite conventional for a book of that size and composition, and with a high budget for advertising. He has said that Grove Press broke even on the 100,000 sale of the hardcover edition "after various expenses were deducted, not including legal defense."

5. From the Grove Press legal packet. This is a reprint of an advertisement in the *New York Times Book Review* and *New York Herald Tribune* of June 25, 1961, and the *San Francisco Chronicle,* May 22, 1961. (See page 252.)

6. Grove Press News Release.

6

1. Grove Press Release, April 25, 1961. See "Stalemate Ends 1st Round of Govt.'s Henry Miller Case," *Publishers' Weekly,* CLXXX (May 15, 1951), 22, for an account of the Upham case.

2. Grove Press Release, June 12, 1961. Under 36 U.S. Code 259a.

3. Miller letter to Rosset, June 3, 1961. This is the first indication that Miller might have gone abroad to avoid unpleasantness and possible prosecution at home.

4. Quoted by Captain Harvey L. Zuckman in "The Law of Obscenity and Military Practice," *Military Law Review,* D.A. Pamphlet 27-100-20, April, 1963, p. 44n.

5. *New York Times,* June 14, 1961.

6. Grove Press Release, Aug. 10, 1961. The Customs Bureau's censorship operations, unlike what happened in the *Cancer* case, are deliberately kept secret, on the grounds that some of the more prurient among us might get curious and attempt to import books

which have been ruled obscene. Two scholars have commented on this operation: "Grant that today Bureau enforcement of the Tariff Act is conscientious, careful and perhaps praiseworthy. Who is to say what will happen tomorrow." James C. Paul and Murray L. Schwartz, *Federal Censorship: Obscenity in the Mail* (New York, 1961), p. 253.

7. Elmer Gertz in *Henry Miller and the Critics,* ed. George Wickes (Carbondale, Ill., 1963), p. 182. Hereafter, Wickes. Barney Rosset reports that seventy cases is a conservative number.

8. William B. Lockhart interview, Dec. 18, 1964, University of Minnesota.

9. See Alfred A. Knopf, "Book Publishing: The Changes I've Seen," *Atlantic Monthly,* CC (December, 1957), 160; Irene and Allen Cleaton, *Books and Battles: American Literature 1920–1930* (Boston, 1937), p. 216; Samuel S. Vaughan, "Why a Book Sells Is Not as Much a Mystery as It Seems," *New York Times Book Review,* Feb. 25, 1962, p. 4.

10. See, too, Thomas J. Wilson, "American Book Publishing: Hazards and Opportunities," *Daedalus,* XCII (Winter, 1963), 83–4.

11. Leonard Schwartz letter to Aaron Sussman, May 22, 1961.

12. Wickes, p. 147.

13. Quoted in E. T. Moore, "*Tropic of Cancer,* the First Three Months," *ALA Bulletin,* LV (October, 1961), 780.

14. Rosset sent Mark Schorer to talk to Frieda Lawrence Ravagli. Although he was under no obligation to offer a royalty, Rosset did, and she accepted. Emphasis added.

15. Emphasis added.

16. By 1968, however, there were at least two pirate editions of Henry Miller's novels in print in the United States.

17. "Censorship Issues and Legal Cases," *Publishers' Weekly,* CLXXXI (Jan. 15, 1962), 68. Emphasis added.

7

1. This is called the "real revolution" by Marshall A. Best, "In Books, They Call It Revolution," *Daedalus,* XCII (Winter, 1963), 33.

2. Raymond Walters, Jr., "There's Something for Everybody," *New York Times Book Review* (Paperback Book Section), Jan.

17, 1960, p. 33. See, also, Peter Yates, "The American Artist," *Arts in Society,* II (Fall–Winter, 1962–63), 48–9.

3. William B. Lockhart and Robert C. McClure, "Literature, The Law of Obscenity, and the Constitution," *Minnesota Law Review,* XXXVIII (March, 1954), 302. Hereafter, L & M, "Law." See, too, Richard McKeon, *et al., The Freedom to Read: Perspective and Program* (New York, 1957), p. 98. "Movies lawyer" Ephraim London remarks: The cheaper the "medium of communication, the likelier it will be censored." The National Office for Decent Literature concentrates on low prices which make books more available to adolescents. William J. Hempel and Patrick M. Wall, "Extralegal Censorship of Literature," *New York University Law Review,* XXXIII (November, 1958), 994. And see Terrence J. Murphy, *Censorship: Government and Obscenity* (Baltimore, 1963), p. 86.

4. Eric Larrabee, "The Cultural Context of Sex Censorship," *Law and Contemporary Problems,* XX (Autumn, 1955), 680 and 679. And see his "Pornography Is Not Enough," *Harper's,* CCXXI (November, 1960), 88–9: "The nature of any censorship . . . is often a function of the anxieties generated by the medium or the milieu which the medium serves." Standards vary among the media. See Murphy, p. 91, and John Roeburt, *The Wicked and the Banned* (New York, 1963), p. 16.

5. L & M, "Law," p. 309.

6. James Rorty, "The Harassed Pocket-Book Publishers," *Antioch Review,* XV (December, 1955), 427.

7. See Walters, p. 2; Alan Reitman letter to me, Oct. 9, 1964; "Censorship Trends: Local, State, National in 1962," *Publishers' Weekly,* CLXXXIII (Jan. 21, 1963), 67; "Tropic Censorship Decisions: A Mixed Collection," *Publishers' Weekly,* CLXXXI (March 5, 1962), 40; and Elmer Gertz, "The 'Tropic of Cancer' Litigation in Illinois," *Kentucky Law Journal,* LI (Summer, 1963), 591.

8. Jordan letter to Lynes, Dec. 7, 1961. Emphasis added. Everything Jordan says checks out. If anything, he understated. See Anthony Lewis, "The Most Recent Troubles of 'Tropic,'" *New York Times Book Review,* Jan. 21, 1962, pp. 4ff.

9. "Widespread Censorship of Paperback *Tropic of Cancer,*" *Publishers' Weekly,* CLXXX (Nov. 13, 1961), 21.

10. Lewis, p. 4. Emphasis added.

11. Gertz, p. 592.

12. Lewis, p. 16.

13. Mathews letter to Pemberton, Jan. 18, 1962.

14. Stuart C. Sherman, "Defending the Freedom to Read," *Library Journal*, LXXXVII (Feb. 1, 1962), 480.

15. Henry Steele Commager, *et al., Civil Liberties Under Attack* (Philadelphia, 1951), p. 8.

16. Robert B. Downs, "Apologist for Censorship," *Library Journal*, LXXXVI (June 1, 1961), 2043. Reviewing Kilpatrick's *The Smut Peddlers.*

17. United Press International story, Nov. 4, 1961. Also, "Group Pressure Cited As Press Freedom Menace," *Freedom of Information Digest*, III (Nov.–Dec., 1961), 8.

18. Alan Reitman letter to me, April 23, 1964. See also "Banning Book-Banners," *Newsweek*, LX (Nov. 26, 1962), 88, for Birch Society activities in this area.

19. By the summer of 1964 both *Tropics* were on NODL's list of "Publications Disapproved for Youth," *NODL Newsletter*, IX (Summer, 1964), 12.

20. Freeman Lewis, *et al.*, "Freedom to Read," *Publishers' Weekly*, CLXXXI (May 21, 1962), 27.

21. William B. Lockhart and Robert C. McClure, "Censorship of Obscenity: The Developing Constitutional Standards," *Minnesota Law Review*, XLV (November, 1960), 10. Hereafter, L & M, "Developing."

22. Mrs. Walter J. Steininger letter to me, May 9, 1965.

23. James Jackson Kilpatrick, *The Smut Peddlers* (Garden City, N.Y., 1960), p. 249.

24. Moore, p. 780. Roland E. Burdick also spoke of the threat to intellectual freedom posed by pressures on schools and libraries in a letter to me, Jan. 18, 1962.

25. Dennis G. Kuby letter to ACLU, May 4, 1962.

26. Esther Featherer, "Pressures on the Libraries," *Freedom of Information Center Publication No. 134,* Columbia, Mo., November, 1964, p. 3.

27. Eric Moon, " 'Problem' Fiction," *Library Journal*, LXXXVII (Feb. 1, 1962), 485ff.

28. Richard J. Neuman, "Who Reads *Tropic*? Or, What Happens When You Leave It Alone," *Newsletter on Intellectual Freedom*, XI (December, 1962), 43.

29. "Censorship Issues and Legal Cases," p. 69.

30. *Censorship*, p. 241.

31. Peter Israel letter to me, Oct. 16, 1964. "All publishers have a stake" in *Cancer*, one author declared in "Tropic Censorship Decisions: A Mixed Collection," p. 40.

32. Most students of the subject agree on this figure. Wickes, p. 147. The Grove Press Release on the Jacobellis decision, n.d., used this number.

33. Reitman letter to me, Oct. 9, 1964.

34. American Book Publishers Council, Inc., *Freedom-to-Read Bulletin*, VI (Fall, 1963), 1.

35. "Tropic Censorship Decisions: A Mixed Collection," p. 40.

36. Rembar letter to me, July 23, 1964. Slough and McAnany report an appeal to the Indiana Supreme Court in *State v. Cuffel*. M. C. Slough and P. D. McAnany, S.J., "Obscenity and Constitutional Freedom—Part I," *St. Louis University Law Journal*, VIII (Spring, 1964), 329n.

37. *Attorney-General v. Book Named "Tropic of Cancer,"* 345 Mass. 11, 184 N.E. 2d 328 (1962).

38. *Zeitlin v. Arnebergh*, 59 Cal. 2d 901.

39. *Smith v. California*, 32 U.S.L. Week.

40. ACLU 44th *Annual Report*, July 1, 1963, to June 30, 1964 (New York, 1964), p. 12.

41. *People v. Fritch*, 13 N.Y. 2d 119, 243 N.Y.S. 2d 1 (1963). One observer wrote in *Publishers' Weekly:* "From a reading of the opinions in the case, it is clear that the majority of the court took personal affront at the book and that they translated their personal feelings of affrontery into action: by slapping the book off sale throughout the state. The judge who wrote the majority opinion called the book 'dirt for dirt's sake' and 'dirt for money's sake,' " R.H.S., "A Summer of Censorship," *Publishers' Weekly*, CLXXXIII (July 29, 1963), 38.

42. *Haiman v. Morris*, No. 61S19718, Superior Court Cook County. Part of the evidence presented in the appeal (the Superior Court decision was in favor of *Cancer*) was an abstract which summarized *Cancer*, chapter by chapter. The summary was preceded by an apology for the scatological writing which the judges would be forced to read. Grove Press's lawyer for the case, Elmer Gertz, wrote me May 25, 1965: "I wish I had an extra copy of that strange abstract of *Cancer* filed by the Corporation Counsel. They have run out of copies, as well they might. It is a rarity. The thinking back of it is characteristic of censors generally."

43. Emphasis added.

8

1. *Kansas City Star,* Aug. 11, 1963. For comment on press apathy in this area, see Morris L. Ernst, *The First Freedom* (New York, 1946), pp. 19–20.
2. Cited in Paul Blanshard, *The Right to Read: The Battle Against Censorship* (Boston, 1955), p. 161. Emphasis added.
3. *Freedom of Information Digest,* III (March–April, 1962), 5.
4. Peter S. Jennison, "Freedom to Read." Public Affairs Pamphlet No. 344 (New York, 1963), p. 18. Emphasis added.
5. Gilbert Seldes, "The Mass Media and the Artistic Climate," *Arts in Society,* II (Fall–Winter, 1962, 1963), 150.
6. Cleveland Amory, "Paperback Pornography," *Saturday Evening Post,* CCXXXVI (April 6, 1963), 10.
7. Kenneth Rexroth, "Empty Zone," *Nation,* CXCIII (July 1, 1961), 15.
8. Alan Reitman letter to me, April 23, 1964. Emphasis added.
9. Oct. 9, 1964.
10. "See No Evil," *Time,* LXXVII (Aug. 25, 1961), 39.
11. *Ibid.* Emphasis added.
12. Hoke Norris, " 'Cancer' in Chicago," *Evergreen Review* No. 25, p. 9.
13. Littlejohn letter to Rosset, Oct. 31, 1961. Emphasis added.
14. *Stamford Advocate,* Aug. 28, 1963.
15. *San Francisco Chronicle,* Aug. 20, 1963.
16. *Star Ledger,* Sept. 13, 1963.
17. Oct. 16, 1961.

9

1. See Catholic population figures in 1960 in Wisconsin from the *Official Catholic Directory.* Roughly 32 per cent. At this time there were 1,347,874 persons of Catholic faith in the state, an increase of roughly 45,000 from 1961. In the critical areas of our study, there were 380,641 in Milwaukee County, and 66,235 in Dane County, where Madison is located, representing roughly 36.7 per cent and 29.8 per cent of the population in those counties,

respectively. These last figures come from the Chancery Office of Milwaukee and Madison.

2. See Wisconsin Revised Statutes, Chapter 136, Section 11, 1849. Much of this information comes from a Legislative Reference Library Report on Obscenity Legislation, *Informational Bulletin* 192, August, 1960—hereafter referred to as LRL—and from an unpublished paper by Mark W. Hopkins, "Legislating Morality in the Wisconsin Press 1849–1957."

3. *Chicago Tribune,* April 10, 1926.

4. *Wisconsin State Journal,* Dec. 12, 1938. A pledge which is still being exacted today in Wisconsin and elsewhere. Other newspapers announced that a "campaign will be started in six weeks." The *Milwaukee Journal,* April 1, 1941, and the *Milwaukee Post,* Nov. 19, 1941, spoke of a campaign. The *Capital Times* pointed out the danger of the Doyne Bill, April 2, 1941.

5. James E. Harpster, "Obscene Literature," *Marquette Law Review,* XXXIV (Spring, 1951), 301–2.

6. *Milwaukee Sentinel,* Oct. 30, 1951.

7. *Milwaukee Journal,* Dec. 9, 1952.

8. *Green Bay Press-Gazette,* May 6, 1953.

9. *Milwaukee Journal,* March 9, 1953.

10. James Russell Wiggins, *Freedom or Secrecy* (New York, 1956), p. 192.

11. Steven I. Cohen, "Constitutional Law—Obscene Literature—Wisconsin Statute Provides Civil Action Against a Book," *Wisconsin Law Review,* MCMLX (March, 1960), 309.

12. The italicized words in this paragraph indicate the addition to the original law by Substitute Amendment No. 1, S., to Bill No. 517, A., July 28, 1961.

13. See Paul Blanshard, *The Right to Read* (Boston, 1955), p. 147; and Hamilton H. Rice, "Youth—Obscenity Problem—A Proposal," *Kentucky Law Journal,* LII (Winter, 1964), 446. Roland E. Burdick of the American Book Publishers Council in a letter to me, Jan. 18, 1962, is on the same side of the argument. Those not so enthusiastic are: Morris L. Ernst and Alan U. Schwartz, *Censorship: The Search for the Obscene* (New York and London, 1964), p. 136, because of the elimination of the "beyond reasonable doubt" phrase of the criminal statutes; and Roger Smith (news editor of *Publishers' Weekly*), who in a letter to me, Jan. 15, 1962, points out that the statute embodies the

use of a "star chamber" for securing a pretrial and hence extra-legal judgment.

14. Cohen, p. 312n, citing Note 59, *Harvard Law Review* 813 (1946).

15. Eric Moon, " 'Problem' Fiction," *Library Journal,* LXXXVII (Feb. 1, 1962), 490. Emphasis added.

16. Lee A. Burress, Jr., "The Pressure of Censorship on Wisconsin Public Schools," *Wisconsin English Journal,* VI (October, 1963), 11.

17. *Ibid.,* p. 6.

18. *Green Bay Press-Gazette,* Oct. 21, 1960.

19. On a national level the American Book Publishers Council noted the same thing in its *Freedom-to-Read Bulletin* of March, 1962, p. 2. Hereafter ABPC *Bulletin.*

20. See Cohen, p. 309; Senate Bill 102 History; and ABPC *Bulletin,* September, 1956, p. 2.

21. Because the national and state CDL offices refuse to answer my letters, I cannot be certain these cities all had chapters formed before or during the campaign. My information comes from news stories and from Mrs. R. V. Anderson, lobbyist for the Wisconsin Federation of Women's Clubs, in a letter, June 4, 1965.

22. *Capital Times,* Aug. 17, 1956.

23. Anderson letter, May 26, 1965.

24. *Capital Times,* March 14, 1963.

25. ABPC *Bulletin,* Fall, 1963, p. 8.

26. *Wisconsin State Journal,* Jan. 21, 23, 1963; Sept. 23, 1964.

27. *Milwaukee Journal,* Feb. 14, 1963.

28. *Sheboygan Press,* July 23, 1964.

29. *Racine Journal-Times,* Oct. 23, 1961.

30. *Wisconsin State Journal,* Nov. 4, 1961.

31. *Racine Journal-Times,* Nov. 4, 1961.

32. Margaret Culkin Banning in *The First Freedom: Liberty and Justice in the World of Books,* ed. Robert B. Downs (Chicago, 1960), p. 320.

33. See the *Wisconsin State Journal,* Jan. 11, 1963.

34. All comes from an interview on Dec. 7, 1961, Madison.

35. William Lockhart and Robert McClure, "Censorship of Obscenity," *Minnesota Law Review,* XIV (November, 1960), 11.

36. From an interview in 1962 by Bob Stevenson and Ron Leys, University of Wisconsin students. Their findings are in the files of

Prof. William Hachten, University of Wisconsin. Hereafter, Stevenson.

37. Stevenson. The same held true in 1965. A "fine-tooth comb" is used on the stands any time anyone presses a complaint against a book or magazine.

38. *Wisconsin State Journal,* Oct. 28, 1964. Emphasis added.

39. From "Transcript of Proceedings," Wisconsin joint Legislative Obscene Literature Commission Public Hearing, Oct. 27, 1964, Madison, p. 53.

40. *Capital Times,* Jan. 10, 1963.

41. From interviews with Edward Nager, assistant district attorney until June, 1964, on Dec. 8, 1961, and Nov. 26, 1964.

42. *Capital Times,* Jan. 10, 1963. Emphasis added.

43. Jones is the past president of the American Society of Newspaper Editors. This article was originally an address delivered during the crucial *Cancer* campaign period, in October, 1961, before the Inland Daily Press Association.

44. *Wisconsin State Journal,* Jan. 11, 1963.

45. Frank E. Forster in an interview, Dec. 8, 1961. See also *Wisconsin State Journal,* Jan. 11, 1963. In a letter to me, W. G. Rice, president of the Madison CLU, said that the CLU opposed the movie committee proposal of the Madison mayor. Dec. 5, 1964.

46. Nager has now become an assemblyman and given up the assistant district attorney's job. He is also executive secretary of the Madison chapter of the ACLU. The new district attorney, Michael Torphy, took over June 1, 1964.

47. W. G. Rice letter to me, Dec. 5, 1964.

10

1. Richard B. Surges letter to me, Dec. 29, 1961.

2. Robert Hess letter to me, Dec. 9, 1964; Leonard Zubrensky interview, Nov. 29, 1964 (Zubrensky is a lawyer and a member of the Milwaukee Chapter of the Civil Liberties Union); Robert Wells letter to me, Dec. 13, 1964 (he is a *Milwaukee Journal* reporter); and Joseph Chobot letter to me, Jan. 27, 1962 (he is a Milwaukee bookseller).

3. "Transcript of Proceedings," Wisconsin joint Legislative Ob-

scene Literature Commission, Public Hearing, Oct. 27, 1964, Madison, Wis. Hereafter, "Transcript."

4. "Minutes," Wisconsin joint Legislative Obscene Literature Commission, June 16, 1964, Milwaukee. Hereafter, "Minutes," June 16.

5. Mary LeMahieu interview, May 31, 1965. She is a Milwaukee native.

6. Donald Olesen interview, June 1, 1965. He is an editorial writer for the *Milwaukee Journal.*

7. Morgan Gibson letter to me, Jan. 19, 1965. See also the *Milwaukee Sentinel,* Jan. 21, 1965, for a story on the Federation of Women's Clubs activities in the obscene arena.

8. Paul Blanshard, *The Right to Read: The Battle Against Censorship* (Boston, 1955), p. 174. See also, Robert B. Downs ed., *The First Freedom: Liberty and Justice in the World of Books* (Chicago, 1960), p. 133; William B. Lockhart and Robert C. McClure, "Censorship of Obscenity: The Developing Constitutional Standards," *Minnesota Law Review,* XLV (November, 1960), 10, which credits the CDL for the rise in police raids, etc.; and William J. Hempel and Patrick M. Wall, "Extralegal Censorship of Literature," *New York University Law Review,* XXXIII (November, 1958), 998. Hereafter cited Downs; L & M, "Developing"; and Hempel, respectively.

9. Lawrence A. Lowell in *Public Opinion and Propaganda,* eds. Daniel Katz, *et al.* (New York, 1954), pp. 13-4. Emphasis added.

10. Hempel, p. 993n.

11. *Ibid.,* p. 1020.

12. John Grams letter to me, June 24, 1965. An instructor at Marquette University, Grams surveyed the station managers for me and asked the secretary of MRTC to send me materials published by that organization.

13. Milwaukee Junior Bar Association, "Report of Literature & Motion Picture Committee," July, 1956, pp. 32-3. Emphasis added. Hereafter, MJBA.

14. Morris L. Ernst and Alan U. Schwartz, *Censorship: The Search for the Obscene* (New York and London, 1964), p. 143.

15. MJBA, p. 15. Unless otherwise indicated the movie commission information comes from this report between pp. 13-22.

16. See Michael Blankfort, "The Screen Writer and Freedom,"

Speeches, Seventh Annual Freedom of Information Conference, Nov. 16–17, 1964, University of Missouri.

17. *Milwaukee Journal,* March 14, 1965.

18. *Ibid.* Emphasis added.

19. *Ibid.*

20. Zubrensky letter to Rice, April 2, 1957. See also the March 26, 1957, letter. Zubrensky was legal counsel for Governor John Reynolds of Wisconsin.

21. "Minutes," Wisconsin joint Legislative Obscene Literature Commission, March 5, 1964, Milwaukee. Hereafter, "Minutes," March 5. Emphasis added.

22. MJBA, pp. 3–4. Unless otherwise indicated, information about the Literary Commission comes from this report, pp. 3–13. This literary commission ordinance, interestingly enough, comes almost a year before the famous St. Cloud, Minn., ordinance. The latter was withdrawn in 1953, after the banning of some 300 paperbacks.

23. Emphasis added.

24. *Milwaukee Sentinel,* Oct. 30, 1951.

25. Other members then were Supervisor Paul Pike Pullen, Mrs. Beulah Thomas, psychiatrist Raymond Headlee, Mrs. Ruth A. Moe, and the Rev. Paul Gia Russo.

26. *Wisconsin State Journal,* Oct. 30, 1951.

27. *Ibid.*

28. *Milwaukee Journal,* Dec. 29, 1952. Emphasis added.

29. *Ibid.*

30. *Milwaukee Journal,* Dec. 2, 1953. Emphasis added.

31. April 2, 1957. Emphasis added.

32. *Milwaukee Journal* editorial, Aug. 11, 1956.

II

1. *Milwaukee Sentinel,* Oct. 15, 1961.

2. Interviews with Perry Hill, June 1, 1965; Donald Olesen, June 1, 1965; and Leonard Zubrensky, Nov. 29, 1964.

3. Ted M. Warshafsky letter to me, Jan. 28, 1965.

4. Hess letter to me, Oct. 30, 1964.

5. Zubrensky interview, Nov. 29, 1964.

6. Surges letter to me, Dec. 29, 1961.

7. William B. Lockhart and Robert C. McClure, "Literature,

The Law of Obscenity and the Constitution," *Minnesota Law Review,* XXXVIII (March, 1954), 320.

8. Surges interview, Jan. 23, 1962, Milwaukee.

9. Theodore Schroeder, *A Challenge to Sex Censors* (New York, 1938), p. 39.

10. Surges interview.

11. *Ibid.*

12. James Donnelley and Robert Gaurke joint interview, Jan. 24, 1962, Milwaukee.

13. William Aschmann interview, Jan. 24, 1962, Milwaukee.

14. Donnelley and Gaurke interview.

15. "Transcript of Proceedings," Wisconsin joint Legislative Obscene Literature Commission, Public Hearing, Oct. 27, 1964, Madison, Wisconsin, p. 175. Hereafter, "Transcript."

16. Divulged in Senator Allen Busby, Oleson, Hill and Zubrensky interviews.

17. Cleveland Amory, "Paperback Pornography," *Saturday Evening Post,* CCXXXVI (April 6, 1963), 10, 12.

18. *Wisconsin State Journal,* May 8, 1963.

19. "Minutes," Wisconsin joint Legislative Obscene Literature Commission, March 5, 1964, Milwaukee. Hereafter, "Minutes," March 5.

20. Emphasis added. Throughout these citations from the transcripts of the hearings, italics unless otherwise stated will be mine. The transcripts are on file in the Legislative Reference Bureau in Madison, Wisconsin.

21. *Manual,* by the way, had been cleared earlier by a Supreme Court decision.

22. James Russell Wiggins, *Freedom or Secrecy* (New York, 1956), p. 191.

23. *Ibid.*

24. Walter Gellhorn, *Individual Freedom and Governmental Restraints* (Baton Rouge, La., 1956), pp. 75–6.

25. Wisconsin distributors seem to have a penchant for censorship. R. E. Peterson in 1955, while representing the Midwest Independent Distributors Association, told an Assembly Judiciary Committee that a state "censor committee of some kind" should be added to the provisions of a bill to bar lewd and obscene magazines in Wisconsin. See the *Sheboygan Press,* May 25, 1955.

26. Erwin Belau of the Des Forgese bookstore, interview Jan. 23, 1962. An anonymous clerk, a student from Marquette Uni-

versity, interview Jan. 23, 1962. (He desired anonymity to avoid possible repercussions.) Manager of Green's Campus Book Store, interview Jan. 23, 1962. Hampels Book Shop, an anonymous woman, extremely hostile, reported no trouble, Jan. 23, 1962. An exception was Mary's Bookstore. Fred Blair in letter to me, June 9, 1965, reported citizen, police, and FBI troubles when it came to his Marxist literature.

27. *State of Wisconsin v. Chabot,* 12 Wis. 2d 110, 106 N.W. 2d. 368 U.S. 15, 82 S. Ct. 136, 7 L. Ed. 2nd 85 (1961).

28. Sheldon Bordow, manager of the City News Center, interview, Jan. 23, 1962.

29. Peter S. Jennison, "Censorship: Strategy for Defense," *Publishers' Weekly,* CLXXXV (March 2, 1964), 58, 61.

30. Letter, April 2, 1957. Emphasis added.

31. Cohen, p. 320.

32. William Randall, telephone interview, Jan. 24, 1961.

33. Eric Moon, " 'Problem' Fiction," *Library Journal,* LXXXVII (Feb. 1, 1962), 496.

34. *Milwaukee Journal,* April 1, 1964.

35. Alec Craig, *Suppressed Books: A History of the Conception of Literary Obscenity* (Cleveland and New York, 1963), p. 204.

36. *Milwaukee Journal,* Dec. 9, 1952.

37. *Ibid.,* May 20, 1955.

38. *Ibid.,* May 8, 1964.

39. *Ibid.,* June 13, 1964.

40. *Ibid.,* Feb. 28, 1965.

41. Kemplin interview, Jan. 23, 1962. A *Journal* reporter who does know of the police censorship is Robert Wells.

12

1. Brennan letter to me, Sept. 30, 1964.

2. The Supplemental Appendix to *McCauley v. Tropic of Cancer,* 20 Wis. 2d 134, 121 N.W. 2d 545 (1963), pp. 102–03. Hereafter, Supplemental.

3. *Wisconsin State Journal,* Oct. 16, 1961.

4. Supplemental, p. 104.

5. "Transcript of Proceedings," Wisconsin joint Legislative Obscene Literature Commission, Public Hearings, Oct. 27, 1964, Madison, Wisconsin, pp. 66, 115. Hereafter, "Transcript."

6. *Milwaukee Sentinel,* Oct. 15, 1961.

7. *Ibid.,* May 21, 1963.

8. *Ibid.,* Oct. 15, 1961.

9. Anonymous clerk at Schwartz bookstore, Jan. 23, 1962.

10. Zubrensky telephone interview, Feb. 16, 1962.

11. Robert Hess letter, Oct. 30, 1964.

12. Host telephone interview, Jan. 24, 1962.

13. Eberhard and Phyllis Kronhausen, *Pornography and the Law* (New York, 1959), pp. 42, 78–9. Surges interview, Jan. 23, 1962.

14. *Milwaukee Journal,* Nov. 28, 1961.

15. William J. Panagis telephone interview, June 21, 1965. Of the Bartell & Panagis firm.

16. See *Milwaukee Journal,* Nov. 2, 1961; the *Milwaukee Sentinel* of the same date; and the *Wisconsin State Journal,* Nov. 11, 1961. Emphasis added.

17. *Wisconsin State Journal,* Dec. 10, 1961. The *Milwaukee Journal* ran a similar account, Dec. 9, 1961.

13

1. John Ciardi in *Contemporary Moral Issues,* ed. H. K. Girvetz (Belmont, Calif., 1963), pp. 240–41.

2. *Ibid.,* p. 241.

3. Robert Hess letter to Elmer Gertz, April 10, 1964.

4. William J. Panagis telephone interview, June 21, 1965.

5. *Kingsley Books, Inc. v. Brown,* 354 U.S. 436 (1957). Among those favoring juries are Alec Craig, *Suppressed Books* (Cleveland and New York, 1963), p. 197; and Terence J. Murphy, *Censorship: Government and Obscenity* (Baltimore, 1963), p. 201.

6. Zechariah Chafee, Jr., *Government and Mass Communications,* I (Chicago, 1947), p. 216.

7. Cited by Harry Whitmore, "Obscenity in Literature: Crime or Free Speech," *Sydney Law Review* (March, 1963), 184.

8. Craig, p. 197.

9. William B. Lockhart and Robert C. McClure, "Literature, The Law of Obscenity, and the Constitution," *Minnesota Law Review,* XXXVIII (March, 1954), 348. Hereafter, L & M, "Law."

10. So wrote Morgan Gibson, poet and member of the University of Wisconsin-Milwaukee English faculty, in "The Milwaukee

Cancer Trial," *Michigan Voices,* III (Winter, 1962), 42–9. Gibson sat through nearly all of the trial and was an expert witness for the defense. In reviewing the witnesses' testimony in the trial, the major source of information is the Appellants' Brief and Appendix; the Respondent's Brief and the Supplemental Appendix to *McCauley v. Tropic of Cancer,* 20 Wis. 2d 134, 121 N.W. 2d 545 (1963). Judge Drechsler's decision is included in the Appellants' Appendix. Hereafter cited simply Appellants' Brief, or Appellants' Appendix; Respondent's Brief, or Respondent's Appendix; Lower Court's Decision, with appropriate page numbers; and *Amicus Brief.* And *McCauley* with appropriate page numbers.

11. *Milwaukee Journal,* May 20, 1962.

12. Respondent's Brief, p. 48.

13. Respondent's Appendix, pp. 105–25.

14. *Milwaukee Sentinel,* May 17, 1962. New York is supposedly more sophisticated than Milwaukee, with Chicago in-between.

15. Appellants' Appendix, p. 135.

16. Respondent's Appendix, p. 125.

17. Gibson, p. 42. See, too, Respondent's Appendix, pp. 125–26; and Lower Court's Decision, pp. 106–07.

18. Respondent's Appendix, pp. 129, 130.

19. Appellants' Appendix, p. 133.

20. Respondent's Appendix, p. 130.

21. Gibson, p. 43.

22. Appellants' Appendix, pp. 135–36.

23. Gibson, p. 44.

24. All of Judge Drechsler's following remarks will be found in Lower Court's Decision.

25. *Ibid.,* pp. 111–12.

26. Emphasis added.

27. 12 Wis. 2d 110, 106 N.W. 2d.

14

1. Appellant's Brief to *McCauley v. Tropic of Cancer,* 20 Wis. 2d 134, 121 N.W. 2d 545 (1963).

2. Emphasis added.

3. *McCauley v. Tropic of Cancer,* 20 Wis. 2d 134, 121 N.W. 2d 545 (1963).

4. Lockhart and McClure, "Censorship of Obscenity: The De-

veloping Constitutional Standards," *Minnesota Law Review,* XLV (November, 1960), 5–121. Hereafter, L & M, "Developing."

5. L & M, "Developing," p. 114, in *McCauley,* p. 552.

6. M. C. Slough and P. D. McAnany, S.J., "Obscenity and Constitutional Freedom—Part I," *St. Louis University Law Journal,* VIII (Spring, 1964), 329.

7. Emphasis added.

8. *McCauley,* Motion for Rehearing, pp. 2–3.

9. Emphasis added.

10. Emphasis added.

11. Emphasis added.

12. As a kind of footnote epilogue, it is interesting to note here that Surges continued in his position until February, 1966, when he resigned to go into private practice. One of the staff members of the district attorney's office, Mr. Gerald Boyle, said in a telephone interview on June 6, 1967, that Surges had done "a great job." Judge Drechsler is still on the bench.

15

1. *Milwaukee Journal,* May 20, 1962.

2. *Press-Gazette,* May 24, 1963. Editor of the paper is Leo V. Gannon. With the exception of this editorializing on *Cancer* and printing suggestions from the local Green Bay censorship group, COMBAT, the newspaper has consistently advocated proper procedures and scored extralegal censorship in its editorial columns. For example, see the editions of Dec. 1, 7, 1960; Feb. 11, March 25, Nov. 1, of 1963. Although I do not know the author of this editorial, its language and thinking is similar to that written to me by Mr. Gannon in a letter, June 2, 1965. At that late date he had not read *Cancer.*

3. *Racine Journal-Times,* May 20, 1963.

4. *Ibid.,* May 21, 1963.

5. Among those carrying anywhere from two to five paragraphs on the decision were: *Eau Claire Leader,* May 21, 1963; *Green Bay Press-Gazette,* May 20, *Kenosha News,* May 20; *Daily Jefferson County Union,* May 21; *Appleton Post-Crescent,* May 21; *Baraboo News Republic,* May 20; *Beaver Dam Daily Citizen,* May 20; *Marinette Eagle Star,* May 20; *Wausau Daily Record-Herald,* May 20; *Beloit Daily News,* May 20. Among those not mentioning

the decision editorially or otherwise: *Sheboygan Press; Fond du Lac Commonwealth Reporter; Waukesha Daily Freeman; Ashland Daily Press;* and *Chippewa Herald-Telegram.* The Madison and Milwaukee newspapers, of course, carried the decision as reported by their own staff, giving it full treatment. In addition to checking editions of these newspapers, Grove Press files and the Legislative Reference Bureau files in Madison were examined with this date in mind.

6. *Milwaukee Journal,* July 17, 1963.
7. *Milwaukee Sentinel,* July 17, 1963.
8. *Milwaukee Journal,* July 22, 1963.
9. *Milwaukee Journal,* May 21, 1963.
10. *Milwaukee Journal,* July 19, 1963.
11. *Ibid.*
12. *Milwaukee Journal,* Aug. 10, 1963.

16

1. *Wisconsin State Journal,* April 5, 1964.
2. *Capital Times,* April 8, 1964. Jack Ladinsky, assistant professor of sociology at the University of Wisconsin, would corroborate this information. I was fortunate in having Ladinsky's full cooperation. He was studying this race under a grant from a research foundation to investigate the structure and strain between popular democracy and judicial independence. Interview, Dec. 7, 1964.
3. *Portage Daily Register,* April 8, 1964.
4. *Capital Times,* April 4, 1964.
5. *Capital Times,* April 8, 1964; and *Wisconsin Rapids Daily Tribune,* March 11, 1964.
6. *Wisconsin State Journal,* March 25, 1964.
7. *Ibid.,* March 24, 1964.
8. *Capital Times,* March 11, 1964. Emphasis added.
9. *Racine Journal-Times,* March 13, 1964.
10. *Stevens Point Journal,* March 13, 1964.
11. Ladinsky calls these figures "reasonably accurate," from the information available, "but well on the shy side, particularly Wilkie's figures."
12. Robert Hess letter to Elmer Gertz, April 10, 1964. Ladinsky agrees.

13. *Capital Times,* March 21, 1964. Ladinsky lends his support to this view. See, too, the Wisconsin Federation Citizens for Educational Freedom, Hales Corners, "News Alert," passed out to Independent School Leaders and Administrators. Such material is available in my files and in Ladinsky's files.

14. United Press International news story, April 2, 1964.

15. William Brissee, in the *Wisconsin State Journal,* March 29, 1964.

16. *Ibid.* The following cited paragraphs on Boyle's campaign efforts come from this source.

17. *Wisconsin Rapids Tribune,* March 13, 1964.

18. *Appleton Post-Crescent,* March 15, 1964.

19. Leonard Zubrensky interview, Nov. 29, 1964. Emphasis added.

20. Ladinsky.

21. *Wisconsin Rapids Daily Tribune,* April 8, 1964; and *Milwaukee Sentinel,* March 16, 1964.

22. *Milwaukee Journal,* April 5, 1964.

23. *Janesville Gazette,* March 24, 1964.

24. *Burlington Standard-Press,* April 2, 1964.

25. *Ibid.*

26. *Kenosha News,* March 26, 1964.

27. Donald Olesen of the *Milwaukee Journal* staff hinted at such affiliations of the Birch Society with the CDL. The *Capital Times* also did so later.

28. Ladinsky.

29. *Milwaukee Journal,* March 11, 1964.

30. *Ibid.,* April 12, 1964.

31. *Wisconsin State Journal,* March 16, 1964.

32. Ladinsky. Zubrensky also said that in one way or another churches aided Boyle.

33. Perlman telegram, March 27, 1964.

34. *Capital Times,* March 30, 1964.

35. Mrs. Walter J. Steininger letter to me, May 9, 1965. Emphasis added.

36. She refuses to tell how many she received, and insists upon anonymity: "It's all past, now."

37. *Wisconsin State Journal,* March 29, 1964.

38. Llewellyn G. Roberts, *Wisconsin State Journal,* March 29, 1964.

39. *Ibid.*

40. At *least* in these places, Ladinsky says.
41. *Capital Times,* April 2, 1964.
42. John Wyngaard, *Janesville Gazette,* April 17, 1964.
43. From the Findings and Conclusions of the Lawyers Non Partisan Committee. Chairman of the committee was Anthony K. Cadden, an archconservative. The report is dated April 2, 1964.

17

1. *Green Bay Register,* March 27, 1964.
2. Elliot Maraniss interview, June 4, 1964. Ladinsky, June 23, 1964. Maraniss is a *Capital Times* reporter.
3. *Capital Times,* March 12, 1964.
4. *Ibid.,* March 16, 1964.
5. *Ibid.,* March 18, 1964.
6. WMTV Editorial Board, "Editorial Comment," WMTV, March 18, 1964, Madison.
7. *Green Bay Press-Gazette,* May 28, 1964.
8. *Janesville Gazette,* April 17, 1964.
9. *Green Bay Press-Gazette,* May 28, 1964.
10. Leonard Zubrensky interview, Nov. 29, 1964; and William B. Lockhart interview, Dec. 18, 1964.
11. *Stevens Point Journal,* April 10, 1964.

18

1. *Grove Press, Inc. v. Gerstein,* 378 U.S. 577 (1964).
2. "Constitutional Law: Is Nothing Obscene Any More?" *Time,* LXXXIV (July 10, 1964), 45.
3. 156 So. 2d 537 (Fla. 1963). For an account, see M. C. Slough and P. D. McAnany, S.J., "Obscenity and Constitutional Freedom—Part I," *St. Louis University Law Journal,* VIII (Spring, 1964), 329. Hereafter, Slough.
4. 173 Ohio St. 22, 179 N.E. 2d 777 (1962)—cited in *Jacobellis,* p. 1677. For an account of the trial, see Slough, pp. 333–34.
5. *Capital Times,* April 2, 1964, for this and previous quotes.
6. Emphasis added.

7. William B. Lockhart and Robert C. McClure, "Censorship of Obscenity: The Developing Constitutional Standards," *Minnesota Law Review*, XLV (November, 1960), 86.

8. *Capital Times*, June 19, 1965.

9. "The Supreme Court," *Time*, LXXXIV (Sept. 11, 1964), 22.

10. *Civil Liberties*, October, 1966, p. 3. See also what the CDL monthly newsletter has to say on the Ginzburg decision in the June–July and September 1966 issues of *The National Decency Reporter*.

APPENDIX

MAJOR COURT CASES BEARING ON OBSCENITY

Adams Theatres Inc. v. Newark, 354 U.S. 931 (1957)
Alberts v. California, 354 U.S. 476 (1957)
Bantam Books, Inc. v. Sullivan 372 U.S. 58 (1963)
Besig v. United States, 208 F 2d 142 (9th Cir.) (1953)
*A Book Named "John Cleland's Memoirs of a Woman of Pleasure,"
    et al. v. Attorney General of the Commonwealth of Massa-
    chusetts*, 383 U.S. 413 (1965)
Burstyn, Inc. v. Wilson, 343 U.S. 495 (1952)
Butler v. Michigan, 352 U.S. 380 (1957)
Commonwealth v. Gordon, 66 Pa. D. & C. 101 (1949)
Commonwealth v. Holmes, 17 Mass. 336 (1821)
Commonwealth v. Sharpless, 2 S. & R. (Pa.) 91 (1815)
Doubleday v. New York, 335 U.S. 848 (1948)
Ginzburg et al. v. United States, 383 U.S. 463 (1965)
Gitlow v. New York, 268 U.S. 652 (1925)
Grove Press, Inc. v. Christenberry, 276 F. 2d 433 (2d Cir.) (1960)
Grove Press, Inc. v. Gerstein, 378 U.S. 577 (1964)
Hannegan v. Esquire, 327 U.S. 146 (1946)
Jacobellis v. Ohio, 84 U.S. 1676 (1964)
Kingsley Books, Inc. v. Brown, 354 U.S. 436 (1957)
Kingsley Pictures Corp. v. Regents of the Univ. of New York,
    360 U.S. 684 (1959)
Manual Enterprises v. Day, 370 U.S. 478 (1962)
Marcus v. Search Warrant, 367 U.S. 717 (1961)

McCormack v. Tropic of Cancer, Superior Court for Suffolk
     County, No. 78441, Nov. 18, 1961
Mishkin v. State of New York, 383 U.S. 502 (1965)
Mounce v. United States, 355 U.S. 180 (1957)
Mutual Film Corp. v. Industrial Commission of Ohio, 236 U.S.
     230 (1915)
Near v. Minnesota, 283 U.S. 697 (1931)
One, Inc. v. Olesen, 355 U.S. 371 (1958)
Parmalee v. United States, 113 F. 2d 729 (D.C. Cir.) (1940)
People v. Richmond County News, Inc., 9 N.Y. 2d 578 (1961)
Queen v. Hicklin, L.R. 3 Q.B. 360 (1868)
*Raymond D. Halsey v. The New York Society for the Suppression
     of Vice,* 234 N.Y. 1, 136 N.E. 219 (1922)
Roth v. United States, 354 U.S. 476 (1957)
Schenck v. United States, 249 U.S. 47 (1919)
Smith v. California, 361 U.S. 147 (1959)
State v. Lerner, 81 N.E. 2d 282 (Ohio C.P.) (1948)
Sunshine Book Co. v. Summerfield, 335 U.S. 372 (1958)
Times Film Corp. v. City of Chicago, 355 U.S. 35 (1957)
Times Film Corp. v. City of Chicago, 81 S. Ct. 391 (1961)
United States v. Bennet, 24 Fed. Cas. 1093 2d Cir. (No. 14571)
     (C.C.S.D.N.Y.) (1879)
United States v. Dennett, 39 F. 2d 564 (2d Cir.) (1930)
United States v. Kennerley, 209 Fed. 119 (S.D.N.Y.) (1913)
United States v. One Book Entitled "Contraception," 51 F. 2d
     525 (S.D.N.Y.) (1931)
United States v. One Book Called "Ulysses," 72 F. 2d 705 (2d Cir.)
     (1934)
United States v. One Obscene Book Entitled "Married Love," 48
     F. 2d 821 (S.D.N.Y.) (1931)
United States v. Thirty-One Photographs Etc., 156 F. Supp. 350
     (S.D.N.Y.) (1957)

SELECTED BIBLIOGRAPHY

BOOKS

Baxter, Annette Kar. *Henry Miller, Expatriate*. Pittsburgh, 1961.

Berns, Walter. *Freedom, Virtue and the First Amendment*. Baton Rouge, Louisiana, 1957.

Blanshard, Paul. *The Right to Read: The Battle Against Censorship*. Boston, 1955.

Broun, Heywood, and Margaret Leech. *Anthony Comstock: Roundsman of the Lord*. New York, 1927.

Carmen, Ira H. *Movies, Censorship, and the Law*. Ann Arbor, Michigan, 1966.

Chafee, Zechariah, Jr. *Government and Mass Communications: A Report from the Commission on Freedom of the Press*. Vol. I. Chicago, 1947.

Chandos, John (ed.). *To Deprave and Corrupt . . . Original Studies in the Nature and Definition of Obscenity*. London, 1962.

Chenery, William L. *Freedom of the Press*. New York, 1955.

Cleaton, Irene and Allen. *Books and Battles: American Literature 1920–1930*. Boston, 1937.

Craig, Alec. *Suppressed Books: A History of the Conception of Literary Obscenity*. Cleveland and New York, 1963.

Daniels, Walter (ed.). *The Censorship of Books*. New York, 1954.

Douglas, William O. *The Right of the People*. New York, 1958.

Downs, Robert B. (ed.). *The First Freedom: Liberty and Justice in the World of Books*. Chicago, 1960.

Ernst, Morris L., and David Roth. *American Sexual Behavior and the Kinsey Report*. New York, 1948.

Ernst, Morris L., and Alan U. Schwartz. *Censorship: The Search for the Obscene*. New York, 1964.

Ernst, Morris L., and William Seagle. *To the Pure: A Study of Obscenity and the Censor*. New York and London, 1928.

Gardiner, Harold C. *Catholic Viewpoint on Censorship*. Garden City, New York, 1961.

Gellhorn, Walter. *Individual Freedom and Governmental Restraints*. Baton Rouge, Louisiana, 1956.

Gertz, Elmer. *A Handful of Clients*. Chicago, 1965.

Girvetz, H. K. (ed.) *Contemporary Moral Issues*. Belmont, Calif., 1963.

Haight, Anne Lyon. *Banned Books: Informal Notes on Some Books Banned for Various Reasons at Various Times and in Various Places*. New York, 1955.

Haney, Robert W. *Comstockery in America*. Boston, 1960.

Hyde, H. Montgomery. *A History of Pornography*. New York, 1964.

Inglis, Ruth A. *Freedom of Movies*. Chicago, 1947.

Iverson, William. *The Pious Pornographers*. New York, 1963.

Kilpatrick, James Jackson. *The Smut Peddlers*. Garden City, New York, 1960.

Klapper, Joseph T. *The Effects of Mass Communication*. Glencoe, Illinois, 1960.

Konvitz, Milton Ridvas. *First Amendment Freedoms*. Ithaca, New York, 1963.

Kronhausen, Eberhard and Phyllis. *Pornography and the Law*. New York, 1959.

Lee, Alwyn. "Henry Miller—The Pathology of Isolation," *New World Writing*. Second Mentor Selection, II (November, 1952), 340–47.

Legman, Gershon. *Love and Death, A Study in Censorship*. Breaking Point, New York, 1949.

Loth, David. *The Erotic in Literature*. New York, 1962.

McCormick, John, and Mairi MacInnes. *Versions of Censorship*. Garden City, New York, 1962.

McKeon, Richard, Robert K. Merton, and Walter Gellhorn. *The Freedom to Read: Perspective and Program*. New York, 1957.

Miller, Henry. *The Air-Conditioned Nightmare*. New York, 1945.

Miller, Henry. *Big Sur and the Oranges of Hieronymus Bosch*. New York, 1957.

—————. *Black Spring*. Paris, 1936.

—————. *Black Spring*. New York, 1963.

—————. *The Colossus of Maroussi*. New York, 1941.

—————. *Henry Miller Letters to Anaïs Nin*. Edited by Gunther Stuhlmann. New York, 1965.

—————. *A Henry Miller Reader*. Edited by Lawrence Durrell. New York, 1959.

—————. *Nexus*. Vol. 1. Paris, 1959.

—————. *Plexus*. 2 vols. Paris, 1953.

—————. *The Plight of the Creative Artist in the United States of America*. Houlton, Maine, 1944.

—————. *Quiet Days in Clichy*. Paris, 1958.

—————. *Tropic of Cancer*. Paris: Obelisk Press, 1934.

—————. *Tropic of Cancer*. 2d ed. Paris: Obelisk Press, 1935.

—————. Obratník Raka, román (*Tropic of Cancer*). V Praze: Nakladem V. Cejky, 1938.

—————. *Tropic of Cancer*. 3rd ed. Paris: Obelisk Press, 1938.

—————. *Tropic of Cancer*. 4th ed. Paris: Obelisk Press, 1939.

—————. *Tropic of Cancer*. 5th ed. Paris: Obelisk Press, 1939.

—————. *Tropic of Cancer*. Medusa edition. Mexico: privately printed, 1940.

—————. *Tropique du Cancer*. Paris: Denoël, 1945.

—————. *Tropic of Cancer*. Paris, 1947.

—————. *Tropique du Cancer*. Paris: Éditions des Deux-Rives, 1947.

—————. *Tropic of Cancer*. Paris: Obelisk Press, 1950.

—————. *Wendekreis des Krebses* (*Tropic of Cancer*). Hamburg: Rowohlt, 1952.

—————. Krebsens Vendekrebs (*Tropic of Cancer*). Copenhagen: Casper Nielsens, 1953.

—————. *Tropic of Cancer* (in English). Tokyo: Keimeisha, 1953.

—————. *Tropique du Cancer*. Paris: Éditions Denoël, 1953, c1945.

—————. *Tropic of Cancer* (in Japanese). Tokyo: Shincho-sha, 1954.

—————. *Tropic of Cancer*. Paris: Obelisk Press, 1954.

—————. *Tropique du Cancer*. Paris: Éditions Denoël, 1956.

—————. *Tropic of Cancer*. Paris: Obelisk Press, 1957.

Miller, Henry. *Tropic of Cancer* (in Norwegian). Stockholm: Central Press, 1958.

————. *Tropic of Cancer*. New York: Grove Press Inc., 1961.

————. *Tropic of Cancer*. Shanghai (pirated edition from Obelisk edition), undated.

————. *Tropic of Cancer*. Vienna: Book Lovers Club (pirated edition), undated.

————. *Tropic of Capricorn*. Paris, 1939.

————. *Sexus*. 2 vols. Paris, 1949.

————. *The World of Sex*. New York, 1959.

Murphy, Terrence J. *Censorship: Government and Obscenity*. Baltimore, 1963.

Nelson, Jack, and Gene Roberts, Jr. *The Censors and the Schools*. Boston and Toronto, 1963.

Paul, James C., and Murray L. Schwartz. *Federal Censorship: Obscenity in the Mail*. New York, 1961.

Perles, Alfred. *Art and Outrage, A Correspondence About Henry Miller Between Alfred Perles and Lawrence Durrell*. London, 1959.

————. *My Friend, Henry Miller*. New York, 1962.

Porter, Bern (ed.). *The Happy Rock: A Book About Henry Miller*. Berkeley, Calif., 1945.

Schroeder, Theodore. *A Challenge to Sex Censors*. New York, 1938.

Schumach, Murray. *The Face on the Cutting Room Floor*. New York, 1964.

Shapiro, Karl. *In Defense of Ignorance*. New York, 1960.

Southern, Terry, Alexander Trocchi, and Richard Seaver. *Writers in Revolt*. New York, 1963.

St. John-Stevas, Norman. *Obscenity and the Law*. London, 1956.

Waples, Douglas, Bernard Berelson, and Franklyn R. Bradshaw, *What Reading Does to People*. Chicago, 1940.

Wickes, George (ed.). *Henry Miller and the Critics*. Carbondale, Ill., 1963.

Widmer, Kingsley. *Henry Miller*. New York, 1963.

Widmer, Kingsley and Eleanor. *Literary Censorship: Principles, Cases, Problems*. San Francisco, 1961.

MAGAZINES

"About Evergreen Review No. 32," *Evergreen Review*, VIII (August–September, 1964), 32.

Amory, Cleveland. "Paperback Pornography," *Saturday Evening Post*, CCXXXVI (April 6, 1963), 10, 12.

"Banning Book-Burners," *Newsweek*, LX (Nov., 26, 1962), 88.

Best, Marshall A. "In Books, They Call It Revolution," *Daedalus*, XCII (Winter, 1963), 30–41.

Brady, Mildred Edie. "The New Cult of Sex and Anarchy," *Harper's*, CXCIV (April, 1947), 312–22.

Burress, Lee A., Jr. "The Pressure of Censorship on Wisconsin Public Schools," *Wisconsin English Journal*, VI (Oct., 1963), 6–28.

Cairns, Huntington. "Freedom of Expression in Literature," *Annals of the American Academy of Political and Social Science*, CC (Nov., 1938), 76–94.

Cairns, R. B., J. C. N. Paul, and J. Wishner. "Sex Censorship: The Assumptions of Anti-Obscenity Laws and the Empirical Evidence," *Minnesota Law Review*, XLVI (May, 1962), 1009–41.

"Censorship Trends: Local, State, National in 1962," *Publishers' Weekly*, CLXXXIII (Jan. 21, 1963), 67–8.

Cohen, Steven. "Constitutional Law—Obscene Literature—Wisconsin Statute Provides Civil Action Against a Book," *Wisconsin Law Review*, MCMLX (March, 1960), 309–24.

Epstein, Jason. "A Criticism of Commercial Publishing," *Daedalus*, XCII (Winter, 1963), 63–7.

Gertz, Elmer. "The 'Tropic of Cancer' Litigation in Illinois," *Kentucky Law Journal*, LI (Summer, 1963), 591–610.

————. "An End to All Censorship," *Nation*, CCI (July 5, 1965), 7–10.

Gibson, Morgan. "The Milwaukee *Cancer* Trial," *Michigan Voices*, III (Winter, 1962–63), 41–9.

Glicksberg, Charles I. "Henry Miller: Individualist in Extremis," *The Southwest Review*, XXXIII (Summer, 1948) 289–95.

Haverstick, John. "Henry Miller: Man in Quest of Life," *Saturday Review*, XL (Aug. 3, 1957), 8.

Heifetz, Henry. "The Anti-Social Act of Writing," *Studies on the Left*, IV (Spring, 1964), 3–20.

Hempel, William J., and Patrick M. Wall. "Extralegal Censorship of Literature," *New York University Law Review*, XXXIII (Nov., 1958), 989–1026.

Highet, Gilbert. "Henry Miller's Stream of Self-Consciousness," *Horizon*, IV (Nov., 1961), 104–5.

Jennison, Peter S. "Censorship: Strategy for Defense," *Publishers' Weekly*, CLXXXV (March 2, 1964), 58, 61.

Kauffmann, Stanley. "Old Shocker Comes Home," *New Republic*, CXLV (July 10, 1961), 17–19.

Kleine, Don. "Innocence Forbidden: Henry Miller in the Tropics," *Prairie Schooner*, XXXIII (Summer, 1959), 125–30.

Krim, Seymour. "Netherworld of Henry Miller," *Commonweal*, LVII (Oct. 24, 1952), 68–71.

Larrabee, Eric. "The Cultural Context of Sex Censorship," *Law and Contemporary Problems*, XX (Autumn, 1955), 672–88.

Legislative Reference Library Report on Obscenity Legislation, *Informational Bulletin* 192 (Aug., 1960), Madison, Wisconsin.

Lewis, Anthony. "The Most Recent Troubles of 'Tropic,'" *New York Times Book Review* (Jan. 21, 1962), pp. 4–5, 16, 18.

Lockhart, William B., and Robert C. McClure. "Censorship of Obscenity: The Developing Constitutional Standards," *Minnesota Law Review*, XLV (Nov., 1960), 5–121.

————. "Literature, The Law of Obscenity, and the Constitution," *Minnesota Law Review*, XXXVIII (March, 1954), 295–395.

Miller, Henry. "From the *New Republic* Mailbag," *New Republic*, CIX (Nov. 8, 1943), 656.

————. "Another Open Letter," *New Republic*, CIX (Dec. 6, 1943), 813–14.

Moon, Eric. "'Problem' Fiction," *Library Journal*, LXXXVII (Feb. 1, 1962), 484–96.

Moore, E. T. "*Tropic of Cancer*, The First Three Months," *ALA Bulletin*, LV (Oct., 1961), 779–80.

Nolan, Michael S. "Constitutional Law: Obscenity Censorship in Wisconsin," *Marquette Law Review*, XLVII (Fall, 1963), 281.

Parkinson, Thomas. "The Hilarity of Henry Miller," *The Listener*, LIX (June 19, 1958), 1021–22.

Rahv, Philip. "The Artist as Desperado," *New Republic*, CIV (April 21, 1941), 557–59.

Rexroth, Kenneth. "Empty Zone," *Nation*, CXCIII (July 1, 1961), 15–16.

Rexroth, Kenneth. "The Neglected Henry Miller," *Nation,* CLXXXI (Nov. 5, 1955), 385–87.

R.H.S. "A Summer of Censorship," *Publishers' Weekly,* CLXXXIII (July 29, 1963), 38.

Rorty, James. "The Harassed Pocket-Book Publishers," *Antioch Review,* XV (Dec., 1955), 411–27.

Seldes, Gilbert. "The Mass Media and the Artistic Climate." *Arts in Society,* II (Fall–Winter, 1962–1963), 150.

Slough, M. C., and R. D. McAnany, S.J. "Obscenity and Constitutional Freedom—Part I," *St. Louis University Law Journal,* VIII (Spring, 1964), 279–357; "Part II," (Summer, 1964), 449–532.

Solotaroff, Theodore. "All That Cellar-Deep Jazz," *Commentary,* XXXII (Oct., 1961), 317–24.

Southern, Terry. "Miller: Only the Beginning," *Nation,* CXCIII (Nov. 18, 1961), 399–400.

"Storm over the 'Tropics'," *Economist,* CC (July 1, 1961), 39–40ff.

Stuart, I. R., and W. G. Eliasberg. "Personality Structures Which Reject the Human Form in Art: An Exploratory Study of Cross-Cultural Perceptions of the Nude," *Journal of Social Psychology,* LVII (Aug., 1962), 383–98.

"Tropic Censorship Decisions: A Mixed Collection," *Publishers' Weekly,* CLXXXI (March 5, 1962), 40.

Vaughan, Samuel S. "Why a Book Sells Is Not as Much a Mystery as It Seems," *New York Times Book Review* (Feb. 25, 1962), 4, 18.

Warshofsky, Fred. "Grove Press: Little Giant of Publishing," Reprint of the March, 1962, issue of *Paperback Trade News.*

Whitmore, Harry. "Obscenity in Literature: Crime or Free Speech," *Sydney Law Review* (March, 1963), 184.

"Widespread Censorship of Paperback *Tropic of Cancer,*" *Publishers' Weekly,* CLXXX (Nov. 13, 1961), 21.

PAMPHLETS

American Civil Liberties Union. "38th–44th Annual Reports." July 1, 1957 to June 30, 1964.

Crowther, Bosley. "Movies and Censorship," Public Affairs Pamphlet No. 332. Public Affairs Committee, Sept., 1962, pp. 1–28.

Jennison, Peter S. "Freedom to Read," Public Affairs Pamphlet No. 344. New York, 1963.

Wickes, George. *Henry Miller,* University of Minnesota Pamphlets on American Writers No. 56, 1966.

DOCUMENTS

Barker, Richard E. "Henry Miller: An Evaluation." Unpublished Master's thesis, Cornell University, June, 1953.

Milwaukee Junior Bar Association. "Report of Literature & Motion Picture Committee." July, 1956.

"Minutes," of the Wisconsin joint Legislative Commission on Obscene Literature, Feb. 11, 1964, State capitol, Madison, Wisconsin.

"Minutes," of the Wisconsin joint Legislative Obscene Literature Commission, March 5, 1964, Milwaukee courthouse, Milwaukee, Wisconsin.

"Minutes," of the Wisconsin joint Legislative Obscene Literature Commission, June 16, 1964, State office building, Milwaukee, Wisconsin.

Neuman, Richard J. "Who Reads *Tropic*? Or, What Happens When You Leave It Alone," *Newsletter on Intellectual Freedom,* XI (Dec., 1962), 43.

"Report of the Wisconsin Legislative Council Committee on Obscene Literature," Wisconsin State Legislature, 1964, Madison, Wisconsin.

"Transcript of Proceedings." The Public Hearings of the Wisconsin Committee of the Wisconsin Legislature to Investigate the Publication and Distribution of Obscene Literature in Wisconsin, Created by Section 13.38, Wisconsin Statutes, Ch. 230, Laws 1963. Coach House Motor Inn, Milwaukee, Wisconsin, Sept. 23, 1964.

"Transcript of Proceedings." Wisconsin joint Legislative Obscene Literature Commission Public Hearing, Oct. 27, 1964, State capitol, Madison, Wisconsin.

INDEX